litzen-Benz, A.L.F.A. 24 HP Corsa Tipo, Peugeot EX5, Bugatti Typ 13 "Brescia", S, Opel RAK 2, Alfa Romeo 8C 2300, Mercedes-Benz W25, Auto Union Typ C, Veritas RS, Cisitalia 360, Lancia D24, Jaguar D-Type, Mercedes-Benz 300 SLR, us 25, BMC Mini Cooper, Alfa Romeo Giulia Sprint GTA, Ford GT40, BRM P83, cia Stratos, BMW 3.0 CSL, Alfa Romeo Tipo 33TT12, Ferrari 312 T2, Lotus 79, BMW BT52, Audi quattro, BMW M3, Lancia Delta Integrale, Ferrari 640 F1-89, Romeo 155 V6 TI, Benetton B194-Ford, McLaren F1 GTR, Reynard 961-Honda , Ferrari F2002, Alfa Romeo 156 GTA, Volkswagen Race Touareg, Renault R25, Schaeffler Audi RS5 DTM, Porsche 919 hybrid, ABT Schaeffler FE02, Robocar

DELIUS KLASING

JÖRG WALZ

THE HISTORY OF MOTORSPORT

FROM THE BEGINNINGS UNTIL TODAY

DELIUS KLASING VERLAG

GERMANY INVEN
CARS, FRANCE C
OF THE 'CONCEPT,
A NOBLE ART
TURNED THE
WHIL

ED THE CONCEPT OF
REATED A SPORT OUT
GREAT-BRITAIN MADE
OF THE SPORT, ITALY
RT INTO A REL'IGION,
THE USA MADE IT A
PROFITABLE SHOW!

Preface | Prof. Dr.-Ing. Peter Gutzmer

◄ Schaeffler Chief Techno-
logy Officer and Vice CEO
Prof. Peter Gutzmer with
Formula E Champion
Lucas di Grassi

___ The history of the automobile couldn't have been written without the history of motorsport. The first automotive designers wanted to pit themselves and their inventions against the competition to prove the efficiency, reliability, durability and emotional resonance of their products. Tackling the challenge of competition is particularly important when the products being trialed herald a new era or technical advancement. And since time immemorial, people don't just enjoy competitions – more than anything, they love to idolize their sports heroes, who are often in the center of marketing campaigns. Time and again, motorsport has roused the creativity and ambition of gifted engineers to maximize the performance and efficiency of power trains, to thrash out the lightweight design and body aerodynamics, to explore the contact of the suspension and tires to the road, all this up to the limits of what is physically possible. At the same time, however, they needed to come up with new and innovative solutions for manufacturing production cars. Today, the world of the automobile is in a phase of the greatest change since its inception more than 140 years ago. In the not-too-distant future, electric drive will supplement and replace the successful and proven combustion engine. Electronic and digital progress has changed the way we use vehicles and live with them. Hence, it's obvious that motorsport must also adapt to this paradigm shift. Hybrid drives with defined energy formulas have been successfully introduced in classic motor racing. Formula E pushes the boundaries even further, with the first single-seater motor racing series run with engines powered solely by electricity. Furthermore, these future-oriented motorsport competitions are being contested in urban regions of the world, in areas where the younger generations in particular like to live – those looking for quality of life and a social environment. As a well-known, innovative company, Schaeffler has always contributed to motor racing directly with its products and support. Joining forces with ABT, the company has also played a trailblazing role in shaping the first German Formula E team. Thus it is particularly pleasing to see the Schaeffler-electric-drive's latest success as part of the ABT-Schaeffler-Audi Sport Team, with whom Lucas Di Grassi won the FIA Formula E World Championship in only its third year of existence – after claiming second place the previous season. Significant and fundamentally new technological expertise was able to be successfully implemented. This knowhow represents the basis for the new Schaeffler electric-drives that will power the automobiles of the future.

Prof. Dr.-Ing. Peter Gutzmer,
Vice CEO of the Executive Board and Chief
Technology Officer Schaeffler AG

Preface

Lucas di Grassi

Thoughts from a driver's perspective

➤ **ABT-Schaeffler pilot Lucas di Grassi talks to Schaeffler co-owner Georg F. W. Schaeffler**

___ Race cars have been at the forefront of technology in the automobile industry for more than 100 years. Race engineers continually drive development forward. They create and build the fastest vehicles on wheels that can be moved by man. This is what makes the sport so incredibly fascinating. In qualifying and at every race, we pilots are constantly taming a wild beast, and yet we also have to push to the limit. It doesn't matter if the race car is powered by a combustion engine, hybrid or electric technology. We simply try to squeeze the last drop out of every single part, out of the tires and the engine. When this works, we're rewarded with a perfect lap on the racetrack. The second fascinating aspect of a race car is the sporting contest against your racing driver colleagues. We all compete under similar conditions in the same environment and at the highest level to see who's the best.

The bottom line is the same in every race series: to move the car at the limit in a competition. But the conditions are, of course, different. In Formula 1, the quality of the race car, especially in terms of aerodynamics, plays a very important role. If you're not sitting in one of the fastest cars, you're not going to be able to fight for victory, no matter how good a driver you are. In long-distance racing, like in the WEC, the philosophy is completely different: The race cars must be fast, but equally, they have to be reliable. A race strategy not only has to work over a couple of laps, but, as in the case of the Le Mans 24 Hours, over the whole day. Sometimes, the driver has to sit in the vehicle for stints of three or four hours, day and night. This is a huge physical challenge for the individual – and ultimately it's a test of motivation and concentration. Formula E has ushered in an entirely new aspect of motorsport: How can I be fast, but at the same time pay attention to the energy consumption of my electric car? The name of the game for every racing driver is to drive as efficiently as possible. It's a very complicated situation, over and above the usual factors in motorsport. Moreover, Formula E races are contested exclusively on the streets of major cities. There's practically no room for error, otherwise you hit the wall and that's the end of your race weekend. None of the essential features underpinning the concept of motor racing has changed: you climb into a car, take it onto the racetrack, and try to drive as fast as possible. These days both speed and efficiency play a major role. There's currently a groundswell of change in the way vehicles are powered in terms of energy – from combustion engines to electric motors. Consequently this path must be followed and we must continue to follow it. In the automobile industry another technology is currently being researched, a technology that could also gain traction in motor racing: autonomous driving. This could change our sport completely. Drivers would no longer need to know how to master their vehicles, or, even more drastic, racing drivers would no longer be needed, period. We would lose the ability to push a car to its limit, because we wouldn't understand the limit. I find this a little scary. Motorsport must not lose its essence. I yearn for a contest in which the driver plays a greater role than technology. The MotoGP is a good example. Motorbikes are, of course, important too, but the rider makes the big difference there. Autonomous driving might be an opportunity. Perhaps a way will be found to combine traditional racing with autonomous driving. But first we have to understand how this new technology could actually enhance our sport. It's imperative that the entertainment factor for fans doesn't diminish. For example, I can imagine autonomous driving playing a role at the 24 Hours of Le Mans. For instance, the driver competes half the race distance, and the vehicle drives itself for the other half. Always swapping. Eventually, instead of needing so many drivers, you'd only need one. This is just an idea, an example of the direction motor racing could take. I believe there are many other ways, directions we can't even imagine at this stage. But I'm completely convinced that motorsport will survive. For instance, no one needs a horse to get from A to B anymore – as might have

been the case hundreds of years ago. But we still have horse riding, for example, show jumping or horse racing. Motorsport in 50 years will certainly have to face similar questions: Is it still necessary? Do we still need drivers? And the answer will be: yes, but in an adapted way.

Lucas di Grassi
Racing driver, passionate innovator and CEO of Roborace

Preface Jörg Walz

◄ **Author Jörg Walz and Le Mans winner Nico Hülkenberg in the Porsche pits**

Spoilt for choice

___ It goes without saying that the Porsche 917/30 from 1973 deserves a place in this book as arguably the most powerful racing sports car and CanAm serial winner. And why is the BMW 3.0 and 3.5 CSL included, but not its rivals, the Ford Capri and Porsche 911 Carrera RSR? Where's the six-wheeled Formula 1 Tyrrell 034 from 1976, and what about the Group C Mazda, with which the Japanese claimed the first Le Mans victory in 1991 for a race car powered by a rotary engine? And, of course, the modern-day NASCARs haven't made the cut, and where are the STW sedans that put up such valiant fights in many national series? Why this car and not that one?

These questions are justified but lead us nowhere. The last twelve decades have seen so many gripping races and competitions, so many interesting and fascinating designs, that to try and include them all in one book could only result in sketchy snapshots. Obviously there is a raft of iconic cars that simply must be mentioned. But what if two of these icons made their debut in the same year? And thus the dilemma begins. The year is simply an indication, but not always for the maiden event. The Bentley Speed Six, for instance, can be found under the year of its fifth Le Mans triumph, and thus makes room for another must: the Alfa 6C 1750. Or instead of the 1750, why not the 1500? But then what happens to the Mercedes-Benz S, from which the SSK and SSKL are derived? The white giants are inextricably linked to the premiere race on the Nürburgring. And in 1927, there's simply no other choice than to mention the circuit in Germany's Eifel region. The year 1970 is the perfect match for another great white, the Porsche 917 – this was the year of Porsche's first outright Le Mans victory. But then there would be no place for the breathtaking winged monsters from the USA. And the Lotus 72 is in the right place in the following year – and certainly more important than the turbine-powered Lotus 56B ... And when the focus turns to the diverse and fascinating divisions of motorsport's disciplines and venues, then the task gets even more complicated. Obviously the Opel Astra V6 4x4 doesn't have the same importance as the McLaren-Mercedes MP4-14, with which Mercedes collects laurels in modern-day Formula 1, but it still represents a technical and sporting pinnacle in France's much-loved Trophée Andros. Had the choice fallen on Mika Häkkinen's world championship winning car, not a word would have been written about the ice-racing series.

A car for every year. This means vehicles from the voluptuous years get a raw deal, whereas the automobiles of the pioneering days – for sheer lack of numbers – seem overrated. And yet, they too mustn't be missed out. They point the way, they explain the foundations and they give us an understanding of today's much-cherished traditions. How could we appreciate the value of classic events, such as the long-standing and greatly celebrated Mille Miglia, if we didn't know its origins? Why does a Le Mans victory still elevate the winner to the motorsport Olympus, and why is there no way around Formula 1? And what electrifies motor racing of the future? A look at the early days and the races of this time helps to understand these questions. And it's fun. And that, dear readers, is what I wish for you. Enjoy!

Jörg Walz

Am Steuer eines ausschliesslich mit
F*A G Kugellagern
ausgerüsteten 6 Cylinder Marmon-Wagens

gewinnt

Ray Harroun

beim

800 km Rennen

in

Indianapolis

den

100,000 MARK PREIS
gegen erste deutsche und amerikanische Marken

MERCEDES-BENZ *siegt*

dreifach
im
„Grossen Preis der Schweiz"

ERSTER: RUDOLF CARACCIOLA
mit einem Stundendurchschnitt von 159,14 km
ZWEITER: HERMANN LANG
mit einem Stundendurchschnitt von 158,96 km
DRITTER: MANFRED v. BRAUCHITSCH
mit einem Stundendurchschnitt von 156,84 km
SECHSTER: CHRISTIAN KAUTZ
Wiederum alle 4 gestarteten Mercedes-b
Alle Wagen waren ausgerüstet mit G

24 STUNDEN LE MANS '82

Dreifacher Porsche-Sieg in der GRUPPE C.

1. Ickx/Bell — Rothmans-Porsche 956
2. Mass/Schuppan — Rothmans-Porsche 956
3. Haywood/Holbert/Barth — Rothmans-Porsche 956
4. Mallock/Phillips/Salmon — Aston Martin Nimrod
5. Yver/Tatty/Gulberg — Ford Rondeau M 379C
6. Buss/Winnen/De Dryver — Ford Rondeau M 382

Bilstein · Bosch · Dunlop · KKK · Schnittfelm · Shell

PORSCHE

2007 - COURSE / RACING

Lisboa 06/01/07 — Dakar 21/01/07
Lisboa – Dakar
1979 — 2007
euromilhões
www.dakar.com

OFFICIAL MAP
Euromilhões Dakar

EUROMASTER

EUROMASTER

DAKAR

BFGoodrich
E CONTROL

11

Vincenzo Lancia, the eventual founder of the eponymous automobile company, is one of the drivers of the FIAT 110 hp Corsa, which tackles the 1905 Gordon Bennett Cup. The capacity of the 110 hp, 1,000 kilogram two-seater is an impressive 16,286 cc. Incidentally, Enzo Ferrari's career also begins as a racing driver.

In 1907, the first permanent circuit dedicated to motor racing is opened in Brooklands, Great Britain. The surface of the 5.23-kilometre oval is so bumpy that the race cars often lose contact with the ground. Still, in 1932, Tim Birken sets a new record with a Blower-Bentley on the outer circuit of the Brooklands track, reaching more than 137.96 mph (220 km/h). The cost back then of building the circuit comes to £150,000.

The Porsche 356 was a classic sports car – in the truest sense of the word. The compact rear-engine coupe is a perfect competition car for professionals and amateurs, whether on ovals, at endurance tests and regularity runs, or at rallies, such as the Tour de Corse.

Even in the early days of motor racing, aerodynamics play an important role. The first considerations, often based on theory, are soon backed up by scientific findings from the wind tunnel. Ford engineers work on the GT40 for the 1967 Le Mans mission.

► The emergence of the all-wheel-drive Audi quattro at the beginning of the 1980s ushers in a new era of rally sport. Very soon it's said that even a trained monkey could win in a quattro. Indeed, the Ingolstadt manufacturer soon realizes that it is better to drive with the best than against the best. For Audi, there is no way around Walter Röhrl. And the opposition immediately switches to all-wheel drive. In this 1981 photo from Sweden, Mikkola/Hertz storm to the new Audi's first victory.

◄ Stirling Moss sticks precisely to the racing line in his Aston Martin DB3S, which is capable of reaching over 250 km/h. The two-seater mounted with a torquey six-cylinder front engine is a typical example of the late 1950s, when Aston Martin wrestles Ferrari and Maserati for the crown of the World Championship for Makes.

➤ The tension before the start. Alas, today's photographers, TV cameras and spectators hardly ever get to see the mental state of the drivers. Helmets became mandatory in Formula 1 in 1952. In 1967, Dennis Hulme introduces a closed integral helmet (like in the photo). In the meantime, drivers' faces are hidden behind bulletproof dark-tinted, mirrored visors.

With a victory at Zandvoort in 1967, a new engine conquers Formula 1. The three-liter V8 from Cosworth is "the preferred power unit" of British Formula 1 racing squads until the start of the turbo era in the 1980s. The four-valve Ford Cosworth with four camshafts and fuel injection is the main power source for motorsport's premier class.

In 1970, Porsche dispatches four of the compact 908/3 on the twisty road course at the Sicilian Targa Florio. The card-suit symbols on the front are intended to quickly distinguish the racing cars painted in Gulf colors. With the Spyder, Siffert/Redman drive to victory. These symbols had actually appeared 50 years earlier at the Madonie course, gracing the four Austro-Daimler Sascha contenders, designed by Ferdinand Porsche.

The Ford Cortina Mk 2 GT with a 1.6-liter, twin-cam, four-cylinder engine comes from the British production of the US marque, which has a presence in England and Germany with specially customized vehicles. In this photo, Peter Huth and his co-driver Ian Grant celebrate their second place at the finish of the 1968 East African Safari Rally.

The NASCAR series is one of the most celebrated and popular sporting events in America. The slipstream duels and tactical maneuvers on the high-speed ovals are very different from the traditional circuit races of Europe. The technical standards, too, are not as innovative as those in Europe. However, knowing the ins and outs of the exciting, tradition-steeped and stable racing series is just as exciting for spectators.

For decades, Formula 1 has represented high-tech. The premier class is constantly searching for technical limits. Exotic materials, elaborate wind tunnels, herculean workforces and countless test kilometers have pushed budgets almost into the stratosphere. The year 2010 brought changes that would cut costs drastically. Modern-day Formula 1 still needn't fear for its high-tech claim. For Mercedes-Benz, the new regulations are a welcome opportunity to make a comeback with their own racing squad. And Michael Schumacher also uses the chance to make a comeback from his resignation.

Sébastien Loëb, from the Alsace region of France, achieves what no other driver has done before. Between 2004 and 2012, the Citroën works driver and his co-driver Daniel Elena are crowned world champions nine times in a row. Their competition cars: Xsara, C4 and DS3 (photo), are based on the WRC regulations.

► In addition to series for automobile manufacturers' factory squads and top international championships, there's an almost endless assortment of series and events for all levels of racing enthusiasts – and for all budgets. Popular among amateur drivers are the long-distance races in which they can share the car, and the costs, and still get plenty of track time. One of these series is the VLN Endurance Cup, with races held on the Nürburgring-Nordschleife, with its season highlight the 24-hour race, as well as the endurance event at Bathurst, Australia. Near-production race cars are regulars on the grid – such as the Audi TT – flying the logos of the Schaeffler brands INA, LuK and FAG.

After the Dakar adventure, as well as the off-road rallies through Africa and South America, Volkswagen discovers a new stage between 2013 and 2016, with the WRC. The sales department is thrilled with the fact that the vehicle fielded looks very much like a production car. The Volkswagen Polo WRC allows VW to market its compact car and to attract a younger clientele to the marque with sporty special editions. Four straight drivers' and manufacturers' titles are the juicy spoils, before Volkswagen – for budget reasons after the diesel scandal – withdraws from the World Rally Championship.

▼ After the end of the Schumacher era, Sebastian Vettel steps up to follow in the footsteps of his idol. In the Red Bull cockpit – hailing from the former Benetton/Renault racing squad from Britain's Enstone – he notches up four world championship titles in a row. The technical mastermind behind this vehicle is the ingenious former March, Williams, and McLaren designer, Adrian Newey. For Vettel, it's as if the RB is tailored just for him. His driving style harmonizes perfectly with the single-seater and its innovative wing concept, featuring a so-called exhaust-blown diffuser, which directs hot gas over the diffuser to create more downforce than the many spoilers, flaps and flics could generate.

▼ Schaeffler invites two very special guests to the legendary Nürburgring-Nordschleife in 2014: The reigning DTM champion Mike Rockenfeller brings his Schaeffler-Audi RS5 to the rollercoaster circuit in the Eifel not far from his Phoenix team's HQ, and rally legend Armin Schwarz comes with his brawny AGM X6 Trophy Truck. The monster truck is, of course, not made for paved roads, however such impressive PR stunts are just another facet of motor racing.

1,160 hp and a beefy 5,600 Nm: that's the impressive specs of the swift giants in the European Truck Racing Championship. Weight 5.5 tonnes, they set another record in motor racing. Nowhere else in circuit racing do higher mechanical forces occur, putting immense stresses on all components. These events regularly attract a full house – year after year, 200,000 spectators flock to the Nürburgring to witness the Truck Grand Prix.

1894 | Peugeot

The race takes off

___ The 126-kilometre motoring competition from Paris to Rouen is recognized as the first international race in the still-young history of the automobile. The combustion engine has not yet become the established power source, as evidenced by the fact that "horseless carriages" with 20 different sources of power compete. Lining up at the event alongside the combustion Otto engines, which will eventually make the breakthrough, are vehicles powered by steam, electricity, gas, compressed air, and even electro-pneumatically-driven cars. Of the 102 entrants who start the race, only 15 will make it to the finish. The Paris newspaper *Le Petit Journal* initiated the race, with the winner receiving 5,000 francs in prize money. In the end there are two winners: A Peugeot and a Panhard et Levassor reach Rouen after 5 hours and 50 minutes.

The Peugeot is an open-wheeled Phaéton mounted with a Daimler engine, producing around three to four horsepower. According to the jury, the winning vehicle is "light and easy to drive", and the average speed achieved is 20.4 km/h. Just three years earlier, a Peugeot accompanied the cycle race from Paris to Brest and back as a support vehicle, but was unable to keep up with the pace set by the racing cyclists. But thanks to strong support from the Peugeot bicycle dealers along the route, who provided tools and jerry cans, the vehicle reached its destination and gave the emerging motor racing scene a decisive boost. ___

1895 | Panhard et Levassor

Media attention from the outset

___ In contrast to the previous year's maiden long-distance drive, the competition from Paris to Bordeaux and back, covering 1,175 kilometers, is an outright race. At almost ten times the distance of the 1894 event, the organizers – the Touring Club de France and media entrepreneurs James Gordon Bennett and William Vanderbilt – stipulate a maximum race duration of 100 hours. More than three million spectators line the route. Émile Levassor, driving a Panhard et Levassor, beats the field of two dozen or so vehicles in 48 hours and 47 seconds – in slightly less than half the prescribed time.

The victor is proud to have broken the previous record set by cyclists. However, Levassor and the second-placed Peugeot, driven by Rigoulot, who reaches the finish line more

The first two vehicles to finish are disqualified

than six hours later, are disqualified, as their vehicles have only two seats. The Peugeot driver Koechlin inherits first place and receives a handsome sum of 70,000 Francs.

Another interesting fact is that while the field is shod with classic carriage wheels (tread made of iron or hard rubber), for the first time one vehicle enters the race fitted with pneumatic tires. Despite setting up many tire service points, numerous defects with the Daimler-powered Peugeot cause the Michelin brothers to miss the cut-off for the allocated time. However, the victory march of the pneumatic tire is now unstoppable.

The two-cylinder Daimler with 1,257 cc, mounted in the Panhard et Levassor, produces around four horsepower at 800 rpm. That's enough to achieve a blistering average speed of 24 km/h. ___

◄ The first competition car was a Phaeton – the name given to the body design of the open four-seater mounted with Daimler engine.

Guests from the new world

The first summit attempt

___ In England, the first London to Brighton race takes place. With the "Emancipation Run", the British celebrate the abolition of the Red Flag Act, in force since 1865, which stipulates that a person

The Emancipation Run marks the end of the Red Flag Act

must walk in front of motorized vehicles waving a red flag in order to draw attention to possible accident risks. Accordingly, the speed at which motorized vehicles travel is slow. With the symbolic burning of the red flag, 33 starters head off for Brighton in 1896. A good dozen of them reach the destination. The American Frank Duryea is the fastest, covering the 90 kilometers from Hyde Park in London to the seaside town in 3:45 hours. Another vehicle in the line-up is the Haynes-Duryea, from the workshop of brothers Charles and Frank Duryea and inventor Elwood Haynes. It is the first automobile featuring a combustion engine that is available in the USA for purchase. With this, Duryea creates a tradition in automobile manufacturing in what is still today the world's largest automotive market. In 1895, the Duryea has already won the USA's first race, the Chicago Times-Herald Race. The 1896 vehicle is an evolution of the previous year's car. The body, wheels and front axle are made of wood, and power is transferred to the wheels via a leather belt. The chassis, however, consists of a steel frame. Also new are the carburetor, and a single lever controlling the steering, shifting, and acceleration.

That same year, the New World's first race on a closed race course is contested at the New York Cosmopolitan Race. Participants have to step out of their vehicles on a steep uphill section and – much to the delight of the spectators – push. ___

___ The 1897 race along the French Riviera from Marseille to Fréjus and up to the Col de la Turbie above the Principality of Monaco, puts Jules Félix and Philippe Albert De Dion in the limelight. Until this time the two have built steam engines and achieved world fame in 1893 as the inventors of the eponymous DeDion axle. Over the 233 kilometers of hilly and flat terrain, Count Gaston de Chasseloup-Loubat knows how to get the most out of his three-wheeled De Dion, which is now powered by a combustion engine.

Climb every mountain – scoring victory on three wheels averaging 30 km/h

After seven hours and 45 minutes, he reaches the finish, averaging around 30 km/h.

In addition to the Count's tricycle, six other De Dion three-wheelers compete, all finishing in the top seven of the motorbike category at this first-ever hill-climb event. In that same year, De Dion mounts a half-horsepower engine on a bike and thus paves the way for the moped. Still, the engineer will eventually focus on four-wheelers. ___

A design defined

___ Shortly before the turn of the century, the motor vehicles with combustion engines coming out of the Panhard et Levassor workshop are the cars to beat. The Parisian designers mount the Daimler engine in the front of the vehicle, thus inventing the "system Panhard" that defines the standard layout to this day – engine in the front, and rear-wheel drive. The more even weight distribution has a positive effect on the handling. The crankshaft of the longitudinally mounted engine transfers power via a gear drive to a layshaft, and from there via chains to the rear wheels. Another new feature is the steering wheel, which replaces the steering tiller.

Amongst other successes, the vehicles from Panhard et Levassor win the 574-kilometer drive from Paris to Bordeaux (René de Knyff) and arguably the most important race of the year, the 1,431-kilometer Paris–Amsterdam–Paris tour. The trip takes the winner, Charron, just over 33 hours, which gives an average speed of approximately 44 km/h.

Germany's first official race is also contested in 1898. The event, organized by the German Sports Association and the Central European Motor Car Club (MMV), runs from Berlin to Potsdam or Leipzig, and back to the capital.

Motorsport claims its first fatality, with the death of Count de Montagnac at the Périgeux-Bergerac-Périgeux competition.   ___

Alternative before the full-throttle era

___ On the Vienna trotting course, 10,000 spectators attend Europe's first automobile race on a closed track. But the emerging automobile is still in its infancy, and it's not yet completely clear where its technical journey will lead. In addition to the rather dominant faction of vehicles with combustion engines, there is also an assortment of electric vehicles, whose low noise is touted as an advantage for taxi services. Designers like the young Ferdinand Porsche appreciate the homogeneous power output of the electric drive, which makes the complicated and laborious gearbox and clutch of that time superfluous. Also interesting is their technical performance, thanks to which the owners of electrically-powered road vehicles set all speed records between 1899 and 1902.

Exceeding 100 km/h for the first time – with electricity

Camille Jenatzy is one of them. And he's the first to break the 100 km/h barrier with an automobile. At the wheel of his cigar-shaped electric automobile, the "red devil" from Belgium, so called because of the color of his hair and beard, sets a speed record of 105.876 km/h. The advantages of the Jenatzy automobile are its aerodynamic shape and its relatively low weight of 1,000 kilos. Strictly speaking, the automobile is nothing more than a large battery with two 25-kilowatt engines, a driver's seat, and four wheels. Due to their short traveling range of 40–60 kilometers, electric automobiles inevitably play no role in the long-distance races of that era. In addition to the record-setting vehicle, Jenatzy develops other electric automobiles, as well as gasoline-electric vehicles (today known as hybrids) and an emerging electromagnetic clutch for use in different race cars.   ___

◄ On its record-setting drive in Paris, Jenatzy's electric automobile, dubbed the "Jamais Contente", is clocked at 105.904 km/h. Incidentally, the restless Belgian is killed in a hunting accident when he imitates the sound of a wild boar while hiding behind a bush – too realistically – and is shot by a hunting buddy.

What else?

Dürkopp – a brand that eventually becomes part of the Schaeffler brand FAG – launches a drivetrain with a chain instead of the previously used slip-prone drive belts. Adler implements the first power transmission using a cardan shaft.

Founded the previous year, the Fabbrica Italiana Automobilindustrie Torino (or FIAT) is ready to face the competition and goes racing. Felice Nazzaro and Vincenzo Lancia are the first factory drivers.

The steering wheel becomes increasingly more common instead of the conventional steering tillers. Powered axles and differentials also become standard technology.

In Berlin, the German Automobile Association holds the first automobile day and also selects a racing committee. Regulations for automobile races are approved and class divisions are introduced.

Harbinger of the new century

___ Out of curiosity – in order to discover which nation builds the best automobile – James Gordon Bennett, the Paris-based son of the owner of the *New York Times*, initiates the Gordon Bennett Cup. The publisher's son commissions the Paris jeweler and goldsmith André Aucoc to create a 17-kilogram perpetual trophy out of silver at a cost of 20,000 Francs. Three vehicles per country are eligible to compete, each no lighter than 400 kilos and no heavier than 1,000 kilograms, and they must have space for two drivers seated side by side. The victorious national federation may host the next Gordon Bennett Cup, on a track between 550 and 650 kilometers long. Each nation is assigned special colors. The French vehicles are blue, the British dark green, yellow for the Belgian racers and white for Germany. This regulation remains in force until the introduction of commercialization with sponsors and advertising.

The maiden race runs over 562 kilometers from Paris to Lyon. The lineup is rather paltry, with only five vehicles taking part. As well as three French na-

With the first international races, the media creates its own events

tionals and Jenatzy from Belgium, there's the Scottish-American Alexander Winton. The Benz, originally entered by Eugen Benz, is withdrawn before the event by his father Carl. Levegh drives his German 7.4-liter Mors in the race, albeit without registering, and reaches the finish between two Panhard et Levassor automobiles.

Victory goes to Fernand Charron in one of the three competing Panhard et Levassors. With a 5.3-liter 4-cylinder engine putting out 24 hp at 950 rpm, and with four gears, cone clutch and without a belt, these cars represent the automobile technology of the new century. The steel-reinforced wooden frame proves to be a good basis for a relatively light vehicle. The sturdiness of the car benefits the leader: while driving 100 km/h downhill and with 15 kilometers to the finish, he collides with a dog, veers off the road with jammed steering, shoots over a ditch, slides between two trees and spins back onto the road. Despite the incident, the former racing cyclist reaches the finish in nine hours and nine minutes at an average speed of more than 62 km/h. ___

Cool headed

___ In 1901, with the first model under the name Mercedes, Wilhelm Maybach creates a vehicle that serves as a perfect example of automobile design. Maybach positions the motor on the front of a frame of pressed steel. The instigator behind the pioneering positioning of the front-mounted four-cylinder is the Consul, Emil Jellinek, who places an order for a number of these models, on the condition they're laid out this way. The designers, Daimler and Maybach, immediately set to work. Jellinek's daughter's name, Mercedes, becomes the eponym for the models from the Cannstatt garage. An innovative feature is the honeycomb radiator mounted in front of the engine, with 8,070 air pipes, a 9-liter capacity and a pumped water system. In a progression that benefits the automobile both in road use and racing, the radiator is facing the driving direction – and this design is still used today.

At work behind the radiator is a 5,973-cc in-line motor, producing 35 horsepower at 1,000 rpm. Weight is shed thanks to the use of aluminum and magnesium, with the motor tipping the scales at 238 kilograms. The side-mounted valves are controlled by two overhead camshafts. Power is transferred to the chain-driven rear axle by means of a coil-spring clutch and a four-speed gearbox. Brake drums on the rear wheels decelerate the vehicle.

The name Mercedes crops up on the winners' lists a total of 27 times at the "Nice Race Week". And although its top speed of 86.5 km/h seems unspectacular by today's standards, the average speed at the La Turbie Hill Climb makes a significant leap from 31.1 to 51.4 km/h. ___

▲ Automobiles in general and race cars in particular are already attracting great interest. The front and rear wheels of the Mercedes are now the same size.

What else?

In Prussia, the first regulations for motor transport are adopted. They soon become the model for further legislations.

◄ At the Nice Race Week in March 1901, the 35 hp Mercedes wins both the 393-kilometer road race and the hill-climb event. Mercedes is only beaten by a steam-powered contender in the "flying kilometer" discipline.

Spyker unveils the first automobile to feature all-wheel drive and brakes on all wheels. The lack of constant velocity joints causes severe jolts to come through the steering wheel and for a long time prevents the breakthrough of this technology.

What else?

Lewess from Britain attempts the first round-the-world trip. On the way from Aachen to Nizhny Novgorod, he is forced to give up when a cylinder breaks.

Mercedes again wins the Nice–La Turbie Hill Climb.

At the wheel of a Napier, Edge wins the Gordon Bennett Cup and, with a Renault, Marcel Renault receives an honorary award from the Austrian Emperor.

In Switzerland, the first attempts to establish automobile liability are undertaken.

Four-wheels win

___ The all-wheel-drive system is a favorite among engineers and therefore is a constantly recurring solution in the search for optimal power transmission. The Dutch vehicle marque Spyker unveiled the first AWD before its breakthrough in rallying in the 1980s, or its emergence in the Grand Prix scene and at Indianapolis toward the end of the 1960s – in fact way before the 1930s and 1940s. At the end of 2000, Spyker resurfaces with a sports car, starts at Le Mans, and from 2006 even competes in Formula 1.

The brothers Jacobus and Henrik-Jan Spijker produce automobiles between 1900 and 1925. The vehicles, initially with two cylinders and cardan-shaft drive, are succeeded in 1902 by the world's first six-cylinder automobiles: with six individual cylinders, an impressive 8,817 cc capacity, all-wheel drive and – another great innovation – brakes on all wheels! In 1906, Jacobus Spijker underlines the performance of this vehicle impressively by winning the hill-climb event held by the Motor Club Birmingham.

The race engine, based on the standard 60 hp model, is said to put out around 80 hp. Power is transmitted via a sophisticated three-speed gearbox to the front and rear axles. However, the braking system proves inadequate for the power output. Reaching 110 km/h, the Spyker is fast, but its braking distance is too long. ___

> **Spyker appears with brakes on all wheels and all-wheel drive**

In 1903, the Gordon Bennett Cup is contested in Northern Ireland. In order to organize the race better, two circuits are joined.

Win on Sunday, sell on Monday ...

___ In Germany, the companies of Gottlieb Daimler (Stuttgart) and Carl Benz (Mannheim) play a leading role in automobile manufacturing. At this stage the two follow their own paths, before merging at the insistence of the Deutsche Bank in 1926. The still-weak market increasingly demands faster, lighter vehicles. Carl Benz errs on the side of caution and decides against motorsport. But the clients take a different view. Marius Barbarou wins the long-distance tour from Paris to Madrid with a vehicle he built himself, based on the Baden manufacturer's design.

Increasing engine power and many race outings are the reason for the competition from Swabia's rising sales figures: true to the motto "win on Sunday, sell on Monday." Mercedes celebrates its greatest victory of 1903 with Camille Jenatzy at the Gordon Bennett Cup. His win in Ireland marks the first great triumph and the breakthrough for the com-

pany founded by Gottlieb Daimler. Benz's financiers take note and push Benz to construct competition vehicles. Six years later, the Lightning Benz is lauded as a shining example. In a rage over this decision, Carl Benz storms out of his company.

The key technical data of the race car with its typically plain body: a four-cylinder, in-line engine with two camshafts, overhead intake valves, upright exhaust valves. Compression: 4.5:1, 9,293 cc displacement and 60 hp. Mixture preparation by means of an updraft carburetor, a low voltage magneto ignition and high voltage system. Four-speed gearbox and coil clutch. Maximum speed: 117.6 km/h. Daimler had, in fact, wanted to field the 90 hp 12.7-liter Mercedes, however a fire in the factory sees the production plant and vehicles go up in flames. Daimler buys the 60 hp race cars back from his customers. ___

Wilhelm Maybach is the technical brain behind the exemplary Mercedes of 1903.

The Emperor's swift guests

The aerodynamic and well-proportioned engine hood makes the Pipe the most elegant starter in the German Gordon Bennett race.

What else?

At the automobile meet in Daytona, Florida, the billionaire Vanderbilt sets a new world record over the mile with a 90 hp Mercedes. He covers the 1,609 meters in 39 seconds and reaches a speed of 148.52 km/h.

___ After Belgium's Camille Jenatzy wins for Germany in his Mercedes at the 1903 Gordon Bennett Cup, Germany becomes the venue for the 1904 race. The German Automobile Club and the hastily established Gordon Bennett Committee, its members drawn from the higher echelons of society, put together a route consisting of an almost 140-kilometer loop in the Taunus region. This route leads from the Saalburg Fort to Usingen, Limburg and Idstein, on to Königstein, Oberursel and Homburg and back to the start. The race runs over four laps, covering a total distance of 564 kilometers.

To cope with demand for places – entries are limited to three per country – elimination heats are held in France and England. For Germany, the Daimler Motors Corporation fields two Mercedes (including the previous year's winner), and the Adam Opel company enters an Opel Darracq. The other participating nations of Austria, Italy, Belgium and Switzerland make a total of seven countries taking up the challenge, under the scrutiny of Emperor Wilhelm II and Prince Heinrich.

The 18-strong field constitutes the largest contingency in the Gordon Bennett Cup's brief history.

The Emperor considers the automobile to be a passing fad

Lining up alongside the white-painted cars from Stuttgart and Rüsselsheim are the green Wolseley and Napier (England), black-and-yellow Mercedes and Daimler (Austria), blue Richard Brasier, Mors and Turcat-Méry (France) and the red-and-yellow Dufaux from Switzerland. The Belgian squad makes a united stand with three yellow Pipe automobiles. They are the most interesting-looking cars in the race, but are the least powerful, producing only 60 hp. Their four-cylinder engines are concealed under an almost streamlined hood. The radiator sits at the height of the wheel hub at the front of the frame. The engine, flywheel and gearbox are also covered. The capacity of the chain-driven Pipe, also featuring an electromagnetic clutch (from the Jenatzy factory), is 13.5 liters, with the nominal rpm at 1,100. The OHV-engine is unique – overhead valves will only later become state-of-the-art technology. The driver and co-driver sit almost directly on top of the rear axle of the 994-kilogram vehicle. While the eventual winner Théry (Richard-Brasier) battles it out with Jenatzy at the front, Hautvast only manages to score sixth (behind three 90 hp Mercedes). Punctures throw his marque colleagues out of contention. ___

Not only do the drivers of that time have to deal with the vagaries of technology, but also with insufficient experience – this applies to drivers, navigators and spectators.

Victory to the four-leaf clover from Paris

___ The sixth and final race for the Gordon Bennett Cup (called simply the "Coupe International" by its founder) is again held in France. After a guest appearance in Germany – thanks to the 1903 Mercedes victory – the 1904-winning Richard-Brasier takes the cup back to France. Lining up to start are cars and drivers from France, Italy, Germany, Austria, Great Britain, and the USA.

In front of around 80,000 spectators, the first cars set off from the starting line in Clermont-Ferrand at 6am on July 5, 1905. Competitors face 550 kilometers of punctures, tire damage, and the eye-burning dust-binding agent Pulveranto. After 7 hours, 2 minutes and 42 seconds, the first contender crosses the line – and is rewarded with 100,000 Francs in prize money. In a repeat of the previous year, a Richard-Brasier wins again in 1905, courtesy of Frenchman Léon Théry and his mechanic Mueller. His steady, precise yet fast driving style earns him the nickname "Chronomètre Théry". The car features a four-cylin-

The Gordon Bennett Cup showcases the classic national colors

der engine and a three-speed gearbox. A bore of 160 millimeters and a stroke of 140 millimeters per cylinder result in a capacity of 11,259 cc, producing 96 hp.

The Richard-Brasier brand was established by Georges Richard and Henri Charles Brasier. Richard began in 1897, with the license to produce Benz, and the Vivinus, which he sold under his name. In 1902, the Mors co-owner merged with Richard.

From 1905, Brasier takes over the Paris-based company (Richard founds the Unic brand, today part of Iveco) and manufactures excellent automobiles until 1930, before the brand with the four-leaf clover in its emblem disappears from the scene.

In 1906, the Gordon Bennett Cup becomes a Grand Prix organized by the ACF. The venue: Le Mans. As in the Gordon Bennett Cup, three vehicles per nation are eligible to compete, and their origins must be easily recognizable through the specific color schemes. ___

▲ The Richard-Brasier tackling the 550-kilometer distance: Its 11-liter, 4-cylinder engine delivers 96 hp at 1,200 rpm via a 3-speed gearbox to the rear axle.

What else?

The Chadwick Six is the first automobile to feature a compressor. The target group of the 75 hp, 100 km/h six-cylinder, which costs between US$ 6,000–8,000, is gentleman drivers keen to drive their own vehicles and leave their chauffeurs at home.

◀ Léon Théry and his co-driver are protected from the wind and dirt spraying up from the road by leather valances. Théry is the most successful Gordon Bennett starter.

The 90 hp produced from the Renault AK 90 CV's 13-liter 4-cylinder engine is transmitted to the rear axle via a cardan shaft and driveshafts. The competition still relies on chain-drive systems.

What else?

Vincenzo Florio is one of the Grand Prix starters. That same year, the Sicilian shipowner will establish the first Targa Florio on his home island.

And the Tourist Trophy on the Isle of Man becomes part of the race calendar.

Marriot achieves a top speed of 205.404 km/h at the third speed meeting in Daytona, at the wheel of a Stanley steam-powered motor vehicle.

With the ACF's Grand Prix, the French village of Le Mans on the Sarthe goes down in motor racing history for the first time. To this day, Le Mans is famous for its 24-hour race.

Great motors for the Grand Prix

___ The year 1906 marks the beginning of a Grand Prix tradition on the 103.2-kilometer Circuit de la Sarthe on the outskirts of Le Mans, that is celebrated to this day. After France convincingly claims the Gordon Bennett Cup in 1905, the French are on the lookout for a new race format. Hence, the French Automobile Club (ACF) launches a new Grand Prix initiative. In addition to the Vanderbilt Cup, the two-day race, with a long leg contested on each day, turns into the motor racing highlight of the year. To be eligible to compete, vehicles must have a maximum weight of 1,000 kilograms (plus an additional 7 kilos for an ignition magneto) and a maximum fuel consumption of 30 liters for every 100 kilometers. Thirty-two vehicles line up on the grid, from the manufacturers Daracq, Panhard, Fiat, Italia, Mercedes, De Dietrich, Gobron-Brillié, Hotchkiss, Clément-Bayard, Richard-Brasier, Vulpès, Grégoire, and Renault. Fiat, Clément-Bayard, and Renault are fitted with new, service-friendly detachable rims, which save time when changing tires. At the wheel

of the winning Renault AK 90 CV is the Hungarian François Szisz. Next to him sits his mechanic Marteau. While the opposition put their trust in chain-drive systems, Renault uses a propshaft, driving the rigid rear axle via a leather-wrapped cone clutch and a three-speed gearbox. The four-cylinder engine with a 12,986 cc displacement puts out 105 hp at 1,200 rpm. The car tips the scales at 990 kilos and reaches 145 km/h.

With a patent-pending turbocharger (1902), unscrewable sparkplugs (1904) and the compressed-air starter (1906), Renault is one of the most innovative leaders in the automotive industry of that time. The alternator arrives in 1914, and 1923 heralds the brake booster.

It takes Renault driver Szisz 12 hours, 14 minutes and 7 seconds to cover the distance of 1,238 kilometers in the first Grand Prix car, achieving an average speed of over 100 km/h on the unpaved country road, tarred by pouring the contents of 500 drums of heavy mineral oil on the surface. ___

1907

Fiat Taunus Corsa

The right car
for every job

No driver can do without a co-driver. Instead of navigating, the "grease monkeys" help with practical matters such as changing tires, refueling, putting the gas tank under pressure, and other maintenance work. Sitting next to Vincenzo Lancia is his mechanic Pietro Bordini. Lancia also establishes the inaugural "Coppa della Velocità" race in Brescia in 1907, following the same format as the Targa Florio.

The Emperor's Prize is won by Lancia's teammate at Fiat, Felice Nazzaro, and his co-driver Fagnano. The Turin driver, whose racing career spans three decades, also wins the Targa Florio and the ACF Grand Prix that same year.

What else?

Motor racing gains in popularity around the world. With the Moscow to St. Petersburg challenge, the first Russian competition is held, covering a distance of 646 kilometers.

The long-distance challenge from Peking to Paris, held between 10 June and 10 August, covers more than 16,000 kilometers. Five vehicles compete, with victory going to Prince Scipione Borghese and his co-driver Ettore Guizzardi.

At Daytona, Mercedes driver Blakely wins the speed trials over 5, 10, and 100 miles. Over 10 miles, he averages 125.32 km/h.

___ The Fabbrica Italiana di Automobili Torino, or Fiat for short, wins the most important races of the year: the Targa Florio, the Emperor's Prize, and the Grand Prix de l'ACF. At the wheel is works driver Felice Nazzaro, who will later establish an automobile brand of the same name. The vehicles differ depending on the requirements, but they are all powered by four-cylinder motors. Fielded at the Targa Florio is the small Fiat 28-40 HP, producing 60 hp and with a displacement of 7,363 cc. At the Grand Prix held in Dieppe, Nazzaro drives a vehicle with a 16.3-liter, 4-cylinder engine putting out 130 hp. With a new consumption formula, which caps the maximum fuel consumption at 30 liters per 100 kilometers instead of the weight formula of 1,000 kilograms, the rule-makers of the French automobile club hope to prevent oversized displacements and want race cars to be closer to production vehicles. But they are largely ignored, as the huge capacity of the Fiat 130 HP demonstrates.

The Emperor's Prize race, on the other hand, is intended for touring cars with a maximum capacity of 8 liters and a maximum weight of 1,165 kilograms. Witnessed by the Emperor himself, the event is contested in the Taunus region not far from Frankfurt and runs over four laps totaling 472 kilometers. Fiat

The Fiat racing drivers Nazzaro and Lancia eventually establish their own car makes

prepares three Taunus Corsa cars for this race. Due to the large number of entries, two elimination heats are run over 236 kilometers, with the best 20 receiving a starting spot at the final race. Not surprisingly, the winning Fiat driver, Vincenzo Lancia (who has also just founded his own automobile brand), and Felice Nazzaro are among the finalists. Nazzaro also wins the main race in 5 hours and 34 minutes, at an average speed of almost 85 km/h, ahead of local heroes Opel. The maximum speed of the 72 hp (at 1,200 rpm) Fiat Taunus Corsa reaches 130 km/h, with a curb weight of 950 kg. The loaded Fiat, with its four cylinders arranged in pairs and a total displacement of 8,004 cc, weighs in at 1,175 kilograms.

That same year, the automobile is put to the test. At the suggestion of the French daily newspaper Le Matin, a challenge is held from Peking to Paris on June 10. From the 62 registered starters, only 11 reach the finish line (in 5 vehicles) after 15,000 kilometers of desert and steppe, dust and gravel. After exactly two months, the 40 hp Itala of the trio under Prince Scipione Borghese reaches the finish line first. Their closest pursuer, in a De Dion-Bouton, arrives in Paris three weeks later. ___

Weatherproof and with an extensive supply of spare parts, the Protos conquers the daunting distance from New York via Moscow to Paris. The team leaves Chicago in early March.

Tools, weapons, and 700 liters of fuel

___ On February 12, the world's longest automobile race sets off from the New York Times building. The route leads from New York via Moscow to Paris. Among the six competing vehicles are the brands Züst, De Dion-Bouton, Motobloc, and Thomas and Sizaire-Naudin, as well as the Protos 17-30 PS driven by First Lieutenants Hans Koeppen, Ernst Maass, and Hans Knape. Koeppen reaches the finish first, after 32,000 kilometers through North America, China, Mongolia, Siberia, and Russia – without Maass und Knape, who drop out before the end of the American stage. Taking their place in San Francisco is the American-German Snyder, who is picked up in Chicago, and Kaspar Neuberger and Robert Fuchs, who travel from Germany to continue on from Vladivostok. They reach Berlin on July 24, and Paris two days later. The four-cylinder Protos with cardan drive is fitted with a 30 hp 4.5-liter power unit. The vehicle differs from the production Protos Touring Car in its reinforced frame made of ultra-strong steel, as well as a double-bottomed floor for the massive fuel reserves. Initially, the German crew carries 700 liters of fuel, eventually decreasing to 520, and 100 liters of oil. With spare parts, tires, tools, provisions, weapons, and sledges, the vehicle tips the scales at 2.7 tonnes.

The removable Dunlop rims prove to be practical, making the necessary tire changes considerably easier. The vehicle is manufactured in Berlin-Reinickendorf, where Alfred Sternberg founded Protos in 1898. In 1908, the company is taken over by the Siemens-Schuckert factory; in 1926 it is sold to AEG and merges with NAG (Nationale Automobil Gesellschaft). A year later the company goes into liquidation. At the destination of this round-the-world challenge, the vehicle is disqualified in an arbitrary decision by the organizers, and is relegated to second place after the American Thomas. ___

During the ordeals faced by the vehicle and its crew, the superfluous ballast is gradually dumped. In Charbin (Manchuria), the Protos looks considerably more stripped down.

Only a bullet is faster

1908 & 1909
What else?

The inaugural Prince Heinrich Tour through Germany is contested from June 5–17, 1908.

In England, a tour of 2,000 miles is run in 1908, with the final 200 miles held on the Brooklands Oval.

In February 1909, a one-kilometer race on ice is contested close to Stockholm.

On March 8, 1909, France's most famous racing driver Lucien Théry dies at the age of 29, of oedema.

___ Between 1909 and 1912, Benz and other automobile manufacturers boycott the annual Grand Prix contested in France due to the preferential treatment given to French manufacturers. This leads to the first interruption in Grand Prix history. However, in the hands of privateers, the vehicles achieve world fame away from Grands Prix. Take, for example, the Benz race car of 1909. In November, Victor Héméry topples the seemingly unassailable 200 km/h mark. On the Brooklands track, opened in 1907, he reaches a speed of 202.7 km/h at the wheel of a Benz simply called the "Grand Prix type". The following spring, Barney Oldfield and his mechanic, protected from battering headwinds only by aviator glasses, achieve a world record speed of 211.267 km/h at Daytona Beach with a somewhat leaner and aerodynamically optimized sister car. Emperor Wilhelm II himself dispatches a message of congratulations. In 1911, a speed of 227.5 km/h is clocked. Oldfield christens

The "Lightning Benz" rapidly achieves world fame

his vehicle "Lightning Benz" and the nickname sticks. It will be ten years before the first aircrafts match the performance values of the "Lightning Benz", and another two years for the first planes to reach the speed of what was for many years the fastest car in the world.

The attractive two-seater, its hawk-like nose giving it an aggressive look, weighs 1.45 tonnes. Some 407 kilograms are attributed to the 21.5-liter four-cylinder in-line engine with paired combustion chambers, producing 200 hp at 1,600 rpm. The combination of heaviness, ponderous torque, ineffective springs at high speed, narrow wear-prone tires, and an unsophisticated frame design, as well as an unprotected seating position, demands a lot of courage and driving prowess from the drivers. Spectators flock in droves to witness the sensational speeds and to revere their heroes behind the wheels. A newspaper headline proclaims: "Only a bullet is faster!" ___

➤ The furious pace of Barney Oldfield on the sandy oval proves to be a spectacular drawcard for spectators.

▼ The engine of the Lightning Benz (aka Blitzen Benz) achieves a staggering 21.5-liter capacity, and puts out 200 hp. The vehicle is a legend to this day.

Showdown in Sicily

___ The 24 HP is the first vehicle to roll off the production line at Anonima Lombarda Fabbrica Automobile, also known as A.L.F.A. From the outset, it's obvious to engineer Giuseppe Merosi's team that the new sporty vehicle from Portello must prove its technical capabilities with motor racing success. The name is an indication of the produced horsepower. In fact, the 4,082 cc, 4-cylinder unit puts out 42 hp. The output of the Tipo Corsa in race trim even reaches 45 hp at 2,400 rpm. The engine block is made of cast iron, the light metal cylinder heads are fixed, with two side valves per cylinder. The force-feed lubrication is part of the advanced automotive technology of the Gründerzeit. The power from the four-speed gearbox is transferred via a cardan shaft to the rigid rear axle suspended on semi-elliptical leaf springs. Drum brakes are also mounted here. The racing version features a chassis with a paneled power unit, two seats and two fuel tanks with a total capacity of 130 liters.

In 1911, the 24 HP Corsa makes its debut at the already well-known Targa Florio. However, at the race on the island of Sicily, spraying mud robs A.L.F.A.-driver Nino Franchini of visibility and victory. His teammate Ugo Ronzoni retires in the third and final lap, exhausted. ___

▲ From day one, motorsport events like the Targa Florio are part of the A.L.F.A. sales and marketing development program.

Looking ahead and back

___ The now legendary 500-mile race in Indianapolis is contested for the first time on a 2.5-mile oval with four slightly banked corners and a track surface constructed from 3.2-million bricks. The racetrack, built in 1909 using Brooklands as a model, is one of the first circuits dedicated solely to automobile races. Initially the track is made of tar and gravel. But when the surface starts to break up at the inaugural event, causing major accidents, the course is immediately paved in bricks. To this day, the finish line, marked by the original bricks, is a testimony to the early "brickyard", which was only changed to an asphalt surface in 1935.

Ray Harroun wins the first-ever Indy 500 after 6 hours, 42 minutes and 11 seconds, with an average speed of just on 117 km/h. He sits at the wheel of a Marmon, which is given the name "Wasp" due to its yellow and black paintwork (see pg. 11 up).

Mounted under the Wasp's relatively streamlined and smoothly-cowled paneling is a 6-cylinder engine with a 7.8-liter displacement generating 105 hp at 1,700 rpm. Top speed is reached at around 140 km/h. Gear shifting is done via a three-speed gearbox. The slim body tapers to the rear, and the spokes of the open wheels are covered for aerodynamic efficiency. Causing a sensation, Ray Harroun competes without the mandatory mechanic at his side and hence enjoys a weight advantage. One of the mechanic's jobs is to observe the opposition and inform the driver of the situation. As a substitute, Harroun fits a rear-view mirror, the first in the history of the automobile. The mirror allows Harroun to keep a close eye on the competition. Also interesting is the fact that the Marmon is the first single-seater, and until 1914 it's the only six-cylinder to win a major race. Incidentally, after the Indianapolis event, motor racing experiences a boom, and an oval tradition is born in the United States. This quickly paves the way for the construction of more Speedways and Superspeedways. ___

The driver and co-driver of the Fiat S.74 almost disappear behind the hulking engine hood and aerodynamic paneling. Behind the crew, the fuel tank and reserve tire can be seen.

1910 – 1912
What else?

No ACF Grands Prix are held between 1909 and 1911 due to the global economic recession.

Ralph de Palma drives the Fiat S.74 1912 at the French Grand Prix. While his teammate Louis Wagner secures second at this gripping race, de Palma retires.

The hulk

___ In 1911, David L. Bruce-Brown launches the Fiat S.74 Corsa's career with his victory at the American Grand Prix in Savannah. Then it's back to Europe in 1912 to contest the revived Grand Prix de l'ACF, which had been abandoned in 1908. The Grand Prix, this time held in Dieppe, pulls the ailing motor racing scene out of a three-year slump. The 1,540-kilometer race is run over two days, with drivers completing 10 laps per day. Lining up alongside Fiat are vehicles from Peugeot, Lorraine-Dietrich, Sunbeam, and Vauxhall. Fiat, however, belongs to the circle of favorites. Eligible to race are open-wheeled vehicles and up to 3,000-cc Voiturettes.

The Fiat spends its racing career in Europe and America

Vehicles with a displacement of up to three liters indeed belong to the smaller capacity category: the Fiat has a volume of 14,137 cc! Thanks to the long-stroke layout (150 x 200 mm bore x stroke), the piston speeds remain relatively low and the engine receives better cooling. At 1,600 rpm, the brawny 4-cylinder unit produces 190 hp. The four-speed gearbox is operated by a gearshift lever mounted externally.

On day one of the Grand Prix, David L. Bruce-Brown crosses the finish line first after around six-and-a-half hours. Alas, he's disqualified the following day for allegedly refueling his car away from the pit area after colliding with a dog, resulting in a punctured fuel tank. Victory is handed to Boillot in a Peugeot, with Louis Wagner taking second place 13 minutes behind him in another Fiat. Back in America, Bruce-Brown is killed while practicing for the 500-mile race at Indianapolis. Fiat again wins the American Grand Prix, which is now contested in Milwaukee, with racing driver Caleb Bragg at the wheel.

Peugeot's victory in Dieppe (and at the Indy 500) heralds a new era of race car design: The more modern construction of the L76, with its lighter design and a smaller engine (7.6 liters), as well as four desmodromic valves per combustion chamber and two camshafts, makes life for cars like the S.74 increasingly difficult.

Still significant today

____ After winning the 1912 Grand Prix in Dieppe, the Peugeot L76 continues its winning streak in Indianapolis. Its avant-garde four-cylinder engine has a displacement of 7,598 cc, which makes it one of the smaller calibers of that time. Still, the vehicle is capable of fighting for overall victory. To improve performance, the combustion chambers of the engine are spherical and vented by means of four valves. It also features two overhead camshafts.

The regulations benefit the lighter competition cars. The ACF introduces new rules for the 1913 Grand Prix, this time held close to Amiens, now covering a distance of 917 kilometers. The rules stipulate that the vehicles must weigh between 800 and 1,100 kilograms. Maximum consumption is set at 20 liters per 100 kilometers. Contesting the event are vehicles from Delage, Excelsior, Itala, Mathis, Schneider, Sunbeam, Opel, and Peugeot. Peugeot

fields a vehicle powered by a 115 hp (at 2,200 rpm) 4-cylinder engine with a displacement of 5,565 cc. Dry sump lubrication is used for the first time. This not only ensures better cooling, it also improves lubrication during cornering and hard braking. At the wheel of the race car, capable of a 168 km/h top speed, the works drivers Boillot and Goux score a double victory. The advances made in the power output per liter of the Grand Prix racer are impressive: while 8 hp per liter of displacement was enough for the Fiat 130 HP to win in 1907, the Peugeot generates almost 20.5 hp per liter. ____

With the introduction of the new consumption regulations for the ACF Grand Prix, the displacement of the Peugeot four-cylinder is reduced by two liters. Grand Prix winner Boillot gets by with 17 of the permitted 20-liter maximum per 100 kilometers.

A great victory before the Great War

___ In 1914, before Germany pulls Europe and half the world into war, Daimler draws attention to the innovative technical abilities of its engineers with a triple victory at the most important race of the year, the French Grand Prix. Four valves per combustion chamber and an overhead camshaft driven by a vertical shaft is the technical legacy of former Daimler engineer Wilhelm Maybach. The four individual cylinders of the 105 hp (at 3,100 rpm) engine tower above the sturdy crankcase. The mixture in the combined 4,483-cc combustion chambers is formed via a piston valve carburetor by means of three spark plugs and two ignition magnets per cylinder.

The power transmission of the Grand Prix car, which is capable of reaching 180 km/h, is achieved by means of a double cone clutch and a four-speed gearbox. The brake pedal actuates a mechanical band brake. Christian Lautenschlager covers the 752-kilometer Grand Prix distance from Lyon at a brisk 105 km/h average in 7 hours, 8 minutes, and 18.4 seconds.

As is customary, the three factory cars make the trip to France and back under their own power. Daimler builds four of these 1,080-kilo vehicles, which are driven by works drivers like Lautenschlager, Otto Salzer, Louis Wagner, and Max Sailer. When war breaks out, one of the vehicles is in England and is confiscated. Rolls Royce engineers use the motor as a model for aircraft engines. But even after the war, the Mercedes Grand Prix race car is still the preferred choice: With a rebuilt Grand Prix car, Count Giulio Masetti wins the 1922 Targa Florio. And the technology of the Mercedes "Grand Prix" is extolled as a paragon for race cars of this era. ___

The first Cannonball

___ Long before the chief editor of *Car & Driver*, Brock Yates, initiates the legendary Cannonball Run in the 1970s – notorious for breaking traffic rules; nothing in common with serious motor racing – the crossing of the vast North American continent lures drivers eager to break records. Participants in the 1908 competition from New York to Paris had only one leg

The name Cannonball stands for 4,800 kilometers in 11 days

(ending in San Francisco) to conquer on the continent, and this took considerably longer than a month. Now, just five years later, Erwin George Baker covers the same route from San Diego to New York in a brief 11 day, 7 hours and 15 minute-sprint, earning himself the nickname Cannonball. On the 4,800-kilometer route from coast to coast, Baker sets 143 new distance records and thus drums up good publicity for his car, a Stutz Bearcat.

Between 1911 and 1935, and again from 1968 into the 1980s, vehicles are manufactured under the name Stutz. The company quickly earns itself a reputation for producing first-class cars. During its early years, when an unhappy customer complains to the Stutz Motor Company about being overtaken by a Mercedes driver, Stutz promptly dispatches Erwin George Baker on another trip across the States.

The Bearcat, inspired by a Stutz Indy racing car, has been part of the model range since the previous year and is built up until 1924. The key features of the swift two-seater, which is capable of reaching 100 kilometers per hour, are: four cylinders, four valves per combustion chamber, a total capacity of 6.4 liters, 50 hp, and a weight of 2,040 kilos. The sprint from zero to top speed takes just on half a minute. To protect the driver from inclement weather, the vehicle features a tiny, round "monocle" windshield. Interestingly, the Bearcat's gearbox is positioned at the rear axle, making it an early example of transaxle design. However, the downside is that customers have to use a lot of pedal power to actuate the clutch. This makes the Stutz a man's car. ___

Old Europe in the New World

While the cannons are booming and the ground in Europe shakes, racing drivers such as Dario Resta in his Peugeot EX5 seek sanctuary and competition in the New World.

____ The vehicles of Frenchman Armand Peugeot conquer the New World. In 1913, a Peugeot L76 (with drums on all four wheels) wins the 500-mile race of Indianapolis. The manufacturer from the environs of Paris will repeat this feat in 1916, at the final Indy race before its cessation due to the war, and again in 1919 at the first post-war Indy 500.

The L76 from 1913 is succeeded by the EX3, which scores its first win at the French Grand Prix and again at the San Francisco round of the Vanderbilt Cup. A new Peugeot EX5 then emerges in time for the race in Santa Monica. The EX5, producing 112 hp (at 2,800 rpm) and reaching just under 190 km/h with four-cylinders and a displacement of 4,494 cc, celebrates its European debut in 1914.

The Vanderbilt Cup is the U.S. equivalent of the Gordon Bennett Cup, and William K. Vanderbilt's attempt to spark great interest in motor racing amongst Americans is successful. He commissions Tiffany to make a trophy that will be awarded to the winner of the annual American Vanderbilt Cup from 1904. The race, which is initially based on Grand Prix rules and later on Indianapolis regulations, becomes so popular that it regularly attracts the greatest names in racing. The final two events are won by Auto Union with Tazio Nuvolari (1936) and Bernd Rosemeyer. ____

Innovative technology
Innovative body

___ For years, the world has been in flames, and the noise of the racetracks has given way to the booms of the battlefields throughout Europe. Yet, there are engineers like the American Harry Arminius Miller who come up with innovations to advance automobile design. In 1917, his shimmering bronze stream-lined vehicle with its aluminum alloy engine, four-valve heads with desmodromic valve control, dual ignition, and dry sump lubrication turns heads. The 4.8-liter, 4-cylinder unit produces 136 hp at 2,950 revs per minute. The Miller Aerodynamic Coupé is given the nickname "Golden Submarine" and is the first streamlined vehicle in America. Even in Europe, there are very few examples – for instance the A.L.F.A. 40/60 HP Aerodinamica with Castagna body, from the year 1914. The aluminum body is wind-tunnel tested. Another innovation is the integrated rollover protection, built at the request of the driver Barney Oldfield after witnessing his friend and rival Bob Burman die in a crash in Corona, California, the previous year. The Aerodynamic Coupé, reaching 170 km/h and weighing in at 725 kilograms, cele-brates its debut in mid-1917 at the Maywood Speed-way near Chicago.

Harry A. Miller is considered one of the most cre-ative minds in the pioneering days of American mo-torsport. In 1923 he fields the first single-seaters at Indianapolis and they promptly win. Notching up more successes in the 1920s and early 1930s, Miller becomes one of the most sought-after race car en-gineers. Of the 54 races it contests, the Golden Sub-marine wins 20 of them, and clinches second and third place twice.

___

Straight-eight
and four cars in
the oval

___ When the guns finally fall silent after four years of war, and the armistice agreement is signed, seven months pass before the start of the first great in-ternational motorsport event, the 500-mile race of Indianapolis. Duesen-berg and Ballot field their new in-line eight-cylinder racers at the oval. The mastermind behind the new Ballot is the constructor Ernest Henry, who designed and built the car within a very short time.

Indianapolis hosts the first race of the post-war era

The regulations limit the displacement to 300 cu-bic inches, which is around 4,917 cc. With 4,894 cc, Henry pushes the boundaries with the long-stroke engine of the Ballot "Indianapolis". As with the long stroke (74 x 140 mm/bore x stroke), Henry is also at the leading edge, with an auxiliary frame for the engine and a four-speed gearbox. This provides ad-ditional stability and leaves the power unit unaf-fected by the flexing of the frame. For durability, the cylinder heads with two overhead camshafts and four valves per combustion chamber is firmly fixed to the engine block – at this time, the seals cannot withstand the potential stresses of high-perfor-mance race engines. The pistons and crankcase are made of aluminum, with the cast-iron block divided into two four-cylinder banks. Taking inspiration from Bugatti's aviation engine, the crankshaft features two units of four crankpins, and central drive. Thanks to dry sump lubrication, the engine safely achieves an impressive 3,500 rpm. The chassis with semi-elliptical springs at the front and rear axles is based on a pre-war design. Ballot budgets 30,000 British pounds for the Ballot quartet to contest the Indy 500.

War silences the race engines in 1918

When the engines rev up again after the war, race car designers benefit from the wartime boom in air-craft construction. The arms race of previous years heralds new insights into metallurgy. This allows the construction of lighter, higher-revving engines. Overhead camshafts be-come standard issue. Aero-dynamics take on an in-creasingly important role. The previously open rear sections of the vehicles now feature a more streamlined design.

Ultimately, the winner is neither the Ballots (un-questionably the fastest vehicles in the race) nor the Duesenbergs (inspired by the powerful Bugatti aviation engines). In a repeat of the 1916 Indianapo-lis race – before it was paused due to the war – vic-tory goes to a Peugeot, Ernest Henry's previous em-ployer.

___

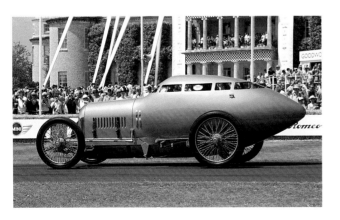

The rise of the small car

After its successful start at the 1921 "Grand Prix de Voiturettes" in Brescia (right), the small Bugatti 13 is nicknamed Brescia. The compact sports car from Alsace turns into a guaranteed winner – for its drivers and the company.

◄ The Type 13 undergoes several technical tweaks. Still, the mechanics of the delicate Voiturette remain fragile, as shown here in the image of the British gentleman driver Raymond Mays at the 1924 hill-climb event in Wales.

What else?

Opel opens its own 1.6-kilometer test track in Hessen, Germany, with a public race.

Opel competes in Brooklands, with success. Opel's outing on the British racetrack marks the first international appearance for German competitors since the end of the First World War.

➤ The birth of the Type 13 took place before WWI. However, the Voiturette doesn't celebrate its greatest triumph until the early 1920s. Friedrich sat at the wheel of a compact Bugatti Type 13 as early as 1911.

___ The world is in a state of upheaval. The waves of the storm that buffeted the entire globe are only just beginning to subside. Hence it's hardly surprising that pre-1914 material is being used in motor racing. The Milan-based company now known as Alfa Romeo fields the 1914-spec Grand Prix A.L.F.A. at the Targa Florio. And after a long break, a race for small 350–500-kilogram Voiturettes with a maximum displacement of 1.4 liters is held at Le Mans. In America, motorsport enjoys a quicker return to normality. After the debut of the new eight-cylinder race cars at the Indy 500 in 1919, the organizers of the oval race introduce a limit on displacement for the years 1920 to 1925. By reducing the cubic inches from 300 to 183, or from almost five liters (4,916 cc) to three, the interest of European customers just might be piqued. For this race, Peugeot develops a four-cylinder car with five valves per cylinder.

The Bugatti, which won the 415-kilometer Le Mans race, seems significantly less imposing. The

With the Brescia, Bugatti begins its sporting rise

400-kilo Voiturette is shod with delicate tires that seem more suited to a bicycle. The model marks the first chapter in the history of avant-garde automobiles from the factory of Ettore Bugatti. The two-seater appeared in 1910, with a two-valve cylinder head, and achieved second place at the 1911 Grand Prix in Le Mans. It was produced up until the start of the war. With his factory in Alsace, the Milan-born Ettore Bugatti suddenly found himself on the wrong side. Bugatti managed to smuggle two of the five new race cars to Italy, while the three remaining vehicles were disassembled and buried on the company premises. After Bugatti's return to Molsheim in Alsace in 1919, the company celebrated its revival on the racetrack. And with the resumption of production, the Type 13 features a 16-valve cylinder head. The small four-cylinder heralds the rise of Bugatti to the sporting Olympus. Victory at Le Mans marks the beginning of a career crowned by innumerable successes, which to this day earns the brand worldwide acclaim. At the wheel of the car sits Ernst Friedrich, Bugatti's engineer, manager, and race driver. In 1921, when he wins the Grand Prix of Brescia run specifically for Voiturettes, the Type 13 is dubbed the Brescia. It is still known by this name today. By 1926, almost 2000 units of this model have been made. ___

The name says it all

___ The term Chitty Chitty Bang Bang came to be associated with a certain type of post-WWI race car, thanks to the book written by James Bond author, Ian Fleming (later turned into an Oscar-nominated movie starring Dick van Dyke and Gert Fröbe). The name Chitty Chitty Bang Bang says it all – or at least represents an entire vehicle species of the early 1920s.

In the years before the First World War, race cars were built with aircraft engines boasting monstrous capacities. After WWI, there was a conglomeration of leftover plane engines. Not surprisingly, manufacturers attempt to utilize war technology in the construction of race cars.

However, it's the lighter race cars with smaller capacities that make the breakthrough at this time. The future belongs to them. By comparison, the Chitty Chitty Bang Bangs, with their dinosaur-like dimensions and weights, seem like relics of a bygone era. Typical of this vehicle type is Chitty Chitty Bang Bang Number One, commissioned by Count Louis Vorow Zborowski and mounted with a 23-liter, 6-cylinder inline engine producing 300 hp, taken from a Gotha bomber. The vehicle is based on a Mercedes touring chassis from 1913 and is completed in 1921. The four-seater is capable of speeds exceeding 100 mph, and that year wins two competitions at Brooklands. The car is so loud that Zborowski, a Kent resident, is banned from driving it within the city walls of Canterbury.

This car is followed up with the No. 2, in which the Count travels to North Africa. It has an 18.8-liter displacement and 230 hp. A third vehicle, featuring modified Mercedes technology, puts out 180 hp. The fourth Chitty Chitty Bang Bang emerges with a 450 hp, 27-liter, 12-cylinder aircraft engine and the gearbox and chain-drive system from the Lightning Benz.

In 1924, Count Zborowski is killed at the Italian Grand Prix in a Mercedes, the same marque in which his father was killed during the Nice Race Week of 1903. The No 4. Chitty Chitty Bang Bang is given the name "Babs" by its new owner, J.G. Parry-Thomas, and in 1926 sets a world speed record for land vehicles with 273.6 km/h. ___

Porsche's first winner

___ Scoring a double victory at the 1922 Targa Florio, the small Austro-Daimler attracts attention. And the average speed set by Alfred Neubauer's "Sascha" in the race car category earns respect. Alfred Neubauer, the future race director of Mercedes-Benz, is joined by Fritz Kuhn from Austro-Daimler's vehicle test division, and Lambert Pöcher. A fourth vehicle is piloted by Count Alexander Kolowrat, nicknamed Sascha, from whom the car gets its name. The technical mastermind behind the Sascha is the young Ferdinand Porsche, who is eager to underline the capabilities of small, light, and more affordable automobiles. After the end of the First World War, the Voiturettes enjoy increasing popularity.

Austro-Daimler's origins go back to 1899, as a subsidiary of Daimler. In 1900, their first automobile was designed, and from 1902, Paul Daimler, the son of Gottlieb Daimler, took over development as the company head. With the 90 hp Mercedes from Wiener Neustädt, the brand contested its maiden race in 1904. The year 1905 heralded one of the first all-wheel-drive vehicles, and the following year Porsche took over as head of development. In 1909, Austro-Daimler parted ways with its German heritage. By the 1920s, Austro-Daimler is manufacturing aircraft engines, commercial vehicles, and armaments, as well as competition cars. Scoring 43 wins and 8 second places from 51 races, Sascha is the most successful of these vehicles. And it has only half the output of the first race cars from Vienna. Producing 45 hp at 5,000 rpm and with a 1.1-liter capacity, it achieves a speed of 144 km/h. ___

◄ The Austro-Daimler "Sascha" is a vital vehicle for the designer Ferdinand Porsche as well as the eventual Mercedes-Benz race director Alfred Neubauer. Standing beside the victorious "Sascha" at the Graz Ries Hill Climb are Ferdinand Porsche and his son Ferry (to the right, behind the radiator). Incidentally, the red paintwork at the Targa Florio is supposed to make Sicilian bandits believe it's a local car.

➤ With its mid-engine, deeper seat position and teardrop shape, the Benz-Tropfenwagen looks like it comes from another planet. Its best results, however, are positions four and five at the Italian Grand Prix.

1921 – 1923
What else?

In 1921, the AVUS (Automobile Traffic and Test Road) in Berlin is opened for general traffic.

In 1921, the inaugural Gran Premio d'Italia is added to the race calendar, along with the revived ACF Grand Prix. This is contested on the outskirts of Brescia Jimmy Murphy wins the French Grand Prix at Le Mans in a Duesenberg.

In 1922, the Italian Grand Prix is contested at Monza on a racetrack built in just 100 days.

▼ The look of the Benz rear-engine race car breaks away from convention. The teardrop-shaped attachment at the front axle is the water reservoir for the radiator on which it is perched.

The creative twenties

___ While single-seater race cars are the norm at Indianapolis, in Europe the first supercharged race car (Fiat 805-405) claims a Grand Prix win. Designers such as Gabriel Voisin and Ettore Bugatti turn their attention to the aerodynamic design of their race vehicles. The Type 32 Bugatti, with its unconventionally smooth body (which even covers the wheels), earns itself the nickname "tank". And in Stuttgart too, streamlining plays an increasingly important role in the design of the new in-house designated Benz RH (RH stands for race car rear engine). The first attempts are made to advance race car construction using scientific insights. The team at Benz is also breaking new ground technologically with the engine layout: in the "Tropfenwagen" (so called for its teardrop shape), the motor is now mounted midship for the first time. In addition, the Tropfenwagen features individual wheel suspension and four external brakes. The Benz engineers push the lightweight boundaries to the edge and drill the entire vehicle, including the gearstick and throttle pedal, with holes.

The aviation designer Edmund Rumpler helps design the Tropfenwagen

Powering the RH is a 1,997 cc, 6-cylinder engine with two overhead camshafts. The motor, fitted with a 4-valve head, produces 90 horsepower at 5,000 rpm. In the days of supercharged engines, this isn't a particularly outstanding achievement. However, the improved aerodynamics allow drivers to match the performance of more powerful vehicles.

The Tropfenwagen celebrates its premiere at the 1923 Grand Prix of Europe held in Monza, finishing fourth against significantly more powerful opponents – the supercharged vehicles of Fiat and Miller. In a time marked by inflation, strikes, and a scarcity of materials, the Tropfenwagen is unable to contest more international events. The economic crisis and the agreement to merge with Daimler work against further outings for the innovative Tropfenwagen. In 1924, the over 160 km/h car is fielded in several national races and is ultimately – fitted with headlights and fenders – converted into a sports car. In total, four Tropfenwagen are built. ___

Simple, stunning, victorious

___ Between 1924 and 1934, the Bugatti Type 35 notches up more than 2,000 victories, making the T35 the most famous racing sports car of its time, and thus contributing decisively to the world fame that the brand still enjoys today under Volkswagen ownership. The Type 35 is a true all-round genius, which it underlines at Grands Prix, sports car races and touring car events in the hands of mainly wealthy works drivers and amateurs. The Grand Prix racer celebrates its debut in 1924 at Lyon. As is customary, the car is driven to the venue and immediately captivates with its unpretentious beauty. Until the creation of the Type 35, no other designer has managed to come up with such a delicate yet powerful race car. The proportions are harmonious; the details, such as the first-ever alloy thick-spoked wheels with inte-

The Bugatti 35 is the world's most successful sports car at the time

grated brake drums, are eye-catching. Another attractive feature is the in-line 8-cylinder engine generating 95 horsepower at 6,000 rpm – still without supercharging. The displacement is adapted to the two-liter formula regulations that are in effect. Other Type 35 vehicles are based on this model, including the T35A, also known as the "Course Imitation". The T35A is a less-expensive touring car version, without pricey aluminum wheels and with a less sophisticated motor (red-banded at 4,000). Thanks to supercharging, the 35B and 35C models produce over 130 hp and up to 180 hp (35B). While the more powerful T35B has a displacement of 2.3 liters, the 2-liter Grand Prix version T35C (C stands for Compresseur) proves to be higher revving. The 35B is also called the TC (Targa Compressor),

➤ Grand Prix cars are already hurtling through the tight Loews curve in Monaco in 1924. This hairpin is still a part of today's Grand Prix track, but has long since been renamed Grand Hotel for the name of the establishment at this location.

◄ From 1925 to 1929, a Bugatti 35 wins the Targa Florio. However, in 1925, Ferdinand de Vizcaya, shown here in this photo, retires, opening the door to victory to his brand colleague Meo Costantini.

What else?

Du Pont develops fast-drying paint, thus making the manufacturing of vehicles faster.

After the Monte Carlo rallies of 1911 and 1912, this event enjoys a renaissance in 1924 and has been a regular fixture on the annual rally calendar ever since.

as it is based on the 1926 Type 35T (Targa) with its capacity increased by 300 cc for the Targa Florio. Eight decades later, the driving performance of the 700-kilo aluminum racer is still remarkable.

The Type 35 celebrates its greatest successes at Grand Prix races. And even though these 500-, 1,000- or even up to 2,500-kilometre races are contested by just one driver, the aluminum body – as stipulated by the regulations – is designed for two occupants. Single-seaters will only emerge in 1931 with the Alfa Romeo Tipo A, featuring two six-cylinder engines assembled side by side. However, because the space for a driver and mechanic is extremely tight, the gear and hand-brake levers are positioned externally on the right-hand side of the RHD. In most cases, the spare wheel is mounted on the left-hand side of the cockpit. The pedalry is no less unconventional: the brake pedal is fitted above the clutch and throttle. This would be hard to imagine today.

In the early 1930s, the starting price for prospective T35C owners will be 40,000 Francs. By the 21st century, these gems will fetch prices between 500,000 and a million Euros, depending on their originality and history. Decisive factors contributing to the illustrious history of the vehicles won't only be the races they contest, but also the drivers who sit behind the thin, large, four-spoke steering wheel: big-league race drivers such as Louis Chiron, René Dreyfus, Jean-Pierre Wimille, Elisabeth Junek, "Williams", Pierre Veyron (whose name was given to the 1,001 hp super sports car from Bugatti), as well as Achille Varzi and Tazio Nuvolari.

In addition to the many drivers who make a name for themselves thanks to their Bugatti victories, the quality of the vehicles from Molsheim in Alsace feeds the reputation of their designer Ettore Bugatti, whose stature has been compared to the patriarch Enzo Ferrari and whose design genius was equal to that of Ferdinand Porsche.

The first world champion

___ Vittorio Jano conceives the design of the first eight-cylinder from Alfa Romeo. The designer had moved to Milan from Fiat in 1923, and immediately came up with sketches for a new Grand Prix race car.

As early as June 1924, the P2 celebrates a win at the Cremona circuit. The speeds reached at its debut are impressive: 158 km/h on average and a top speed of 195 for the flying kilometer. However, clinching the title at the inaugural World Manufacturer's Championship in 1925 is the greatest triumph. Alfa Romeo takes home the title ahead of Duesenberg and Bugatti. At this time, only four venues host the world championship rounds. As there is no obligation to contest all races, victories at the European Grand Prix (Spa-Francorchamps) and Italy (Monza) are enough for the Milan contingent to win the title. At the Grand Prix de l'ACF, contested at Montlhéry, Antonio Ascari, father of the eventual Ferrari champion Alberto, is killed in an accident with the P2. Alfa Romeo withdraws its cars from the race. As a consequence, the 500-mile race at Indianapolis is contested without the works team from northern Italy. Proud of securing the title, Alfa incorporates the golden laurel wreath in its emblem.

Under the long front hood lies a two-liter eight-cylinder engine with a fixed cylinder head and supercharger. Initially, the motor, with a 6:1 compression ratio, puts out 140 hp at 5,500 rpm, and ultimately 155 horsepower. This is comparable to a specific liter output of 78 hp. The 750-kilogram lightweight monoposto accelerates up to 225 km/h. Over the next few years, until 1929, the six P2 built for open formula racing feature different designs for the rear. One variant has the spare wheel mounted longitudinally into the tapered tail of the world championship-winning vehicle, while another version has the wheel fixed transversely behind a massive fuel tank. ___

Alfa Romeo proudly incorporates the golden laurel in its badge

Vittorio Jano will go down in history as one of the greatest designers, creating vehicles including the Alfa Romeo 6C 1750 and the 8C 2300, the P2 and P3, as well as various Lancia models and Ferrari's Dino engines.

What else?

From 1925, the circuit of Montlhéry, just outside Paris, becomes the venue for the French Grand Prix.

Pete de Paolo is the first to complete the Indianapolis 500-mile race in less than five hours, thus breaking the 100-mph mark.

The eight-cylinder supercharged race car wins two of the three Grands Prix of 1924. The following year, the car is victorious twice, enough for Alfa Romeo to claim the inaugural World Championship title.

The Indianapolis victory of 1914 and the successes of the "Golden Twenties" represent the heyday of the French make Delage, before it disappears from the market in 1935 due to the Great Depression.

Hot-shoe masterpiece

What else?

For Grand Prix racing, a 1.5-liter regulation is introduced. The minimum weight of the vehicle is set at 600 kilograms.

___ As early as 1922, the V12 conceived by Delage proves to be one of the most innovative and superior cars of the two-liter era – especially when, in 1925, it receives a power boost, thanks to supercharging. For the 1926 season, capacity is reduced to 1.5 liters. In addition, the minimum weight is set at 600 kilograms with the minimum width of the optional one- or two-seater body prescribed at 80 centimeters. Delage creates the eight cylinder 15-S-8.

A drawback for the pilots of the Albert Lory-designed Delage is the unfavorable position of the exhaust pipes on the right – they roast the drivers' legs and feet. Moreover, the pilots are almost overcome by exhaust fumes. Even the most tenacious and blister-tormented among them have to occasionally take a break to cool off and grab some fresh air during the race, which runs over hundreds of kilometers. The Delage wins the Grand Prix of England on the Brooklands circuit. Sharing driving duties are Robert Sénéchal and Louis Wagner. Robert Benoist, too, takes a turn at the wheel of the unusually flat and sophisticated Delage 15-S-8. Everything that spins in the engine uses ball- or roller

A combustion engine yields over 100 hp per liter for the first time

bearings as a pivot; the vehicle is equipped with no less than 60 bearings. The twin-compressor straight-eight with dual overhead camshafts in a fixed cylinder head is the first race engine with a power output exceeding 100 hp per liter – it's a sensational 110 hp/l. Ultimately, the drivers can call on 165 hp at 6,500 rpm. For the 1927 season, the cars are revised, with the exhaust moved to the left side of the engine. Thus the problems of excruciating heat and toxic fumes are relegated to the past, and output increases to 170 hp. With this, the 15-S-8 proves unbeatable.

Aside from the Bugatti Type 39A, the Delage represents the most convincing design for the 1.5-liter formula, which will be in force until 1927. From 1928, the engine size must correspond to a vehicle weight window of between 550 and 750 kilograms. From 1929, the weight is increased to at least 900 kilograms, however, fuel consumption is limited to a maximum of 14 kilograms. For Delage, this vacillation ultimately heralds the end of the factory engagement in Grand Prix races. The race cars are acquired by private drivers, and the marque turns its attention to building upmarket road cars. ___

Records and victories
for a heavyweight

The mighty Mercedes-Benz win the inaugural race on the Nürburgring in 1927 (left). In its stripped down version, the technically refined sports car becomes the SS. The power plus, by means of a compressor, turns it into the SSK. The lightweight version is given the name SSKL.

◄ And at the Klausen Pass Hill Climb (photo) and the Mille Miglia, Mercedes-Benz joins the winners' ranks courtesy of the robust SSK.

What else?

The inaugural 1,000-mile Brescia-Rome-Brescia takes off. Until 1957, the Mille Miglia will be regarded as one of the world's greatest road races. The victorious OM-crew, consisting of Minoja/Morandi, takes around 21 hours to cover the distance. Eleven years later, it takes Biondetti/Stefani less than twelve hours with their Alfa Romeo 8C 2900 B. The average speed increases from 77.2 km/h to 135.4 km/h.

___ June 1927 marks the inauguration of the Nürburgring, Germany's first permanent racetrack. Mercedes-Benz sends Adolf Rosenberger and Rudolf Caracciola to contest the maiden race with the recently completed S model. It's the only factory-run car in the field. Nevertheless, the young Caracciola's victory is impressive; he wins the nearly 400-kilometer race in just under four hours. At the German Grand Prix, contested over 500 kilometers, Mercedes-Benz S wins again. And the following years, the road to victory at the 'Ring is the exclusive domain of the sports cars from Stuttgart. In the years 1927 and 1928 there's hardly a weekend when the S-pilots fail to bring home the laurels. The year 1928 alone yields 53 wins.

The father of the Mercedes S is Ferdinand Porsche, who is working for Daimler-Benz at this time. Using the model K as a basis, he creates the soon-to-be-legendary S. The letter S stands for Sport, and the car features a flatter frame with holes drilled in the cross members to reduce weight. The straight-six power unit has moved 30 centimeters towards the middle of the vehicle.

Thanks to a lower height, and the position of the center of gravity, the vehicle in its various body variants enjoys excellent road-holding qualities. The 6,789 cc vertical-shaft engine with overhead camshafts produces 120 hp at 3,200 rpm without supercharging, and 170 hp with a supercharger actuated. A horizontal carburetor converts up to 30 liters of fuel into a combustible mixture to cover 100 kilometers. Drivers of the two-seater sports version, which is capable of achieving 170 km/h, readily accept this, and rave about the phenomenal throttle response of the hefty vehicles, some weighing 1.7 tonnes, many reaching even 2 tonnes. Obviously, the S is anything but a delicate racer.

In 1928, the S, equipped with a dual ignition system (magnet and battery), as well as two spark plugs per combustion chamber and now producing 170 hp (alternatively 225 hp), serves as the baseline for the "Super Sports" (SS). The performance data are identical to the S, however the capacity increases to 7,068.5 cc. Moreover, the balance of the crankshaft has improved and the oil reservoir grows from 8 to 15 liters. In the hands of sportsmen such as Caracciola and Malcolm Campbell, it will turn into a winner, for instance at the Tourist Trophy races of 1929 and 1931. Caracciola's priceless factory vehicle produces 190/250 hp. And although the Great Depression puts a halt to Mercedes' factory outings, well-heeled privateers fly the flag.

The father of the Mercedes-Benz S is none other than Ferdinand Porsche

Next comes the SSK, featuring a short wheelbase and the ultra-strong "elephant" compressor that pumps the engine up to 240/300 hp. Riddled with holes to reduce weight, 125 kilograms lighter, and costing 40,000 Deutschmark, is the SSKL (super/sport/short/light), with which Caracciola will win the Mille Miglia in 1931. In 1932, Manfred von Brauchitsch will win there again, this time with the streamlined SSKL, dubbed "Zeppelin on wheels", created by the aerodynamicist Reinhard von Koenig-Fachsenfeld. ___

Explosive idea

The first secret trials of the rocket-powered, speed-trial vehicle take place in April 1928 with the RAK 1 on the Opel track south of Rüsselsheim. On Berlin's AVUS, the RAK 2 pilot Fritz von Opel achieves a speed of over 230 km/h in May 1928 – as witnessed by large numbers of spectators and journalists.

Driving the rocke[...]re on Opel's race track in Rüs- is a great adven[...]11, 1928, it takes the black Opel Fritz von Opel.[...]econds to catapult from zero to he philosophi[...]ished onlookers witness the car the future of [...]ard by a dozen rockets, although cles and spa[...]re up. The masterminds behind the manned spa[...]Opel founder's grandson, Fritz von [...]sionary Max Valier, [...]nufacturer Friedrich [...]r. At the wheel is Opel [...] race driver Kurt C.

[...]een to aim higher. On [...]ountdown to stage two [...]Opel launching the RAK 2 on Berlin's

Wha[...]

The In[...] The RAK 2 is powered by 24 solid-fuel Trial i[...] technical specs: 24 solid-propellant time[...]h a caliber of 80 mm, each packed with over[...]acked gunpowder. Length 500 mm, jet ters[...]5 mm, nozzle opening 90 mm. The aver- run[...]t per unit of propellant is 250 kg. This Mi[...]e streamlined vehicle with lateral stabiliz- Be[...]s has 120 kg of explosives on board – is[...]to pulverize entire neighborhoods. Luckily, [...]ng goes without incident. Von Opel ignites [...]kets via a foot pedal, and the RAK 2 is cata- [...]to 236 km/h. However, the profile and selling [...]side wings, adjusted by the driver, generate [...]cient downforce. Beyond 230 km/h, the car's [...]axle loses contact with the ground. Fritz von

Opel manages to bring it under control at the last minute, and gives attending journalists, who are highly enthusiastic about rocket propulsion, a glimpse of possible future projects with manned rockets ... dreams that, in 1928, are greeted with plenty of headshaking.

In the racing scene, the rocket-powered Opel

Handling 120 kilograms of explosives requires utmost concentration

remains an exotic species. Further rocket-powered projects are attempted with railway cars and aircraft. In the RAK prototypes, rocket technology has proven itself for the first time, opening the door to still-theoretical possibilities for space travel. For Opel, this foray into rocket technology is a one-off. The Great Depression demands concessions, and in 1929 General Motors takes over the Rüsselsheim-based company. For Opel, this now means concentrating on the core business of automobiles. Fritz von Opel, however, will go on to realize his vision on his own: In 1939, the first series production jet aircraft lifts off; in 1961 the first men travel to outer space, and the first moon landing takes place eight years later. —

Effortlessly easy

___ After Vittorio Jano's conceptions are included in the design of the hugely successful Grand Prix P2 vehicle, his ideas flow on to the 6C 1500 touring car, which is offered for sale from 1927. The new model is relatively compact. Thanks to its low frame, semi-elliptical springs and exemplary brakes, it displays direct and agile handling characteristics previously unheard of. It's no surprise that the 6C 1500 enjoys great success at many races. Manning the cockpit at the first victory is none other than Enzo Ferrari.

In 1929, the 1.5-liter is followed by a new model with increased capacity and more power, which is given the designation 6C 1750. Like their little brother, the sporty versions feature a straight-six power unit with two camshafts driven by a vertical drive shaft, as well as dry sump lubrication. They are available with or without a compressor. The Sports, later called Gran Turismo, and Super Sport, later dubbed Gran Sport, Bbialbero-versions deliver 55 and 64 hp to the crankshaft at 4,400 rpm. With a compressor they even reach 80 hp and 102 hp respectively.

Following long-standing Italian tradition, the 6C

The lightness of the nimble 6C serves as a benchmark for many vehicles

1750 features different bodies. For racing, the lightweight Spider body from Zagato turns out to be a winner. All up, the vehicle weighs just 840 kg. In 1933, the capacity of the six-cylinder engine is again increased to now yield 1,917 cc. It takes no time at all for the 1750 Alfa Romeo to notch up its first race successes. After winning in 1928 at the wheel of the 6C 1500, Giuseppe Campari follows up with another victory in 1929 with the new 6C 1750. The triumph at the Mille Miglia also marks the start of the 1750 racer's long winning streak. The following year sees 30 of the Alfa 6-cylinder vehicles line up among the 135-strong "Mille" field. And at the wheel of the 6C 1750, now called Gran Sport, factory driver Tazio Nuvolari scores another victory for the 1750 after a gripping duel with his team colleagues Campari and Varzi. These three wins are the first of eleven that the Milan brand achieves on the ca. 1,600-kilometer round-trip road race from Brescia to Rome and back. Of particular note is that Nuvolari achieves an average of over 100 km/h at that time. ___

With the Alfa Romeo 6C 1750, Alfa Romeo offers a compact, powerful and nimble vehicle that immediately appears in the winners' lists of major races. This image shows Tazio Nuvolari and Giovanni Battista Guidotti, who follow in the footsteps of Campari/Ramponi at the 1930 Mille Miglia. Campari/Ramponi won this road race for Alfa Romeo in 1928 with a 6C 1500, and in 1929 with a 6C 1750.

What else?

The Principality of Monaco is the venue for the first-ever Monaco Grand Prix, and also hosts a second major motorsport event with the Monte Carlo Rally.

Stylishly superior

Drivers have to lend a hand in the pits at the Le Mans 24-hour race. Bentley wins the prestigious race a total of six times.

___ When the "Bentley Boys", Glen Kidston and Woolf Barnato, cross the finish line at Le Mans on 22 June, 1930, they have covered almost 2,931 kilometers. Scoring five of the first eight wins at what is today the world's longest-running 24-hour classic, it almost seems that victory at Le Mans is the sole domain of Bentley. With the triumph of the three-liter Sport in 1924 and 1927, followed up by the 4.5-liter from 1928, victory in 1929 and 1930 goes to the Speed Six, with its 6,597 cc displacement divided between six inline cylinders. Tom Birkin, arguably the most colorful of the "Bentley Boys", competes in the four-cylinder Blower-Bentley (4.5 liters with supercharging), which proves to be swift, but fails to reach the finish.

However, the Speed Sixes are lauded for their durability, torque, and – thanks to innovative camshaft drive – superb running characteristics. The 182 units of the Speed Six racers that are built

The role of the Bentley Boy Barnato extends far beyond driving duties

are recognizable by their small radiators with green badges, and from early 1929 they join the 140 hp Standard Six. Thanks to classic tuning, the Speed Six receives a power boost to 200 hp. Four valves per cylinder, a light alloy crankcase and a dual ignition system with ignition coil and ignition magnet, as well as a dry-plate clutch and drum brakes all round, are standard for all 6.5-liter cars. The company founder, W.O. Bentley, calls "Babe" Barnato "the best driver that Bentley ever had." Indeed, the Bentley Boy scores three straight Le Mans victories between 1928 and 1930, and until today is the only competitor to win Le Mans at every one of his attempts. However, his role within Bentley is far more important than that of any other driver; ultimately, the wealthy Captain Woolf Barnato helps pull Bentley out of its dire economic straits in 1926 and takes over as CEO. ___

Although the start numbers are painted on the body and radiator, several event organizers, for instance at the Brooklands 12-Hour race of 1930, insist on the first standardized number plates, as shown here on the right-hand headlight of the victorious Speed Six driven by Barnato/Clement.

What else?

Maserati wins the Grand Prix of Monza and San Sebastian. Hence, another marque joins the circle of Grand Prix victors.

A car for all occasions

As a four-seater, the 8C 2300 is good for outright victories at the 24 Hours of Le Mans (right); the two-seater variant with a body suitable for road use wins the Mille Miglia and others. Unburdened by headlights and fenders, and with an aerodynamic shroud on the radiator (left), the two-seater with the designation "Monza" can be fielded at Grands Prix.

In 1932, Tazio Nuvolari wins the Monaco Grand Prix with a works Alfa Romeo 8C 2300 Monza campaigned by the Scuderia Ferrari. For the 318-kilometer race distance, he needs 3 hours and 32 minutes.

What else?

Alfa Romeo mounts a pair of 1750 cc six-cylinder engines side by side in the front of the Tipo A model. The twelve-cylinder single-seater, also featuring two linked gearboxes, puts out a respectable 230 km/h. The vehicle celebrates its race debut over ten hours at the Italian Grand Prix, at which two "Monza" racers lock out the first spots. Setting up the Tipo A proves complicated, and the Tipo B is already waiting in the wings (see 1932).

___ The 8C 2300 is regarded as Vittorio Jano's masterstroke. The eight-cylinder automobile cannot hide its close ties to the 6C 1750 from 1929, however, the housing for the two overhead camshafts is now made of weight-saving aluminum, thus lowering the center of gravity. With a bore of 65 mm and stroke of 88 mm, the eight-cylinder yields 2,336 cc. Initially, 142–165 hp is produced at 5,000 rpm. The race cars are fielded at races by the Alfa Romeo works team as well as the Scuderia Ferrari. When Alfa withdraws its factory-run outings in 1933, Ferrari takes over the race cars, but not before the bore has been raised to 68 mm leading to an increased capacity of 2,556 cc. Thus, the output of the 8C 2600 "Monza" receives a boost to 178 hp with a top speed of 225 km/h. The 2.9-liter 8-cylinder, which is closely related to the Tipo B power unit, marks the pinnacle, and will power a new model from 1936.

Its six-cylinder brother, inspired by the P2 world-championship car, turns out to be a winning racer. However, the success story written by the eight cylinder sibling is considerably more impressive. The first victory comes at the 1931 Targa Florio, traditionally contested in Sicily in springtime. A fortnight later, Tazio Nuvolari wins again – this time at the Gran Premio d'Italia at Monza. Thus the Grand Prix version of the 8C 2300 gets its nickname. Between 1931 and 1934, the 8C 2300 wins the 24 Hours of Le Mans four times in a row. During its maiden season, the 8C 2300 nets no less than 17 outright victories for Alfa Romeo. And it continues its winning ways through to 1938. Incidentally, Enzo Ferrari notches up the last victory of his

active racing career at a hill-climb event in June 1931, at the wheel of the 8C with the chassis number 001.

Different frame and body versions for the racing models of the eight-cylinder sports car also quickly arrive on the scene. Spectators get to see the vehicle with and without fenders, with and without headlights, with one, two, or four seats. Complying with the Le Mans regulations of the time, there's a four-seater with a long chassis, while the legendary "Monza" version features a short 2,750-mm wheelbase. Then there are the Corsa models, which are fielded at the Mille Miglia and the Targa Florio.

As a touring car, the 8C 2300 tackles rallies, with many valuable technical features flowing into the design of the Tipo B monoposto. It also proves suitable as a Gran Turismo or sports car for road use – equipped with different, mostly sporty and elegant bodies. With this balancing act between diversity and motor sport, the Alfa Romeo 8C 2300 comes to a crossroads. In the future, Alfa Romeo will manufacture sports cars specifically for each racing category. This makes the Alfa Romeo 8C 2300 a car for all occasions. ___

The Alfa Romeo 8C 2300 proves to be a true universal genius

The star of the early 1930s

___ The German Grand Prix of 1935 is intended to clearly demonstrate the superiority of German engineering. Auto Union and Mercedes line up on the grid at the Nürburgring with a formidable contingent. And indeed, it seems at first as if Caracciola will win the race for Mercedes, but the Auto Union, driven by Rosemeyer, moves into the lead, only to be thrown back by a puncture. "Caratsch", too, is hampered by problems. Suddenly the dark-red Alfa Romeo is the spearhead of an armada of Silver Arrows. Nuvolari comes into the pits to refuel, but his fuel system is faulty. When Nuvolari finally rejoins the race, he's running ninth. Putting in a last-ditch sprint, he ploughs through the field to rank second. In the last lap, Nuvolari also overtakes the Mercedes pilot von Brauchitsch, who's struggling with deteriorating tires. This race goes down in history as one of the greatest Grands Prix ever.

This triumph marks the end of the successful career of the Tipo B, which has netted wins at more than two dozen major races between 1932 and 1935.

With the Tipo B, Alfa campaigns a single-seater for the first time in Europe. In order to position the driver's seat as low as possible in the chassis, the engineers come up with a new layout for the transmission, in which the two cardan shafts deliver power to each wheel on the rear axle. The suspension at the front axle is initially rigid, but is replaced with an independent front suspension from 1935.

The Tipo B celebrates its debut with Tazio Nuvolari's victory at the Italian Grand Prix of 1932. Rudolf Caracciola also belongs to the circle of winners. Initially, the straight-eight with two four-cylinder blocks and twin supercharging had a displacement of 2,600 cc and developed 215 hp at 5,600 rpm. Soon, the power unit of the single-seater, fielded initially by the factory and later by the Scuderia Ferrari, who took over the role of works squad, would yield 2,905 cc (255 hp) and 3,165 cc (265 hp). This displacement would eventually exceed 3,800 cc and develop 330 hp. ___

▲ With the appearance of the Silver Arrows and the introduction of the 750-kilogram formula, the monoposto from Milan is pushed more and more into the background. After notching up successes early in the 1934 season, Tazio Nuvolari manages to beat the formidable opponents from Germany one last time at the 1935 German Grand Prix. The image shows the start of the Swiss Grand Prix of 1934.

◄ In the 1930s, journalists asked their questions directly to the vehicle. The photo shows second-placed Louis Chiron in 1935, surrounded by journalists, in his 3.2-liter Tipo B.

▲ Jean-Pierre Wimille is one of the drivers who sticks with Bugatti. However, the marque's time in Grand Prix racing is over.

New but already obsolete

What else?

In Hans Stuck's *Auto-Buch*, published in 1933 under his own name, he describes the essential characteristics a racing driver must possess: presence of mind, a keen eye, a fit body, sporting ambition, a robust constitution, courage and energy, composure and consideration, humor and mastery. Not a lot has changed to this day ...

___ Unveiled in late summer 1933, the Bugatti Type 59 is the last in a long line of racing cars to emerge from Ettore Bugatti's premises. The 300 hp Type 53, with its 4.9-liter engine and all-wheel drive built specifically for hill climbs, made its debut the previous year. With this technically superior car, Achille Varzi managed to beat his eternal arch rival, Tazio Nuvolari, at the Klausen Pass race in 1932.

The chassis of the Type 59 shares similarities with the 16-cylinder Type 45, and features almost the same wheelbase and track dimensions as the Type 35. The body, too, resembles previous Grand Prix Bugattis. But the impression is deceptive: The Bugatti 59 is an entirely new design. And it's interesting to note that Bugatti dared take this step just as the new Grand Prix regulations, with a minimum vehicle weight of 750 kilograms, were coming into effect.

Although it is a completely new development, by the time the Bugatti 59 is launched, it is already technically obsolete. The body is wide enough to accommodate two people, but at those Grands Prix contested on circuits, only the driver's seat is required.

In spite of appearances: The Type 59 is a new design

The Bugatti 59 debuts with a 2.8-liter engine, but shortly afterwards, at the Monaco Grand Prix of 1934, it receives a displacement boost to 3.3 liters. Technically, the power unit of the Grand Prix vehicle has been adopted from the Type 57 SC road-going touring car. The opposition puts its trust in thoroughbred race engines. To keep the company solvent, Ettore asks his 25-year-old son, who works within the company, to stop participating in motor racing and instead focus on the production car business. Four of the Type 59 cars are sold to England; one road-going sports car goes to King Leopold of Belgium.

From 1935, the new 50B engines are mounted into the Type 59 chassis. The most powerful of the three versions puts out a good 400 hp. In addition to a raft of successes at sports car races, the vehicle scores second place at the 1936 Vanderbilt Cup, and wins the "Coupe de la Commission Sportive", as well as the Prescott Hill Climb of 1939. In 1946, the Type 59/50B enjoys a renaissance at the first post-war race, the Prisoners' Cup at the Bois de Boulogne park in Paris.

Shiny silver

___ Legend or fact? The story of the Mercedes W25 race car, built to comply with the 750-kilogram regulation introduced from 1934, goes like this: In spring that year, at the technical scrutineering for the Eifel race, the Mercedes mechanics discover to their horror that the car is one kilogram over the pre-scribed weight. 751 kilograms. What should they do? Pull out of the Nürburgring event? "This would paint us in a bad light ...", recalls works driver Manfred von Brauchitsch. Apparently, this quip gives the mechanics the idea to strip the paint off the car. Legend has it that the W25 is freed of its paint ballast overnight and turns up on the grid on Sunday morning in its shiny new aluminum outfit – and is victorious. This marks the birth of the Silver Arrows. The strange thing, though, is that no one from that time can verify this story.

Until 1936, the constantly upgraded W25 wins 16 races, and in 1935 makes Rudolf Caracciola the German and European champion. The performance stages of the 5,800 rpm, 3,360 cc, supercharged straight-eight engines of those days: 354 hp,

398 hp (W25 A) and 430 hp (W25 B). Equally as im-pressive as this data is the engine sound, along with the howl of the compressor. For the 1935 season, the displacement is increased to 4,310 cc and a sec-ond compressor is fitted (W25 C). Now, the motor produces 462 hp. "Caratsch", Luigi Fagioli, and von Brauchitsch can now shift through five gears and, thanks to stiff competition from the also-silver Auto Union racers, receives another injection of power – boosting the horsepower to 616 hp. In the meantime, this model, conceived for the 1936 season, accom-modates twelve cylinders. At 300 kilograms, the en-gine is too heavy for circuit racing, but is still a top contender for time trials, which have become the trend. The completely paneled speed trial vehicle reaches speeds of up to 362 km/h.

At the Grands Prix of Monaco and Tunis, the Silver Arrows from Stuttgart again eclipse the increasingly dominating opposition from Saxony. The race car is the W25 producing 449 hp with a single supercharg-er. But the W25's days are numbered. ___

▲ The Mercedes-Benz W25 scores victories in its maiden year of 1934 and dominates the 1935 Grand Prix season. The photo shows the Mercedes of Manfred von Brauchitsch (#6) at the start of the Inter-national AVUS race.

▼ The performance of the Mercedes-Benz W25 increases from its initial 354 hp, to 398 hp, 430 hp, and ultimately up to 480 hp.

The power of two

Although the Bimotore is designed in-house by the Scuderia Ferrari, it receives the blessing of Alfa designer Vittorio Jano. Second place at the AVUS remains its best result.

___ In the mid-1930s, in its fight to the top of Grand Prix racing, Alfa Romeo comes up with a whole range of different race cars. The Tipo B, developed straight from the two-seater 8C 2300 Monza, has already proved its worth with victories. The spectrum of the Tipo B's supercharged eight-cylinder engine ranges from an initial capacity of 2.6 liters with 215 hp, to 2.9 and 3.2 liters up to 3.8 liters (330 hp). However, in the face of its German rivals' growing power, the Tipo B loses more and more ground.

But Alfa Romeo still has a string in its bow: For the 1935 season, the 8C with a 3.8-liter engine is fielded in the renamed European Championship. The over 4,000 cc 12C emerges the following year. And the showpiece is the Bimotore, capable of reaching over 320 km/h, which the Milanese are keen to pit themselves against the might of the Silver Arrows at the high-speed racetracks of Tripoli, Tunis, Berlin, and Reims. The Grand Prix race car generates its power from 16 cylinders. Mounted at the front and rear are supercharged, 270 hp, 3,200 cc eight-cylinder engines. Combined they yield a capacity of 6,330 cc and produce 540 hp. Power from both

The Bimotore is a desperate attempt to beat the Silver Arrows

engines is supplied to the clutch positioned at the front engine. A shaft delivers the torque from the rear engine through the gearbox to the front. The differential is positioned behind the three-speed gearbox. From this, two prop shafts deliver power to each of the rear wheels. The front axle is shod with 5.5 x 20 inch tires, with the rear wheels measuring 7 x 21 inches. For those tackling the speed trials, the Bimotore receives a clear plastic windshield and an aerodynamic fairing from the driver's headrest tapering to the rear. Thus, Tazio Nuvolari reaches 321.5 km/h on the autobahn.

The technical mastermind behind the Bimotore is the long-standing Ferrari employee Luigi Bazzi, who keeps tabs on everything concerning the Scuderia Ferrari-made car. The Bimotore debuts at the Tripoli Grand Prix in 1935, but is outperformed by Mercedes and Auto Union. And again on the Berlin Avus track, the second-placed Chiron has to succumb to Fagioli's Mercedes. In the end, the vehicle proves too cumbersome and unwieldy, and the excessive fuel consumption and tire wear are almost beyond belief. ___

Perched between the two supercharged straight-eight engines and surrounded by up to 240 liters of fuel, the drivers, who can only be described as daring, reach speeds of up to 320 km/h.

1936

Arrival of the midship engine

▲ The Type C's 16 cylinders produce up to 520 hp. This makes the 824-kilogram lightweight capable of achieving 340 km/h. The photo on the left shows the streamlined Type C in the brick-paved banked corner at the AVUS racetrack. With the Auto Union R (time trial car), also powered by 16-cylinders and aerodynamically shrouded, Bernd Rosemeyer even surpasses the 430 km/h top speed on the autobahn near Darmstadt, before his fatal accident.

◄ 1936 is a big year for the Auto Union Type C. Of the events in which it competes, it wins three of the five Grands Prix, half of the circuit races, and all the hill-climb events. Incidentally, a new limited slip differential from ZF prevents the previously notorious wheelspin of the inside rear wheel, when cornering.

▼ The narrow bucket-shaped seat is wrapped by the 200-liter fuel tank. Even a radiator is squeezed into the short front.

___ From a technical perspective, the Type C is unquestionably the jewel in the crown of the Grand Prix cars designed for the 750-kilogram ruling. Without driver, tires and fluids, the 750-kilo mid-engine car, with its aluminum tubular frame, represents systematic lightweight design, which more resembles an aircraft than a race car. In the notoriously difficult-to-control vehicle, the driver takes his place in a simple seat positioned behind an oversized, vertical steering wheel, surrounded by 200 liters of high-octane racing gasoline. Behind the driver sits a 16-cylinder Roots supercharged engine with crankcase and cylinder heads made of cast aluminum. The unbridled horsepower tortures the tires fitted on delicate spoked rims, with the width of the rubber more suited to a bicycle. And indeed, this proves to be problematic. Through the rotational force, the wheels' circumference changes and therefore the tires are unable to withstand the rigors of a 500-kilometer Grand Prix.

The Type C inherits its traits from the Types A (1934) and B (1936) and is fielded in 1936 and 1937. All hark back to the P-car project, the concept of which engineer Ferdinand Porsche offered for sale to the German industry at a price of 75,000 Reichsmark. Twelve Type C cars are built for the 1936 and 1937 seasons, and are also given streamlined bodies for speed trials. Over the years, the displacement of the 16-cylinder goes from 4.3 to 6 liters, with the record-attempting models reaching up to 6.3 liters. The torque of the 6-liter Type C is stated as 850 Nm. Its output lies at 520 hp at 5,000 rpm, enough to

Bernd Rosemeyer and Hans Stuck shine racing the mid-engine cars

propel the race car to 320 km/h. The speed trial power unit even develops 560 hp. Bernd Rosemeyer, the only person capable of taming this difficult racer, turns a lap time on the 22.8-kilometer-long Nordschleife in under ten minutes. In 1936, the record-setting vehicle achieves speeds of up to 389 km/h. The following year, Rosemeyer promptly breaks the 400 km/h barrier with a speed of 406 km/h.

On the plus side of the Type C ledger are many victories at Grands Prix, hill-climb events, and other competitions. Rosemeyer, who is married to the legendary aviator Elly Beinhorn, dies in an accident during a record attempt in 1938, but his triumphs on the Nordschleife make him immortal. "King of the Mountains" Stuck continues to excel at various hillclimbs with the Type C. At times, his Type C race car is shod with twin tires for improved grip. Having reached the pinnacle of motor racing with the European Championship, Stuck adds the German road and hill-climb titles to his list of accolades.

When the three-liter formula comes into effect in 1938, the twelve-cylinder Auto Union Type D is unveiled, and the era of 16-cylinder mid-engine vehicles draws to an end. Apart from the successor's laurels, many years will pass before mid-engine single-seaters again claim victory in Grand Prix racing. ___

➤ The nimble roadster turns out to be an ideal racer at regularity runs and trials on easy terrain. It also serves as a good baseline for a raft of race car designs, which prove successful in motor racing during the first post-war years.

▲ The two-seater, six-cylinder sports car feels at home on all types of terrain, whether that's at rallies (top, on the Côte d'Azur), circuit races (center) or road races, like the Mille Miglia (below). Huschke von Hanstein and Walter Bäumer win the "Mille" with the coupé in April 1940. Visible in the background is the huge timekeeping board, intended to give spectators at the start/finish a clear overview of the race.

What else?

Mercedes-Benz and Auto Union again tackle the AVUS races with streamlined race cars. The race distance is shorter than Grand Prix events, as the tires can't withstand the high speeds and steep curves.

1937 is the final season in which the 750-kilogram formula is contested. The 5.6-liter supercharged 8-cylinder engine of the newly launched 610 hp Mercedes-Benz W125 marks the performance pinnacle.

Brilliant sports Car

___ With his victory at the sports car race on the Nürburgring in the summer of 1936, BMW factory driver Ernst Henne shines a light on a new sports car from Munich, or more accurately, Eisenach. The new BMW 328, manufactured between 1937 and 1939, quickly evolves into Germany's most successful and beloved sports car.

In Hitler's Germany, the Silver Arrow pilots from Auto Union and Mercedes are commandeered by the party as heroes. Indeed, most in the motorsport scene are appropriated by the party. They find themselves either in the NSKK (National Socialist Motor Corps) or (like Hans Stuck, Bernd Rosemeyer, and Huschke von Hanstein) in the SS (Schutzstaffel). In contrast to private drivers, their membership comes with the advantage of factory-maintained vehicles. This proves interesting for manufacturers such as BMW, as they too receive a good slice of the generous subsidy cake from the state.

The roadster, with its distinctive sleek shape, is mounted with the 2,971-cc, straight-six engine of the BMW 326, but features a new cylinder head with a V-shaped-valve configuration designed for the sports car. These are actuated by means of push rods and rocker arms via a lateral camshaft. Three Solex downdraft carburetors take care of the fuel mixture. Output lies at 80 hp (at 5,000 rpm). The power unit, front-axle wishbones and rigid rear axle are fixed to a tubular frame with box cross members. Hydraulic drum brakes are responsible for deceleration. The swift BMW 328, capable of 150 km/h,

tips the scales at 830 kilograms. Fuel consumption is given at 14.5 liters over 100 km. On request, BMW supplies the vehicle with a 100-liter fuel reservoir. Until the start of the war, 426 of these sports cars are manufactured. At customers' request, several of them receive sheet-metal paneling from coachbuilders such as Gläser, Wendler, and Drauz. Most of them leave the BMW premises as standard "open two-seater sports cars". Bayerische Motoren Werke (BMW) offers the roadsters for 7,400 Reichsmark. For the 500-kilogram chassis, the price is 5,900 RM.

In cooperation with Touring coachbuilder in Milan, a lightweight, streamlined coupé is created for the 1939 24 Hours of Le Mans with the Superleggera design typical of the Italian bodybuilder. With this car, Prince Max von Schaumburg-Lippe clinches victory in the two-liter class and fifth overall. Another eminent international race is the Mille Miglia. The event isn't contested in 1939, but for the race in the spring of 1940 – Italy is not yet involved in the war – BMW prepares five vehicles: three new open race cars, a race sedan featuring a streamlined body courtesy of Professor Wunibald Kamm, and the Le Mans-Coupé. Fritz Huschke von Hanstein and Walter Bäumer achieve outright victory over the shortened 927-mile Mille Miglia race. Fitted under the light-alloy body of the 700-kilogram factory racer, achieving 200–220 km/h, is a 122-hp race engine powered by an alcohol-gasoline-benzol mixture.

> **Thanks to the 328, BMW receives state-subsidized motorsport funding**

1938 | Mercedes-Benz W154

Demonstration of power

___ For the past four years, the silver vehicles from Saxony and Baden-Württemberg have been shining bright. However, it's only towards the end of the 1930s that the designation "Silver Arrows" appears in the news and in everyday conversations. According to the recollections of former Mercedes race director Alfred Neubauer, the 750-kg racers were perhaps lacking in the mighty and impressive appearance. But this changes with the arrival of the three-liter supercharged vehicles for the 1938 season. The new W154, driven by Caracciola & Co, that is unveiled is low and elongated and produces 468 hp. This inevitably contravenes the rule-makers' intention of reining in the power escalation of previous years. However, in Hitler's Germany, party members and companies who use the drivers predominantly for propaganda purposes, have their sights firmly set on prestige, competition, and on giving a demonstration of technical expertise: essentially, a demonstration of power on the race tracks of Europe. Hence, for the time being, the performance explosion continues unchecked.

No longer having to keep to the 750-kilogram ruling, the obviously heavier twelve-cylinders are fielded against the eight-cylinders. The curb weight of the single-seater with two compressors comes in at 850 kilograms, or 981 kg including tires, water, oil, and fuel. The maximum output of the four-valve V12 with a V-angle of 60° and a displacement of 2,962 cc develops at 8,000 rpm. For speed trials, however, the men under the direction of Alfred Neubauer fall back on the 736 hp W125 R.

➤ The 485-hp Mercedes-Benz W154 wins the first three races of the 1938 season. And in 1939, the 3-liter 12-cylinder dominates at three of the five Grands Prix contested. At the 1939 Grand Prix of Belgium at Spa-Francorchamps, Hermann Lang wins, with his teammate Manfred von Brauchitsch taking the checkered flag in third after almost 500 kilometers and almost three-and-a-half hours of racing.

The images of the Grand Prix grid in a year in which the gleaming silver German cars dominate. Here, three W125 lock out the first row. The large radiator grille with extensions to each side reveals the version from the 1938 season.

The rules limiting maximum weight to 750 kilograms, which have been in effect for the past four years, lead to massive leaps in progress in terms of lightweight solutions. Moreover, the ongoing pressure from competition accelerates the development and use of limited slip differentials, coil springs, De-Dion axles, hydraulic shock absorbers, double-shoe brake drums, different dimensions of tires on the front and rear axles, special coolants with ultrahigh boiling points, and performance-enhancing fuel. The fuel mixture consists of acetone, benzol, ether, and cooling alcohol. Only the experts know the exact recipe of this highly explosive brew. And the specialists have to prepare plenty of it: over 100 kilometers, the supercharged monsters guzzle a good 160 liters of the stuff.

Aside from the relatively weak brakes, the biggest concern of this time is the narrow tires – their de-

The fuel mixture consists of acetone, benzol, ether, and alcohol

velopment hasn't kept pace with the cars' enormous outputs. Despite extensive tests with different diameters (19 and 21 inches), the tires barely survive the 100 race kilometers and are frequently the cause of accidents. For this reason, the qualities needed in Grand Prix drivers in the late 1930s are primarily the same as for today's top long-distance drivers. The Grand Prix distances cover more than 500 kilometers, e.g. the Grand Prix of Tripoli, contested in the Italian colony Libya over 525 kilometers through the scorching African heat, at which Mercedes pilots Manfred von Brauchitsch, Rudolf Caracciola, and Karl Lang achieve a triple victory. All up, Mercedes wins six of the nine races that the Stuttgart squad contests in 1938. Two victories are clinched by Rudolf Caracciola, who also scores another five podium results and is crowned European Champion for the third time. ___

What else?

Bernd Rosemeyer is fatally injured in his Auto Union during a record attempt. The cause of the accident is the strong, gusting crosswind, which blows his aerodynamically sophisticated speed trial car off course.

For the 1939 race season there is a simpler, lighter bodyshell made of aluminum. The radiator grille shrinks to a narrow slit (left). The W125 driven by Richard Seaman goes up in flames after an accident (far left). The accident costs the Englishman his life.

A long, illustrious life

What else?

Exasperation with the overpowering Silver Arrows leads race organizers (e.g. of the Libyan Grand Prix held in Tripoli) to put their money on the new 1.5-liter formula for Voiturettes. Mercedes-Benz reacts and stealthily designs a 1,500 cc race car in just six months. The W165, mounted with a supercharged 1.5-liter 8-cylinder engine, scores a double victory.

Bugatti manages one last major victory: Wimille/Veyron win the 24 Hours of Le Mans with a Bugatti 57C. Two years earlier, the 3.2-liter, supercharged, 8-liter sports car had already pipped the competition at the post.

____ With the introduction of a new Voiturette regulation for race cars with a capacity up to 1,500 cc, the governing body puts a cap on the power explosion in Grand Prix racing. Alfa Romeo, Maserati, and other manufacturers hastily design new race cars. In Portello, the single-seater, developed in Modena in 1937 at the urging of Alfa's race director, Ferrari, receives the designation Tipo 158 (1.5 liters, 8-cylinders). The "Vetturetta" is given the nickname "Alfetta". Initially, the smaller single-seaters compete against racers with larger capacities. The big class goes predominantly to silver, with red dominating the modern "Vetturette". Soon, the Italian races and the Grand Prix of Tripoli will run exclusively for 1.5-liter single-seaters. For these races, Mercedes creates just one 1.5-liter W165 (two-stage supercharging, 256 hp at 8,000 rpm, 718 kg), with which Lang and Caracciola beat their Italian rivals.

Technologically interesting is the transaxle design, with the straight-eight in the front and the four-speed gearbox and differential package at the rear axle. This ensures an ideal axle load distribution, and thus is beneficial to the driving dynamics. At work behind the three-part radiator grille (until its first major modification in 1939), is 195 hp at 7,200 rpm and a compressor. Two camshafts control the 16 valves. A frame of oval tubes constitutes the chassis and supports the individually suspended 18-inch wheels. Touring contributes the aluminum body. As another weight-saving measure, the

> **Enzo Ferrari initiates the 1.5-liter vehicle, but leaves Alfa Romeo after a dispute**

170-liter fuel reserve is divided into two tanks. The Tipo 158, capable of achieving 232 km/h, weighs in at 620 kilograms.

In 1940, twenty-two 1.5-liter cars compete in Tripoli. Four of them come from Portello. Alfa Romeo wins and matches the previous year's lap record. In the meantime, the 1,500 cc engines put out 215–220 hp (at 7,500 rpm). At this point, Italian motor racing also stops for the war, which the well-hidden factory-Alfa safely survive. In 1946, the cars are retrieved and prepared for new race challenges. And with the once-proud race cars from Nazi Germany all destroyed or confiscated, or at least unfit to compete again, the small Alfa enjoys its role as favorite when it resumes its racing activities. For the next five years, the swift Alfetta, with top speeds of 270 km/h, prove almost unbeatable!

Modifications are made in 1947, and it is predominantly the engine that benefits. The unit now features a two-stage supercharger and produces 275 hp (at 8,500 rpm). With this, the Tipo 158 continues on from its pre-war winning streak and achieves a raft of extraordinary successes in 1947 and 1948. Alfa Romeo doesn't race in 1949, but in 1950 returns with great success to Grand Prix racing, run from this year on as Formula One World Championship. All race victories that year go to Alfa Romeo and, thanks to its Tipo 158, now 350 hp with a top speed of 290 km/h, Nino Farina is crowned first-ever Formula One World Champion. ____

➤ The Alfetta's brilliant design seems to be blessed with the best DNA. Its origins are noble enough to bring home Formula One World Championship titles in 1950 and 1951.

Ferrari incognito

____ Young Enzo Ferrari launches his career as a racing driver for CMN and Alfa Romeo. But he soon realizes that his talent lies elsewhere. When he establishes the Scuderia Ferrari in the winter of 1929/1930, the squad proves formidable and becomes the official Alfa Romeo factory team. In 1938, Alfa Romeo takes back the reins and Enzo Ferrari, as race director, is summoned from Modena to Milan. However, tempers quickly flair between the successful factions. Ferrari leaves Alfa Romeo within the year. During his brief term in Milan, Ferrari sets the course for the 308, 312, 158 (Alfetta) models as well as the 512, which is no longer fielded.

Ferrari comes to an arrangement with his longstanding backers, which outlines the resurrection of his Scuderia within the next four years, but he's prohibited from competing in any races. For this reason, he founds the Auto-Avio Costruzioni. Under this company, Ferrari conceives two sports cars and fields them at the 1940 Mille Miglia. One of them is piloted by the young Alberto Ascari and Minozzi. The other is manned by (Marchese) Lotario Rangoni (Macchiavelli)/Enrico Nardi.

The "815" is the understated designation of the forerunner of the legendary sports cars that will bear the name of the Commendatore after the war. In his memoirs *Piloti, che gente ...* Enzo Ferrari retrospectively describes the vehicle as the Ferrari 815 and thus the first Ferrari. The numbers indicate the engine specs: 8 cylinders and a 1.5-liter capacity. The 54-kilogram Superleggera body of aluminum-magnesium-alloy is built by the Carrozzeria Touring coachbuilders in Milan. Many components from Fiat are fitted under the dark-red body: chassis, rear axle, and gearbox as well as the eight-cylinder engine made of two joined and capacity-reduced Fiat Balilla-1100 engines. The 1,496 cc power unit produces 72 hp, propelling the 815 up to 170 km/h.

Enrico Nardi attempts the first test run, which takes him from Modena to the Autostrada and on unpaved tracks through Emilia Romagna. At the new edition of the Mille Miglia in 1940, now under the title of "primo Gran Premio di Brescia" due to the changed layout, Ascari temporarily holds the lead and sets a lap record. ____

The Marquis Lotario Rangoni Macchiavelli and Enrico Nardi (#65), as well as Alberto Ascari and Giovanni Minozzi (#66), pilot the two so-called "Autoaviocostruzioni tipo 815 spider Touring" at the 1940 Mille Miglia, in the year where the tradition-steeped event is run in a loop over a shortened road course. Neither of the cars reaches the finish.

Beach racing with production cars

1940 & 1941
What else?

Like the Mille Miglia, the 1940 running of the Targa Florio is contested in an unusual format on a shortened track: The race for the 1.5-liter vehicles is run on a 5.7-kilometer circuit in Favorita Park at Palermo. The total distance is just 228 kilometers.

In 1941, Floyd Davis and Mauri Rose win the last pre-war Indy 500 with a Wetteroth-Offenhauser. Later that year, the Americans join the war effort, which now spreads around the globe and throws the world into upheaval.

___ While war is raging in Europe, the Americans continue to race. After two Maserati victories at Indianapolis, at last a U.S. designer wins thanks to Floyd Davis and Mauri Rose with a Wetteroth-Offenhauser. Rex Mays is crowned 1941 AAA Champion with a Stevens-Winfield. Other racetracks, too, host heated duels, including Daytona Beach as part of the now popular Beach Road Race.

Since 1936, the coast of Daytona has also been the venue for stock cars – production vehicles reserved for beach and road racing. Joining the action right from the outset is Bill France, a man who will make a name for himself by founding the NASCAR series, today the world's most popular touring car championship. The seed is planted in the early 40s at Daytona. The Daytona 500, which has been contested on the eponymous Superspeedway since 1956, is still regarded today as the most important NASCAR race. Thus, the idea of modern motor racing with production cars takes shape. According to legend, the origins of stock cars lie in the days of Prohibition. At that time, alcohol smugglers used conventional yet souped-up vehicles, with significantly increased load capacity at the rear axle, to smuggle bootleg whiskey in hidden tanks over the federal state borders.

However, the cars that compete in pre-war Daytona are a far cry from these moonshine-haulers. The

The origins of NASCAR lie in whiskey smuggling and Daytona's race tradition

3.2-mile racetrack for the inaugural Beach Road Race consists of two straights running down the beach and back along the parallel highway, with two curves connecting them. In 1936, Bill France is one of the 28 starters. He competes with a borrowed Ford and hopes to take home the handsome sum of US$ 5,000. The race, however, is red-flagged after 200 miles due to deeply-rutted curves and the incoming tide. On top of this, numerous vehicles are demolished. The tricky terrain demands a great deal of skill, and with so many cars stuck in the corners, becomes virtually impassable. Bill France finishes in sixth place. When Daytona refuses to hold another race, the American takes over the event and begins to organize the following year's race. Using clay, he has the corners piled into banks and shortens the race distance to 50 miles. Gradually, the event establishes itself and in 1953 will become a major fixture on the calendar.

In 1940, 40,000 spectators flock to the beach. The race proves so popular that it's held twice the following year. In July, lawyer and amateur racing driver Carl D. "Lightning" Lloyd Seay finishes the first race – after two rolls – in fourth, before going on to win the second outing in August. His car is one of the thousands of 81A Standard 2 passenger coupés that Ford produced in 1938, with 85 hp from its 3.6-liter V8 engine. ___

➤ Stock car racing – motor racing with predominantly standard vehicles – is often a fun event. The early days of the series are dominated by drivers who previously earned their living by smuggling illicit alcoholic drinks.

1944 | Maserati 4CL

Sixteen valves for a change

___ The Maserati 4CL is conceived in the year 1939, but it's not up to the task of beating the Alfetta. For many years, however, the four-cylinder Grand Prix car proves a worthy opponent to the technically superior Tipo 158 from Alfa Romeo. A total of 15 of these cars are built.

The type designation denotes the number of cylinders (4 Cilindri) and the typical Maserati valve drive with small steel latches (Linguette) between the camshaft and valve stem. The cast-iron engine block is fixed to the double camshaft head and, without sealing rings, is connected to the light-alloy crankcase. With four valves on each cylinder, the 4CL is dubbed "the 16-valver." These 16 valves guarantee a very high gas exchange and the best possible performance of the compressor. The unit, with the bore-to-stroke ratio of 78 x 78 square millimeters, develops 220 hp at 6,600 rpm.

Aluminum transverse beams sit on the steel cross members. This frame is regarded as both the end and the pinnacle of traditional frame design. The front wheels are sprung independently by torsion bars, with a rigid rear axle sprung by leaf springs. The 4CL weighs in at 630 kilograms with a top speed of 235 km/h. With the "Aerodinamica" body from Pininfarina, built specifically for the speed trials and the Tripoli Grand Prix, even 250 km/h is possible.

In 1946, Maserati experiments with two-stage superchargers following the successful attempts by Alfa Romeo to increase boost. With the introduction of round beams in the design of the final 4CL frame, the stiffness and thus the handling of Ascari's racer improves noticeably. This proves advantageous to the 4CL (T) and, between 1947 and 1950, turns it into a stronger rival for the Alfetta. The T stands for Tubolare, indicating the tubular space frame now forming the backbone under the thin aluminum body.

The four-cylinder engine roller-bearing crankshaft is now charged by two compressors and has been boosted to 290 hp. Initially the engines are cast iron; eventually they will be made of aluminum. Within four years, 29 of the 4CL (T) leave the factory in Modena. Maserati only expands its range from 1946, and only with models for road use, such as the 1500 Gran Turismo (A6). ___

1945 | Simca Huit

Racing to better times

___ With the competitions from Paris to Rouen in 1894, and from Paris to Bordeaux the following year, it was the French who were the driving force behind motor racing. And after the end of the Second World War, Paris is once again the place where it all starts anew. Weapons have been silent in Europe since May 8, however, it's not until September 2 and the surrender of Japan that peace returns to the South Pacific. A week later, engines again roar into life, with the first races held in Paris' Bois de Boulogne.

Lining up to start are, inevitably, pre-war vehicles. The 4.7-liter supercharged Bugatti 59/50B, with which Jean-Pierre Wimille convincingly wins the Prisoners' Cup, has underlined its full potential at numerous races since 1935. Ettore Bugatti himself witnesses the last victory of his brand. A signature feature of the Bugatti 59 is its so-called "piano wire wheels" which use splines between the brake drum and rim, making them very easy to change. The "Coupe de la Libération" goes to Henri Louveau in a Maserati 4CL 1500.

The race for automobiles up to 1,500 cc is the very first event of the post-war period. Amédée Gordini wins the "Robert Benoist Trophy" at the wheel of a relatively new Simca Huit, which won the up to 1,100 cc class in 1939, as well as the index classification at the 24 Hours of Le Mans. At that stage, the name Gordini didn't mean much to anyone, however this changes. The Gordini company will stop making race cars in the mid-1950s, and instead join Renault to turn their cars into winners at rallies and races. The small Simca features an aerodynamic body with covered wheels and is given the name "tank". At Le Mans, Gordini averages over 120 km/h with the 1,087-cc four-cylinder contender; in Paris he achieves almost 95. The production version of the Simca Huit at its unveiling in 1937, and its market launch in 1938, is basically a facsimile of the Fiat 1100. Putting in a record-breaking drive over 10,000 kilometers, Simca underlines the performance capabilities of the new model: Averaging 115.14 km/h, the Simca smashes eight records and consumes less than eight liters over 100 kilometers. ___

Six months after the end of the war, engines rev up again

➤ Stanguellini is one of many Garagisti who build their own sports cars based on Fiat models and then race them successfully.

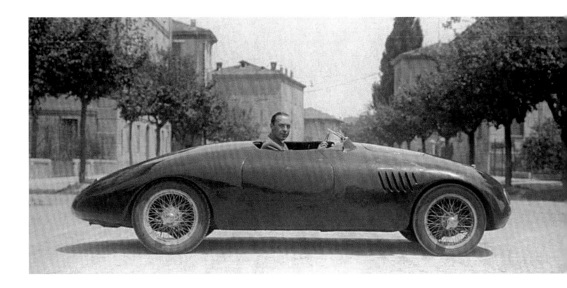

1944 – 1946
What else?

The first race in Germany is the Ruhestein Hill Climb, on 21 July. Hermann Lang wins in the streamlined BMW 328 that won the 1940 Mille Miglia, ahead of Alexander von Falkenhausen in a standard BMW 328. In September, another race is held in Karlsruhe. Here, von Falkenhausen wins the race car category, with Karl Kling clinching the sports car classification.

In May 1946, the Indianapolis race takes off again on the 2.5-mile oval. After 200 laps, George Robson wins the first post-war Indy 500 with an Adam-Sparks.

In Switzerland, too, normality returns with the resurrection of the Grand Prix of Nations in 1946 in Geneva. Giuseppe "Nino" Farina wins with an Alfa Romeo 158. The race director of the Alfa Romeo squad is Giovanbattista Guidotti.

Great little cars

___ After the first race in Paris' Bois de Boulogne, the racing bug bites once again, especially in Italy, hence new cars are quickly put on their wheels in many factories. The most prominent designer is Enzo Ferrari who, after the Auto Avio Costruzioni 815, turns his attention to building sports cars that will bear his own name. Also taking up the challenge are the racing workshops of Abarth, Cisitalia, Conrero, Dell'Orto, Ermini, Giannini, Moretti, Minardi, Siata, and Stanguellini. Like Ferrari with his "815", almost all of them help themselves to the shelves at Fiat. Reassembled, optimized for racing, and equipped partly with the car bodies of reputable coachbuilders, the grids look very interesting indeed.

In the Stanguellini workshop, the dream of its own race car comes true

With successful performances for the Fiat 1100 Stanguellini, and the Stanguellini 1100 Sport at such races as the Circuito di Modena and the Coppa Nuvolari, in 1946 the sports car manufacturer from Modena stakes its claim to actively shape Italian motor racing history. Beneath the banana-shaped, extremely simple, flat body lies vamped-up production technology from the Fiat spare-parts stock. The Fiat 508 Sport "Balilla" acts as an organ donor. The driver sits on the left of the completely covered chassis. A flat windshield made of clear plastic offers the only protection. However, a closed variant is also available. In 1946, Stanguellini wins the Italian Sports Car Championship. At national and international races held in Italy in 1947, the now in-house designed 1100 Stanguellini, featuring a light, stiff, steel tubular frame, dominates its class. Class wins for the over 1.5-liter contenders also often go to the Stanguellini from Modena. Francesco Stanguellini establishes the foundations for racing. He started out in 1900, as a bicycle manufacturer and a Fiat automobile dealer, before making a beeline for motor racing. His son Vittorio launched his racing career in 1935, with a Stanguellini based on the 500 Topolino and the 1100 Balilla. ___

1947

Ferrari 125 S

Birth of a legend

A vehicle bears the name Ferrari for the first time. On March 12, 1947, the 125 S leaves the factory premises for its first test. The first Ferrari victory comes on May 25. Franco Cortese wins the race held in Rome (photo left). The photo on the right shows the original vehicle in the Ferrari museum at Maranello.

◄ "Spinner" center lock technology is also well suited for racing in other categories. The increase in displacement from 1.5 to 1.9 liters turns the 12-cylinder into the Tipo 159. With a 2-liter capacity, it becomes the Ferrari 166. Note the handkerchief fastened over the mouth as a breathing mask.

What else?

The German motor racing scene begins to flourish again with races in Hockenheim, Munich, Braunschweig, and Hamburg, as well as the "Rund um Schotten" and the Eggberg Hill Climbs.

___ With the silencing of the guns, the automobile and racing scene outside of destroyed Germany enjoy a revival. As early as 1945, the first big race takes place in the Bois de Boulogne in Paris, witnessed by crowds of spectators. Pre-war race cars that have survived the turmoil of the past few years more or less unscathed, can now return to their original purpose – motor racing. But new vehicles are already in the pipeline. Enzo Ferrari begins preparing, selling, and racing vehicles that now bear his name and the famous "Cavallino Rampante", the prancing horse. The first model to appear on the scene in 1947 is an open sports car with the designation 125. Like the 815, a steel tubular frame is hidden beneath the open light alloy body. Under the detachable rear lid sits the 75-liter fuel tank. In the center there is room for two people. The driver sits behind a large and prominent wood-rimmed steering wheel. In front of both occupants, an imposing cluster of dials on the dashboard provides information about the fuel level, fuel and oil pressure, water and oil temperature, as well as revs. The rev counter with a telltale needle is redbanded at 8,000 rpm. The 1.5-liter 12-cylinder motor, conceived on the drawing boards of designers Gioachino Colombo and Luigi Bazzi, who had already achieved fame at Alfa Romeo with Ferrari, produces its maximum output of 72–90 hp at 6,000 rpm. Incidentally, the pair responsible for the technical development and production, Guiseppe Busso and

Attilio Galetto, are also former henchmen. The engine block, oil sump and cylinder heads of the V12 are made of aluminum.

Typical of Ferrari at that time, the designation 125 denotes the capacity of each cylinder. Pilots rave about the engine. Velvety, powerful, spirited, and high-revving, recalls Franco Cortese. However, he's not particularly enthusiastic about the usable rev band and the constant shifting of the five-speed gearbox. Concealed under the compact 3.45-meter-long, almost 1.5-meter-wide body is an independent suspension. Mounted on the front axle, the 15-inch wheels and drum brakes are suspended on transverse links and semi-trailing arms with transverse leaf springs and hydraulic shock absorbers. At the rear, the rigid axle hangs on longitudinal leaf springs along with dampers.

The Ferrari 125 Sport celebrates its debut on May 11 at Piacenza, Italy. A fortnight later at the "Gran Premio di Caracalla" in Rome, Cortese scores the first win for a Ferrari and thus establishes a legend that continues far beyond Ferrari F1 pilot Schumacher's streak of victories and titles. Two of the 125 S are built, with some engines rebored to two-liters during the season (and logically receive the designation 159). The 1,903-cc power unit develops 118 hp at 7,000 rpm. The development then flows straight into the Ferrari 166 with a displacement of 1,995 cc producing up to 140 hp, which quickly carries the sporting fame of the fledgling marque around the world.

The 125 marks the birth of a tradition that continues to this day

A chapter of post-war history

___ With the currency reform, there's a noticeable upswing in the market. The German Mark replaces black market activities. Overnight, the shop shelves are restocked with goods. But the decades-long divide through Germany deepens. The Soviets order the blockage of the transit route to and from Berlin. In terms of automobile construction, the allies lift the order restricting German automobile manufacturers to building only vehicles up to 1500 cc. In Italy, the fledgling and successful motor racing company Ferrari now supplies the first sports cars to private customers. And Great Britain again hosts Grand Prix races.

In Germany, this won't happen until 1950, but in the meantime the first tentative attempts are made to distract people from their daily travails with thrilling motorsport. Hence, in the late summer of 1947, the first "Eifel Trophy Race" is held on the still-damaged Nürburgring. For the entry price of five Reichsmark, spectators receive coupons for wine, bread, and sausage. That same year, businessman Lorenz Dietrich, racing driver Georg "Schorsch" Meier, and ex-racing driver and BMW engineer Ernst Loof join forces to start building race cars, with the help of 15 former BMW employees.

The Veritas is Germany's first post-war Grand Prix racer

As the founding of companies is not yet permitted, this is done under the pretext of a working group, from which Veritas GmbH emerges in 1948.

The technical basis of Veritas vehicles consists of available and recyclable parts from second-hand BMW 328 vehicles that were "probably buried somewhere", as racing driver Karl Kling recalls. With

➤ Concealed under the aerodynamic aluminum body is a tubular frame, and the familiar mechanics of the BMW 328. The eventual Mercedes works driver Karl Kling and the publisher Paul Pietsch are amongst the most prominent of Veritas' victorious pilots.

What else?

Nine race events make up the German motor racing calendar. New are the races in Cologne and Nuremberg. Aside from events in Hockenheim and at the Nürburgring, a long-standing racing tradition begins at the Norisring.

The Targa Florio experiences a revival. A total of 83 vehicles take up the race over 1,080 kilometers on the tradition-steeped Madonie course. Igor Troubetzkoy (alias "Principe Igor") and Clemente Biondetti win with a Ferrari 166.

At the first post-war Mille Miglia, Biondetti/Navone also win with a Ferrari 166.

◄ The Veritas cuts a significantly more professional figure than the many makeshift constructions of the early post-war era. The Veritas Arbeitsgemeinschaft (working group) factory is housed in a derelict mill in Messkirch.

Cockpits these days are spartan work places. There's nothing superfluous here.

a rickety lorry, Loof traipses the length and breadth of Germany to collect parts. Once the stockpile of used frame components dries up, Veritas begins building its own frames. The suspension, the two-liter, straight-six engine and other elements are still sourced from BMW's inventory. The sleek form of the light-alloy body is reminiscent of the BMW 328s that contested the 1940 Mille Miglia sporting the Carozzerria Touring body. Veritas is not the only race car manufacturer to recycle the 328 parts.

Alex von Falkenhausen, who also has close ties to BMW, is the man behind AFM sports cars. AFM disappears from the scene in 1951 due to financial difficulties. And Veritas, too, only survives until 1953. But prior to this, racing drivers including the former Mercedes Silver Arrows pilot Karl Kling, who will be signed up to race for the team again in the mid-1950s, score a string of successes, for example at the Hockenheimring, where "Schorsch" Meier clinches a convincing maiden victory for the Veritas RS. Kling becomes the first title holder of the new German Sports Car Championship with the Veritas

RS. The RS abbreviation stands for Rennsport (racing sport). These two letters denote a 1,000 kg two-seater with a tubular frame and a revamped engine now producing around 120 hp. By the end of 1948, a total of 17 race cars are built in the small Veritas workshop. And, of course, they are all road legal. After all, it's still common for competitors to drive their racing cars to the tracks. Following on from the Veritas RS are Formula 2 cars which, in the early 1950s, regularly line up in packs to compete. When BMW forbids Veritas from using its motors from Munich, the RS is mounted with the unreliable Heinkel power unit. And the road coupé proves to be a flop. Thus, Veritas remains a brief chapter of early post-war history. ——

What might have been?

___ In the spring of 1949, guests at the Turin Motor Show are astonished when they visit the Cisitalia stand and discover an avant-garde Grand Prix car packed with technical innovations. The 718-kg mid-engine single-seater is said to manage 300 km/h and, thanks to driver-activated all-wheel drive, effortlessly transfers 385 hp to the road. The 1500-cc 12-cylinder boxer engine revs to 10,600 per minute, with the engine output at 250 hp, thanks to hemispherical combustion chambers and super-charging. The man behind the Cisitalia is racing driver and industrialist Piero Dusio. The Compania Industriale Sportiva Italia, or Cisitalia, is founded during wartime. With the assistance of Fiat employees Dante Giacosa and Gianni Savonuzzi, the monoposto D 46 (initially 201) emerges shortly afterwards, and in this, acclaimed drivers such as Nuvolari, Taruffi and Chiron reassert themselves in the winners' lists.

But Dusio wants more. The Cisitalia boss has Grand Prix ambitions. Via Carlo Abarth and Rudolf Hruska, he gets in touch with Ferry Porsche. In 1947, Dusio commissions the construction of a revolu-

tionary Grand Prix race car with a supercharged, 12-cylinder mid-engine and all-wheel drive. Porsche Jr. consents. With chief designer Karl Rabe and former Auto Union development engineer Eberan von Eberhorst, Porsche sets to work. Porsche's design office already has relevant experience, with its construction of mid-engine Grand Prix cars for Auto Union – experience that the still-fledgling Cisitalia brand doesn't have on the Grand Prix stage, compared to the big players Alfa Romeo, Maserati, and soon, Ferrari.

Ultimately, however, Dusio lacks the courage and money to advance into Formula 1. And so the Grand Prix Type 360 race car becomes a museum artifact. Cisitalia eventually achieves fame thanks to another museum exhibit: in the 1950s the coupé successor to the 1948 1100 Spider will be classified as a work of art. The Cisitalia 202 GT takes its place in the New York "Museum of Modern Art" as the first of just six vehicles to receive this honor. The two Cisitalia 360 are on show today in the museums of Porsche and Donington. ___

The compact single-seater features a supercharged 1.5-liter 12-cylinder mid-engine and all-wheel drive. But funds dry up before its race debut in Europe. The Cistalia reaches South America and races there.

As well as Ferry Porsche, the successful engineer Rudolf Hruska, who will eventually go to Fiat and Alfa Romeo, becomes involved in the project. The photo shows the supercharged 12-cylinder.

Tackling Formula 1 with proven technology

1949 & 1950
What else?

In 1949, the Rallye Monte Carlo and the Gran Premio di Monza again get the green light. Thanks to Juan Manuel Fangio, Ferrari wins the Italian Grand Prix contested with Formula 2 race cars. With 230 entries, the Rallye Monte Carlo receives an unprecedented number of registrations.

From 1949, the Le Mans 24 Hours and the Freiburg-Schauinsland Hill Climb are again contested. And there are many class winners on the mountains. Hans Stuck is the fastest with a Formula 2 AFM. At Le Mans, victory goes to Chinetti/Selsdon at the wheel of a Ferrari 166 MM.

____ Guiseppe Farina and Juan Manuel Fangio dominate the newly created Formula One World Championship with their Alfa Romeo Tipo 158 "Alfetta". The race distance is now 300 kilometers, or over at least three hours. The two Alfisti are tied three-all for wins on racetracks, some of which only just pass muster. The Alfa race cars are upgraded pre-war designs that are still far from extinction. After a year's hiatus, the Milanese emerge with a new evolution of the Tipo 158. The technical framework hails from the pre-war era and is still standing the test of time. As a result, first and foremost, the racers of Farina, Fangio, and Fagioli receive a decent performance boost that ultimately develops 350 hp. This is enough for 290 km/h. After introducing the sports saloon 1900, the coffers of the company, which shifts gear from a small-volume producer to an automobile manufacturer, are once again flush. Towards the end of the season, the Ferrari 125 S, a sibling of the 1947 Ferrari sports car sharing the same designation, faces new and serious opposition. Thus the path for the evolution of the Alfetta is paved. The Tipo 158 undergoes a complete makeover during the winter break so that Fangio can debut the vehicle, now dubbed the Tipo 159, at the Swiss Grand Prix. He wins. Under the slightly modified body is a reinforced tubular space frame. The suspension and powertrain of the race car are adapted to the performance. Thanks to two-stage supercharging, the 8-cylinder inline engine with a capacity of 1,479 cc produces 425 hp. Over the course of the season, this will even reach 450 hp

Formula One World Championship ushers in a new era of motor racing

at 9,500 rpm. And the speed increases accordingly: with a top speed of 305 km/h, the Tipo 159 breaks the 300 km/h barrier.

The new Alfetta immediately proves a success. Its power stands up to high-speed tracks, and the handling copes well with twisty circuits. In 1951, Fangio claims the world championship title with the Tipo 159 – but Ferrari, too, nets its first Formula 1 successes. The switch of F1-engine regulations to two-liter aggregates reinforces Alfa Romeo's decision to withdraw from the premier class of motor racing.

____

➤ The transaxle design with the gearbox mounted at the rear axle ensures a well-balanced weight distribution of the front-engine vehicle, which, with a power boost to 425 hp, makes Giuseppe Farina and Juan Manuel Fangio Formula One World Champions.

The mother killer

___ Alfa Romeo dominates the fledgling Formula 1. However, the Milan faction faces opposition from Central Italy. At the Monaco Grand Prix of 1950, Ferrari lines up to contest the premier class for the first time, on a stage on which the Maranello squad still plays today. The maiden season yields the burgeoning company three podium results, however Ferrari's achievement is a far cry from that of its former team and employer, Alfa. Like Alfa, Ferrari relies on a 1.5-liter supercharged engine, which develops up to 300 hp in the Ferrari 125 single-seater.

Ferrari zealously throws itself into revamping the Alfetta, which the company designed before the war. In Milan, Alfa Romeo upgrades its Alfa Romeo Tipo 158 into the Tipo 159. This won't make things any easier in the upcoming season. In Modena, an assistant convinces Colombo (who soon returns to Alfa to modernize the Alfetta), engine designer Aurelio Lampredi, and team principal Enzo Ferrari that there is still untapped potential in the 4.5-liter normally aspirated engine. The high consumption of the supercharged race car – up to 150 liters over 100 race kilometers – is the Achilles heel of the supercharged 1.5-liter Grand Prix vehicle. This presents an opportunity for the naturally aspirated competition with its 4.5-liter displacement. This becomes obvious when Raymond Sommer repeatedly takes the lead with the technically outdated Talbot Lago at the Belgium Grand Prix, while the supercharged cars are in the pits refueling. Hence, the "Commendatore" gives the go-ahead to build the Ferrari 375 F1. In 1950, the new power unit, which grows steadily in displacement, finds its feet in the 275 F1. At the Grand Prix of Barcelona, which is not

➤ On July 19, 1952, Alberto Ascari will lap the entire field at the British Grand Prix at Silverstone with his Ferrari 500 F2 and, with six victories under his belt, will earn the world championship title. The 500 F2 is the 4-cylinder successor to the 375 F1, in which, in 1951, Froilan González beats the previously dominant supercharged Alfa Romeo also at Silverstone.

◄ "I've killed my mother …" Enzo Ferrari's alleged words at Silverstone after González defeats the Alfetta, which Enzo Ferrari created.

part of the world championship calendar, Alberto Ascari and Dorino Serafini then clinch the first (double) victory in the autumn of 1950, with a Grand Prix Ferrari.

Twelve cylinders with 375 cc each yield a 4.5-liter displacement. The long-stroke power unit has a compression ratio of 11:1. Breathing through three Weber 40 carburetors and ignited by 24 sparkplugs, it's good for 360 hp. Gearshifts are done via a four-speed gearbox, which feeds the power via a limited slip differential to the De Dion rear axle controlled by Panhard rods. The front suspension consists of wishbones with hydraulic shock absorbers, attaching the front wheels to the space frame independently. With this, Scuderia seems well prepared to tackle the 1951 season. Alas, at the start of the new race season, the red squad from Maranello has to admit defeat once again to Fangio's supercharged Alfa. The breakthrough only comes at the beginning of the second half of the season, when the 375-pilots Froilán González and Alberto Ascari clinch three

With the 375, Ferrari lays the foundation for its F1 career

straight wins. Enzo Ferrari – as legend has it – emotionally claims to have killed his mother (after all, he spent his early years as a designer at Alfa Romeo). In a heart-stopping finale, the decision goes down to the wire between Ascari and Fangio, between Ferrari and Alfa Romeo. Ferrari has to surrender, for now. The lifespan of the 375 is short. The end of the 1951 season also signals the end of the current engine regulations. Due to a lack of spectators and a lack of competitive race cars with supercharged 1,500-cc or 4.5-liter normally aspirated engines (Alfa Romeo has withdrawn), the two-liter regulations from Formula 2 are applied to Formula 1 from 1952. Here, too, Ferrari is excellently positioned. The 500 F2 with the 2-liter, 4-cylinder is fast, reliable, and thanks to its De Dion rear axle, also blessed with great road-holding qualities. With this vehicle Alberto Ascari is crowned world champion in 1952 and 1953 and brings the world championship titles home to Ferrari.

____

What else?

Peter Walker and Peter Whitehead achieve the first Le Mans win for the marque from Coventry at the wheel of a C-Type Jaguar XK120 C.

Porsche scores a class victory at Le Mans in the 751-1100 cc category with the aerodynamically optimized 356. This success marks the start of a long Le Mans tradition for the sports car manufacturer from Stuttgart.

◄ The 12-cylinder unit of the 375 develops 350 hp with a displacement of 4,493 cc. With this, González and Ascari win the last three races of the 1951 Grand Prix season and conclude the year in positions two and three, behind the Alfa pilot Fangio.

Knock knock

What else?

Formula 1 now fields racing cars built in compliance with Formula 2 rules. The two-liter, 4-cylinder Ferrari proves unbeatable, and Alberto Ascari convincingly scores the world championship title.

Mercedes-Benz again steps onto the international stage of motor racing. At Le Mans, the Stuttgart company fields the new 300 SL, now with gull-wing doors, and promptly wins the 24-hour race. Hermann Lang and Fritz Riese, along with Theo Helfrich and Norbert Niedermayer, secure a double victory for the racing squad managed by Alfred Neubauer and engineer Rudolf Uhlenhaut. Porsche repeats its class win of the previous year with the 356.

___ A diesel race car first turned heads in 1931, when Dave Evans tackled the entire 500-mile race without a pit stop in his Cummins Diesel Special. It was the first time that any Indy-500 racing driver had covered the distance nonstop. Twenty years later, the Cummins Diesel Special makes a comeback at Indianapolis. At the initiative of engine builder Don Cummins and engineer Neve Reiners, the first turbo-diesel-powered race car is conceived. It celebrates its debut in 1950, but retires after a quarter of the distance. In 1952, however, the diesel again writes history, this time thanks to Fred Agabashian, who claims pole position in the single-seater. This marks the first-ever top qualifying time for a diesel, and with an average of 222.11 km/h. Unfortunately, Agabashian is unable to make the most of his pole position. While running in the lead, his vehicle is sidelined with a clogged turbocharger in lap 71 of 200.

The six-cylinder diesel engine from the Cummins factory is dubbed the 3.0 L6 6401 and is routinely mounted underfloor for use in buses. Accordingly, its capacity is 6,751 cc. Out of this displacement it produces 350 hp at a low 4,000 rpm, typical for a diesel engine. The turbocharged diesel unit is positioned as a front mid-engine in a Kurtis chassis, however, for the first time, Frank Kurtis offsets it to the left-hand side of the chassis. This gives the Cummins Diesel Special a weight-distribution advantage in the left-hand banked turns of the oval, which is run anticlockwise. This vehicle layout quickly becomes the norm, with the chassis from Kurtis

gaining huge popularity in the Indy scene. Company founder Frank Kurtis began designing race cars in the 1930s. Under the name Kurtis-Kraft, his vehicles go on to win the Indy 500 five times between 1950 and 1955.

Without any pit stops, a diesel races for 500 miles from pole position

Between 1950 and 1960, the Cummins Diesel Special is the only diesel-powered race car in history to compete in Formula 1 – the Indianapolis 500-mile race is a points-scoring round of the newly established F1 championship. The reason is that Formula 1, contested mainly in Europe, is keen to be given world championship status. Hence the sport's governing body compromises by accepting different technical regulations. However, the Americans are not particularly interested in taking the title and limit their Formula 1 commitment primarily to the Indy 500 round. At the same time, most Europeans also stay away from Indianapolis. And because different circuits require different technology, from 1961, the long-distance classic on the oval, and F1 run on classic circuits, strike out on different paths. ___

Freddie Agabashian
Indianapolis Motor Speedway
-1952-

The front opening, protected by mesh wire, feeds cool air to the engine; the air inlet on the engine hood provides air to the three Weber dual carburetors; the oval holes between the headlights and the radiator cool the internal brakes of the sports car, which is capable of achieving 265 km/h.

Victories and fierce duels

___ In conjunction with the first successes of the innovative Aurelia B20 (the transaxle layout is just one detail), Lancia also works on a thoroughbred race car whose successes are expected to make a lasting impact on the marque's corporate image. The D20, with independent suspension, internal brake drums, and a race engine based on the Aurelia-V6, now with four overhead camshafts, debuts at the 1953 Mille Miglia. It finishes third behind Marzotto's Ferrari 340 MM and Fangio's Alfa Romeo 6C 3000 CM. Next up is the 24 Hours of Le Mans, and, after experiencing the sweltering heat of the closed coupés, a Spider is requested. The roof is quickly removed, and just two weeks after Le Mans, the Spider emerges in time for the Gran Premio dell'Autodromo di Monza, now with the designation D23. Under the hood with its characteristic air scoop sits the tried-and-true, extremely compact, 2,962-cc V6, which develops 217 hp at 6,500 rpm. With the roof gone and the wheelbase shortened by half a meter, the 800-kilogram D23 is 50 kilograms lighter than the D20 coupé. The first victory comes at the Grand Prix of Portugal, which at this time is also open for sports cars.

At the same time in Turin, a 3,284-cc power unit is being worked on, which, thanks to its finely balanced crankshaft, puts out 265 hp at 6,500 rpm. The wheelbase is shortened, however, and the gearbox is now positioned behind the rear axle. It's housed with the differential and delivers the power to a single rigid drive shaft. With its harmonious front layout, the Spider is dubbed the D24 and weighs around 60 kg more than its predecessor. Laden with fuel, oil, water and driver, it tips the scales at 1,050 kg.

Meanwhile, Juan Manuel Fangio has joined the Lancia driver lineup. The D24's debut as part of the 1,000-kilometer race on the Nürburgring is followed by the internationally acclaimed Carrera Panamericana. This race runs for five days in eight legs over 3,077 kilometers through Mexico. Like the "Mille", the "Targa", and other road races, the Carrera runs over poorly-marshaled public roads. Lancia deploys 5 vehicles and 20 mechanics. Fangio, Bonetto and Taruffi receive a D24 each. Their teammates Bracco and Castellotti have to make do with the D23. With a view to durability, prior to the event, Lancia reduces the capacity of the D24's 6-cylinder, normally-aspirated engine to 3,099 cc and the output to 230 hp at 6,250 rpm.

Right from the outset, the red Spiders from Turin take the lead, which leads to fierce duels within the team that rage over hundreds of kilometers, ultimately resulting in the death of Bonetto while fighting with Taruffi. After this, the company boss Gianni Lancia forbids any clashes between his pilots, and the "Carrera" concludes with a triple victory to Lancia. Thanks to his swift yet careful driving style, the Argentine Formula 1 champion Fangio reaches the finish ahead of Taruffi and Casellotti. While Lancia increasingly devotes it energies to Formula 1, victories at smaller events, as well as at the Mille Miglia and Targa Florio, round out the winning streak of 1954.

The Lancia D24 comes after the D20 and D23. The 3.3-liter 6-cylinder sports car is significantly more successful. The D24 celebrates its premiere in 1953 at the 1,000-kilometer Nürburgring race, but is defeated by the 4.5-liter Ferrari. Still, after spending many laps in the lead, its debut shows promise. At the Carrera Panamericana (above and center), Lancia notches up a triple victory. The photo below shows the Lancia D24, with which Pierro Taruffi and Eugenio Castellotti contest the 1954 Coppa della Dolomiti. Shortly before, Taruffi wins the Giro di Sicilia, and Juan Manuel Fangio wins the Mille Miglia.

Well-engineered racing machine

___ "We build and sell normal automobiles, not race cars," states Jaguar boss William Lyons in 1953, when he fails to see a particularly strong response to the Le Mans successes of 1951 and 1953. True to the motto "quit while you're ahead", he's also keen to avoid rising costs. However, the 1953 victory of the C-Type (in-house designation XKC), a close relative of the standard road-going XK 140 sports car, puts Jaguar in the limelight: Jaguar has proved to be extremely innovative, and has been instrumental in advancing disc brakes, today a standard feature in automotive design. And fuel tanks made of plastic have long since found their way into mass production.

Lyons could have been using the flexibility of Germany's former Chancellor Konrad Adenauer as an example, when he famously quoted: "What do I

What do I care about my chitchat from yesterday ...

care about my chitchat from yesterday?" Indeed, after careful consideration, the Jaguar boss builds a new race car for the 1954 endurance racing season. After C comes D, and this time a purebred race car is conceived right from the outset: the racer features an aluminum bodyshell, optimized with the help of a wind-tunnel-tested 1:10-model. Concealed under the body is a box-shaped monocoque riveted together from sheets of aluminum alloy – albeit with the front and rear suspension from the C-Type, adopted from the XK 140. Moreover, the vehicle also features power-assisted disc brakes all round and aluminum rims! Compared to conventional wire-spoke wheels, these are lighter, sturdier, and, like the brakes, come from the tire supplier Dunlop. The shorter wheelbase and length make it more compact than the C-Type.

➤ The D-Type wins the 24 Hours of Le Mans three times straight from 1955 to 1957.

What else?

Mercedes-Benz celebrates its comeback to Grand Prix racing with the W196. Juan Manuel Fangio and Karl Kling finish the first Formula 1 race for the Stuttgart squad in July 1954 on the Reims circuit with a double victory in their streamlined, covered single-seater.

◄ The D-Type also becomes a favorite amongst American sports car racing drivers. Aluminum rims now replace the spoked wheels.

The technical basis of the C-Type engine is adopted from the XK120. The otherwise new design of the race car earns Jaguar its first successes at Le Mans.

The straight-six engine with two overhead camshafts is a well-proven unit – now however lowered in height with dry sump lubrication and a 14-liter oil reservoir. Three Weber 45 dual carburetors take care of the mixture preparation. And thus, the 3,442-cc power unit produces 245 hp at 5,750 rpm. Eventually, the motor receives a capacity boost to 3.8 liters. There is an eye-catching large vertical stabilizer directly behind the driver's head, providing the race car (capable of reaching 261 km/h) with aerodynamic stability on straights.

The successor to the crown is finished in time for Le Mans. However, teething problems (clogged fuel filters as well as problems with brake lines and gearbox) throw a small spanner in the works of the Jaguar, with drivers Rolt/Hamilton crossing the finish line after 24 hours just 105 seconds behind Gonzalèz/Trintignant in their Ferrari. However, from 1955 to 1957, there is no stopping the British Racing

Green sports car on its path to victory at the endurance classic. And ultimately, even though the Jaguar no longer features state-of-the-art technology – as the race driver and journalist Paul Frère finds out driving the D-Type at Le Mans – the key to success is still a well-engineered racing machine.

Incidentally, the "D-Type 3.5 liter" from 1955 appears on the price list of the German importer at 36,500 DM. This is ten times more expensive than a Beetle of that time, and the exclusive XK 140 Roadster costs only half.

Good times and bad

▲ Parallel to Mercedes' successful Formula 1 outings, the brand takes the title in the World Sports Car Championship for Makes thanks to the 300 SLR. Mercedes wins the Mille Miglia, the Tourist Trophy (left and right), and the Targa Florio.

What else?

The motor-racing season seems to be under a cloud: Even before the tragedy at Le Mans, Formula 1 pilot Alberto Ascari and two-time Indianapolis winner Bill Vukovich are killed. Lancia withdraws from motor racing and gives its six innovative D50 to Scuderia Ferrari. Even before the Le Mans accident, Mercedes-Benz has already decided to retire from racing, and a number of event organizers around the world step down from their positions. In Switzerland, a ban on circuit racing is still in place today.

◄ Stirling Moss and his co-driver, British journalist Denis Jenkinson, achieve the fastest time at the Mille Miglia and reach the finish after 1,597 kilometers in just ten hours and seven minutes.

___ Even though the lines and the name suggest an affiliation with the family of the gull-wing 300 SL sports car, the silver bodyshell of magnesium alloy conceals purebred Formula 1 technology. Instead of the straight-six engine with mechanical fuel injection of the SLR, at work here is the inclined straight-eight motor of the world-championship-winning W196 Formula 1 race car. In the sports car, the power unit develops 309 hp. Accordingly, it receives the internal code name W196S. Additional technical delicacies include fuel injection, positive-control valves (desmodromic) without valve springs, independent torsion bar suspension, and internal brakes to reduce unsprung masses.

The three-liter M196, as the engine is called, is regarded not only as one of the most technically complex units, but also as one of the most successful: ten victories (from twelve races) go to the credit of the 2.5-liter Formula 1 machines, raced for the first time in 1954, with the 300 SLR winning five of six races. Describing the technical superiority of this design, columnist Laurence Pomeroy writes: "Figuratively, one may say that if the BRM looks like a typewriter, the four-cylinder Ferrari is the equivalent of an abacus and the Untertürkheim cars rate as an electronic calculating machine."

With its legendary triumphs at the Targa Florio, the Tourist Trophy, and the Mille Miglia, the 300 SLR becomes an icon among racing cars – especially the red #722 car. The starting number represents the time, 7.22am, that Moss/Jenkins take off on their flying trip from Brescia to Rome and back. While Juan-Manuel Fangio unwaveringly keeps his nose in front of Stirling Moss in Formula 1, the Briton regularly relegates his rivals to finish behind him in the 300 SLR – especially at the "Mille", where his co-driver, journalist Derek Jenkins, provides him with important navigation tips for the trip with "pace notes", which will eventually become indispensible in rallying. After a driving time of just ten hours and seven minutes, the 300 SLR arrives back in Brescia. This represents an average speed of over 157 km/h – on 1,600 kilometers of public roads, through narrow twisty cities, and with service breaks!

For the Le Mans 24-hour race, the one- or two-seater SLR (depending on its intended purpose), receives a new type of "air brake", a kind of flap intended to assist the drum brakes. However, instead of causing a stir with its technology at the long-distance classic, the Silver Arrow is embroiled in arguably the darkest moment of motor racing history: In the crash involving the SLR and an Austin Healey, pilot Pierre Bouillon, alias "Levegh", and 81 spectators lose their lives.

The year 1955 concludes with a convincing title win for Mercedes-Benz thanks to the W196 and W196S in the Formula 1 World Championship and the World Sports Car Championship for Makes, but the Le Mans tragedy puts a halt to the company's works-run motor-racing activities. ___

The 300 SLR heralds great wins, but also huge tragedy

1956 | Porsche 550 A

David versus Goliath

▲ The Porsche 550 enjoys success around the world, whether at the Carrera Panamericana (top), the Mille Miglia (center), the Targa Florio (right), or at the Nürburgring (bottom).

What else?

Bugatti launches its final Grand Prix race car at the French Grand Prix. However, the Type 251 with its transversely mounted eight-cylinder mid-engine turns out to be a flop.

Significantly more successful is the Maserati 250 F with its front-mounted engine, with which Moss wins at Monaco and Monza, and Fangio becomes 1957 F1 world champion after three wins.

➤ Umberto Maglioli hands Porsche its first outright win at a world championship round. In 1956, the Italian keeps the larger-capacity competition at bay on the twisty Madonie course of the Targa Florio.

___ Tipping the scales at almost 530 kilos, this car is a real flyweight, however its 1.5-liter capacity from four cylinders and 135 hp output certainly doesn't make it a favorite at international sports car races. Still, Umberto Maglioli is an ace at making the most of the flounder's 240 km/h maximum speed. On June 10, 1956, he wins the Targa Florio against the more powerful opposition from Maranello and Modena. One lap equals 72 kilometers, running from Cerda in the mountains not far from Palermo, and back down to the coast. The challenge is to survive the ten laps on public roads, all of which are cordoned off for the race. And so, not only do Maglioli and his fellow combatants have to deal with the challenges of the circuit and the ticking stopwatch, they also have to avoid dogs, mule carts, and other obstacles. With an almost 15-point advantage, the compact Porsche beats the competition and hands the Stuttgart brand its first overall victory in the World Championship for Makes. The 550A celebrates its debut in May 1956 in the hands of Maglioli/von Trips with a class victory at the 1,000-kilometer race on the 'Ring. Interestingly, this is the same day that the large rear wing appears "above" Michael May's 550 – an aerodynamic modification that will eventually flow into Formula 1. A raft of class wins at events like the "Mille" and the "Carrera" round off the successes of the flat two-seater. Thus, the small 500 earns fame at the "Carrera", a name that will later be used to distinguish the sports cars from Stuttgart.

The 550A launched in 1956 is an evolution of the Porsche 550, unveiled three years earlier as the first Porsche to be developed exclusively for racing. The mid-engine sports car comes from the same drawing board as the first sports car of Beetle-designer Ferdinand Porsche, which now bears his name for the first time. Like the Porsche No. 1, the 550 features an aluminum body and an air-cooled four-cylinder boxer engine mounted in front of the rear axle. The power plant, designed by Ernst Fuhrmann, with four overhead camshafts, represents the pinnacle of flat-four engines. The motor's camshafts are driven by vertical drive shafts, allowing an impressive 7,000 revs per minute. However, the vertical shaft engine is so complicated to set up that Fuhrmann later calls it a "folly of youth".

In its design, the 550A is a purebred race car, built on a tubular space frame instead of the previously used platform-type format of the Beetle and Porsche 356. The skeleton of the 550 was a ladder-type flat chassis. For better accessibility, the rear can be eas-

Pros and amateurs alike choose the compact Spyder

ily accessed and the front-mounted fuel tank is fitted with a quick-release tank cap. Aside from the Spyder body, aerodynamically efficient hard-top 550 race cars also tackle the Le Mans endurance classic.

Around the world, the 550 and 550A become popular amongst seasoned amateur racers – the likes of Hollywood legend James Dean. Alas, tragedy strikes the young actor and hobby racing driver in his 550. While driving to a race at Laguna Seca, he is killed at the wheel of a 550 Spyder on September 30, 1955. ___

➤ Ferrari wins Le Mans with the Testa Rossa in 1958, 1960, 1961, and 1962. At an auction in 2007, the 1962-winner TRI/LM of Gendebien/Hill (cockpit photo) fetches almost seven million Euros. In 2010, the original version from 1957 (right photo) yields an auction price of over nine million Euros.

Red-headed wonder

___ Testa Rossa means redhead – the name given to the race car from Maranello that follows the 500 Mondial. This designation goes back to the red-painted DOHC cam covers adorning the two-liter, four-cylinder inline engine of the 500 Testa Rossa in 1956. From 1957, the Testa Rossa, designed by the technical team under ex-Alfa Romeo engineer Vittorio Jano, also receives the twelve-cylinder engine conceived on the drawing board of another former Alfa Romeo engineer, Gioachino Colombo. He is the mastermind behind successful race cars such as the Alfetta Tipo 158 and 159, which competed for the first time in 1938 and clinched Formula One World Championship titles in 1950 and 1951. The power unit mobilizes 2,953 cc at 7,200 rpm to develop an impressive 300 hp, and thus a phenomenal specific output of 100 hp. Six Weber dual carburetors take care of the mixture preparation of the Ferrari, capable of a 270 km/h top speed. The four-speed gearbox no longer sits at the differential in the rear (transaxle design), but is directly bolted to the engine.

The doors, prescribed by the rules, are fake.

Like its four-cylinder sibling, a delicate tubular space frame with two distinctly shaped side members forms the skeleton of the lightweight 800-kg sports car. Underneath its thin aluminum skin is room for the power unit, two occupants if necessary, a fuel tank, and – depending on the layout – two versions of rear axle: the factory pilots compete with independent suspension, while customers have to settle for a rigid axle. As the 250 Testa Rossa variant, the front-engine sports car becomes one of Ferrari's most successful cars. After its premiere in 1957 at the 1,000-km race on the Nürburgring, it will ultimately net a string of victories in 1958 in-

◄ While the 250 Testa Rossa is designed as a thoroughbred race car, the 250 GT is suitable for racing, as a Grand Tourer, and for use on public roads. Still, a number of these coupés, in Italy often referred to as Berlinettas, have found their way to the race-tracks of the world.

What else?

Juan Manuel Fangio achieves his fifth Formula 1 title (the fourth in a row) and thus sets a benchmark that will remain unbeaten for decades. It is only equaled in 2002, by Michael Schumacher.

Due to the Suez crisis and the resulting fuel shortages in France, the Monte Carlo Rally is canceled at short notice. The finite nature of fossil fuels becomes evident for the first time to the automotive scene.

cluding in Buenos Aires (double victory to Phil Hill/Peter Collins in front of Wolfgang von Trips/Luigi Musso/Olivier Gendebien), Sebring (Hill/Collins and Musso/Gendebien) at the "Targa" (Musso/Gendebien), and at Le Mans (Gendebien/Hill), to secure the Manufacturers' World Championship title. At its debut, Ferrari lets no less than seven racing drivers to prove themselves at the three-spoke wooden steering wheel. One of the aspirants is the German racing driver Wolfgang Graf Berghe von Trips.

A great deal of its popularity can be attributed to the incomparable design – sweeping fenders that open up towards the cockpit flanks, the headlights covered by Plexiglas. The protruding oval radiator inlet gives the impression of wanting to dash on ahead of the car. And in fact, with this shape, body designer Sergio Scaglietti has conceived an ideal airflow around the large brake drums. As well as the two seats, the regulations of the time are also responsible for the fake doors – after all, the also-mandatory roof doesn't have to be on during racing.

Until 1960, the 18 Testa Rossa 250 built in Maranello prove themselves against their rivals from Porsche, Aston Martin, and Maserati – including another Le Mans triumph and World Championship for Makes title in 1960. In the meantime, to improve the directional stability of the sports car, Pininfarina modifies the design of the front-engine vehicle for the 1959 season and creates a harmonious, conventional front section out of the radiator, fenders, and headlamps. Further modifications and an increased capacity add two more Le Mans victories to its list of achievements.

Mid-ship miracle

___ 1958 begins with a surprising victory for Stirling Moss in a Cooper T43 Mk II powered by a four-cylinder engine producing around 175 hp, designed by Coventry Climax. Cooper unveiled the T41 mid-engine single-seater for Formula 1 and 2 at the end of 1956. And already in 1957, the compact mid-engine cars attract attention in the field of F1 front-engine vehicles. The tiny single-seaters look distinctively different to the traditional front-engine giants. Moss' performance in Argentina marks the breakthrough to a perfectly balanced mid-engine car.

Maurice Trintignant underlines Cooper's excellent result with a win at the Monaco Grand Prix in the modified successor. The 194-hp 2.2-liter Climax power unit is now tilted to the left and mounted deeper in the chassis. This creates room for a new gearbox and ZF differential.

On fast tracks, the weak but lightweight 380-kg Coopers don't have a chance against the more powerful opposition, but they certainly put up a good fight to yield podium results. This lays the foundation for further successes, with Cooper achieving two world championships with Jack Brabham.

With the new, now 2495-cc Coventry Climax FPF engines fitted in the T51, Brabham immediately snatches victory at the season opener in Monaco. This is followed by a win at Aintree as well as podium spots at Zandvoort, Reims, and Monza. At the British Grand Prix, 16 racing drivers put their trust in Coopers. Bruce McLaren notches up a win at Sebring. Stirling Moss wins the races in Portugal and Italy. After missing out on the title in 1956 and 1957, he also walks away empty-handed in 1958 – and again in 1960 in the mid-engine car. Thus, Stirling Moss becomes famous for being the most successful pilot without a Formula 1 World Championship title.

Jack Brabham, however, repeats his title win in 1960 with five victories: Initially with the T51, from May with the Cooper T53, now with a lower, slimmer design and 240 hp. By 1961, the front-engine dinosaurs are extinct. There is no longer a way past the mid-engine design. ___

What else?

NASCAR introduces an award for the "Rookie of the Year." The first title winner is Shorts Rollins.

With the end of the Mille Miglia, another road race disappears from the scene. The Targa Florio, however, remains on the calendar until the 1970s.

◄ Cooper has established a new design style in Formula 1. The delicate mid-engine single-seaters emerge on the stage in the early 1960s and represent a new standard. The comparison with the Mini gives an indication of the dimensions of the Formula 1 race cars of that era.

▲ The green sport cars from Newport Pagnell are the first race cars to feature permanently mounted pneumatic car jacks. Today, pneumatic jacks are standard features.

What else?

Jack Brabham wins the first of two consecutive world championship titles with the Cooper-Climax and thus underlines the superiority of the new vehicle layout.

▼ The double victory at the 1959 Le Mans 24 Hours is just one of many triumphs in the DBR1's most successful season.

Martin, Aston Martin

___ The DBR1 seems to be the perfect car for the demanding Nordschleife of the Nürburgring. Between 1957 and 1959, the open sports cars from Newport Pagnell win the 1,000-kilometer race three times in succession, thanks to the victorious driver pairings of Tony Brooks and Noel Cunningham-Reid, Stirling Moss and Jack Brabham (1958) as well as Moss and Jack Fairman (1959). As was customary until the 1980s, Grand Prix greats like Moss and Brabham give well-paid guest appearances at sports and touring car races.

At its debut in 1956, the sports car, designed by Aston Martin engineer Ted Cutting, still had a long way to go. At Le Mans, following the serious accident the previous year, the capacity of new prototypes was capped at 2.5 liters. Accordingly, the new DBR1, named after the company founder David Brown, had a capacity of 2493 cc. However, its maiden outing wasn't exactly cause for celebration, with the racer retiring in the last hour of racing.

In 1957, the DB 3S again won its class. The two DBR1, powered by 3-liter 6-cylinder engines, again retired. For them, the 24-hour race was over after ten and twelve hours respectively. And in 1958, the DBR1 once again failed to reach the flag. Success only comes in 1959: The DBR1 crews of Roy Salvatori and Carroll Shelby, and Maurice Trintignant and Paul Frère, achieve a double victory with a convincing

> **The DBR1 proves the theory that "beautiful race cars are also good race cars"**

lead far in excess of 300 kilometers ahead of the third-placed Ferrari. 1959 turns out to be a bountiful year for the DBR1, with the Tourist Trophy win and the manufacturers' championship crown.

Green paint is applied to the thin-paneled aluminum body, which rests on a delicate tubular space frame supported by a ladder-type chassis with twin tubular members. Also attached to the frame are longitudinal control arms at the front and the De Dion rear axle. For the suspension of the 801-kilogram two-seater, torsion bars are fitted to the front and rear. Under the hood sits the latest evolution of Aston Martin's six-cylinder inline engine. From 2992 cc, the dual camshaft engine with two spark plugs per cylinder and three Weber dual carburetors produce 250 horsepower at 6,000 rpm. With this, 254 km/h is possible.

The recent success at the Sarthe may have contributed to the sports car from Newport Pagnell becoming the preferred automobile of the British royal family. Whatever the case, the cars have achieved success since 1913 under the name Martin, and from 1922 under the name Aston Martin. ___

A cage like spaghetti

___ The shine of the 1957 season quickly fades. Only a few years after Fangio claims his fifth F1-title with Maserati and hands Ferrari the crown of the Manufacturer's World Championship, Maserati owner Orsi finds himself in financial difficulties. Despite this, Maserati still knows how to make headlines.

The "Birdcage" and the Maserati "Spaghetti" are nicknames given to the graceful, lightweight designs in which Stirling Moss and Masten Gregory net more successes. The Tipo 60 and the Tipo 61, as the Birdcage is correctly called, owe the nickname to the chassis design. Under the low-slung, slender aluminum body, a tubular space frame serves as the backbone. What's special is the way it's constructed. The frame consists of 200 steel tubes of exceptionally small diameters. Cleverly welded together in triangles, the frame weighs a mere 30 kilograms. Thus, the two-liter Tipo 60, unveiled in 1959, tips the scales at just 585 kilograms. And even the Tipo 61, almost as lightweight at 600 kilograms, with its 2,890-cc straight-four engine, makes effortless work of its 250 hp, reaching a top speed of up to 300 km/h.

The way in which the six Tipo 60 and seventeen Tipo 61 vehicles are realized is impressive: To reduce the front surface area and thus drag, the engine is tilted 45 degrees to the right. Only the two 48 dual carburetors with their open air inlets make it necessary to fit a flat air scoop over the engine. The wide, low windshield allows a view into the extraordinary structure of the car.

At its premiere race in 1959 in the Bahamas, Carroll Shelby, who will eventually earn himself a name as the Cobra and Mustang "whisperer", sits at the wheel of the Tipo 60. And after the two-liter contender dominates its class during the season, a need for more displacement becomes apparent. No one understands how to draw attention more than Lloyd "Lucky" Casner. The chronically cash-strapped team boss comes up with a new way to source funds: He spontaneously involves racing fans, who pay five dollars for a car sticker, team pass, and a monthly magazine. ___

A total of 22 units of the so-called "Birdcage" race car are created in the Modena workshops of the Officine Alfieri Maserati S.p.A. Today, Maserati belongs to Ferrari, and the marque's own racing series for classic sports cars is a favorite haunt for expensive vintage vehicles.

Flat-out on salt

1960 marks the last time the Indianapolis runs as part of Formula 1.

In 1961, the U.S. Grand Prix is held at Watkins Glen. This time, well-known Formula 1 teams and drivers line up to compete. Innes Ireland in a Lotus 21 beats Porsche pilot Dan Gurney.

___ Donald Campbell inherits a love of speed from his father, speed record-setter Sir Malcolm Campbell. The Briton not only continues his father's work, but also his motor sport tradition. The yearning to go as fast as possible is as old as the automobile itself. Records already played a role in the late 19th century: Jenatzy was the first person to shatter the 100 km/h barrier, and the Lightning Benz was the first to break the 200 km/h mark.

Record attempts on the German autobahns reached their limit at a speed exceeding 360 km/h, and ultimately ended with the tragic death of the Auto Union driver Bernd Rosemeyer. The actual cause of the accident is still unknown. However, regardless of whether it was a gust of wind or a deformed aluminum body that rendered the aerodynamics ineffective, it soon became clear that public roads were simply too narrow for record attempts. This opened the way for record hunters to travel to the Bonneville Salt Flats in the U.S. state of Utah, where, in 1935, Malcolm Campbell smashed the 300-mph mark, reaching almost 485 km/h in the "Bluebird". This marked Campbell Sr.'s ninth land speed record since 1924. For this achievement, King George V bestowed a knighthood on him in 1931.

In contrast to his father's displacement monster – the last member of the normally aspirated family – Donald Campbell puts his faith in the CN7 powered by a 5,000 hp supercharged gas-turbine. However,

The Campbell family pushes the boundaries on land and water

the gas-turbine drives all the CN7's wheels via two gearboxes. Richard Noble's jet-powered "Blue Flame" and "Thrust", which will achieve speeds exceeding 1,000 km/h and 1,227 km/h respectively, are "earth-bound rockets". Through helping with the "Bluebird", Noble gains expertise that will assist him in setting the existing record in the late 1990s. He is responsible for the braking system, which consists of three independent almost 17-inch discs and air brakes. The body is made of two layers of aluminum panels using honeycomb composition materials.

In 1961, comprehensive repairs are necessary after an accident, and this turns into a stopgap year for the CN7. Fitted with a new cockpit cover and a stabilizing rear fin, the vehicle is fit and ready for the 1963 attempt. Donald Campbell reaches almost 650 km/h, but the record doesn't hold for long. Americans Bill and Bob Summers set a new record with a speed of 658.649 km/h in 1965 with their "Goldenrod" powered by four engines; a record that is still in effect today for wheel-driven vehicles. In 1967, Donald Campbell is killed during a water speed record attempt. ___

➤ Campbell's Bluebird still follows the template of classic automobile design. It is, after all, a wheel-driven vehicle. Later, speed-record cars are earthbound rockets propelled by jet engines.

Colin Chapman (with trophy) was regarded as an ingenious designer all his life. His strokes of genius make Lotus a world championship winner again and again. One of his maxims is light-weight design. With racing driver Jim Clark, he has a kindred spirit in the team. Clark achieves the first of two world championship titles for Lotus in 1963 with the Lotus 25-Climax.

Lightweight winner

___ The Lotus 25 bolsters the reputation of Colin Chapman's workshop as a breeding ground for technical ideas. With the vehicles presented over the 1962 season, Lotus plays a part in the breakthrough of monocoque design in single-seaters. This method of construction, in which the chassis is made of riveted aluminum panels, revolutionizes the design of race cars. It remains standard until the emergence of the carbon-fiber era in the 1980s.

Compared to the conventional tubular space frame used until the arrival of the Lotus 25, the bathtub-like monocoque with bulkheads, bracing, and trussing has many advantages: It's lighter, with more torsional stiffness, and also safer, as there are no more tubes, which could deform in the event of an accident. The side pontoons allow space for the fuel tanks made of rubber. The entire chassis now weighs a mere 30 kilograms, and the increased rigidity enables the engineers to build a vehicle that is even more compact.

Climax-V8 engines are usually used to power the Lotus. But even the eight-cylinder units from BRM are mounted in the chassis behind the Lotus F1 pilots. In 1961, the F1 governing body lowers the maximum capacity from 2.5 to 1.5 liters. Thus, even into the 1964 season, the Lotus 25 has a displacement of 1,496 cc. The engine develops a good 200 hp at 9,800 rpm. The V8 from Coventry Climax proves to be a good choice, as, thanks in no small part to the Lotus 25, it turns into the most successful power unit in the 1.5-liter era of Formula 1, until 1965. From 1963, a low-pressure fuel injection system from Lucas replaces the previously-used four Weber dual carburetors, and over time the engine output of the Climax motor grows from the initial

190 to 213 hp. The complete vehicle tips the scales at just 450 kilograms and stands on cast light-alloy wheels, which in turn help to reduce the unsprung masses. Thanks to rapid groundbreaking construction and technological advancement, the 1.5-liter vehicle quickly eclipses the performance of the former 2.5-liter days.

The 25 celebrates its debut at the Grand Prix in Zandvoort and, just a month later, Jim Clark scores the first win at Spa-Francorchamps. Notching up more successes in England and America, Clark and Lotus even find themselves in a position to fight for the title against BRM pilot Graham Hill. When the Scotsman retires while holding the lead at the finale, the path is clear for Hill to snatch the title. Lotus 25 pilots notch up a total of 14 victories. In 1963, no less than seven triumphs go to Clark, who wins the first of two world championship titles and the first of seven constructor titles for the team from Hethel, a well-known race squad that exists up until 1994.

The single-seater weighs just 450 kilos and stands on cast-aluminum wheels

As the Lotus 33 (new numbering begins with the introduction of new, wider Dunlop tires), the Lotus 25 also takes the step into the three-liter era of Formula 1, beginning in 1966, and it will remain there until 1967. In 1965, a title is added for both Lotus and Clark.

___

The Lotus 25 is the most distinctive design in the Grand Prix era of these delicate, elegant "cigars". Replacing the tubular space frame, Chapman implements a light and rigid monocoque out of riveted aluminum panels.

What else?

Porsche clinches its only Formula 1 victory at Reims. At the wheel sits Dan Gurney. Of technical interest is the use of specially designed disc brakes with internal brake calipers, and the air-cooled flat-eight with four overhead camshafts, driven by vertical drive shafts.

Sought-after gems

___ The Ferrari 250 LM (for Le Mans) represents the jewel in the crown of the model line with the three-liter V12, which has enjoyed exceptional success for more than a decade. Along with the models 250 S Berlinetta and 250 MM, built in 1952 and 1953 for the Mille Miglia, as well as the 1963-debuting 250 P and 250 LM mid-engine sports cars, the family portrait gallery consisted of no less than 25 different 250 models. Included in the ancestral lineup are super sports cars à la 250 GT Berlinetta "lusso", a direct relative of the racing car, as well as purebred racers such as the 250 Testa Rossa, 250 GTO, and 250 LM.

At the beginning of its career, the 2,953-cc, 60°-12-cylinder engine develops 200 hp (at 7,000 rpm). The 850-kilogram 250 S Berlinetta lightweight, with its engine fed by three Weber 36 carburetors, reaches speeds of 230 km/h. As with the 250 Testa Rossa (1957), 250 GT LM (1961), and 250 GTO (1962), 300 hp is now possible – with the same displacement and an increase of around 500 rpm. Fuel preparation is by means of six Weber 38 carburetors. The weight class remains identical, only the GTO weighs 30 kilograms more, with the 250 P 90 kilograms lighter. The GTO is capable of reaching 280 km/h, the 250 P and the 250 LM as its derivative come close to the magical 300 km/h barrier with around 290 km/h. After the homologation of the prototype, the 1964-successor 250 LM is mounted with a rebored 275 power unit producing 320 hp with a capacity of 3,286 cc.

Homologation proves to be quite an obstacle. Already in 1962 there are problems with the classification of the GTO. And now the sport's governing body refuses to accept the 250 LM as a GT with its midship-mounted engine – and therefore the suc-

➤ True to the motto "better is the enemy of good", Ferrari develops a mid-engine version of the 250. As the 275, it wins at the Sarthe in 1965 in the hands of Masten Gregory and Jochen Rindt, before the dawn of the Ford GT40 era. Ferrari originally wants to homologate the 250 LM as an evolution of the 250 GTO, which generates some controversy. In fact, the mid-engine is based on the 250 P prototype, which wins Le Mans in 1963 and 1964 (as the 275 P).

◄ With the Ferrari 250 GTO (O stands for Omologato) the motor racing world experiences the first edition of a homologation special built specifically in compliance with the regulations. The homologation series legalizes the introduction of numerous improvements to details compared to the already successful 250 GT. The GTO nets many victories.

What else?

Eric Carlsson wins the Rally Monte Carlo for the second time with a Saab 96. At work under the tear-shaped compact car is a noisy two-stroke engine with three cylinders and 80 hp. At the other end of the scale are the three 250 hp Ford Falcons with their brawny 4.2-liter V8 engines.

cessor to the GTO. Hence, the 250 LM is relegated to the prototype category with machines up to five-liters. Thus, the front-engine GTO, which was built parallel to the 250 LM, continues winning the world championship crowns of 1961, 1963, and 1964. However, the 250 LM also makes headlines: In 1965, Masten Gregory and Jochen Rindt achieve the ninth and, to date, final Ferrari victory at Le Mans.

The V12 with dry sump lubrication is housed longitudinally in front of the rear axle behind the two narrow bucket seats. As a result, the 250 LM, as the first mid-engine GT from Maranello, mutates into the progenitor of an entire line of Ferrari mid-engine sports cars. Concealed under the aluminum body resting on a tubular space frame is independent suspension, with double wishbones at the front and a trapezoidal-link rear axle. Disc brakes

at the front and rear are responsible for deceleration. The front brake discs are visible behind 15-inch Borrani spoke rims. At the rear, they lie between the engine and the non-synchronized five-speed transmission at the differential to reduce unsprung masses.

Amongst collectors, the Gran Turismo Omologato, or GTO, are traded like the famous Blue Mauritius. The lightweight sports car conceived by Giotto Bizzarini, aerodynamically designed by Carlo Chiti, and built by Sergio Scaglietti before being further developed by the young Mauro Forghieri, fetches prices of up to 22 million francs. In the early 1970s, a second-hand more or less road-legal race car in good condition could change hands for less than 30,000 francs. Its 250 LM successor, of which only 32 are built, is one of the most sought-after gems and thus yields particularly high returns. ___

Until the end of the 1960s, the red Mini pockets 19 overall victories on the international stage. The most successful driver is Finland's Rauno Aaltonen, who understands how to keep even the 190 hp Porsche at bay – for example at the 1967 Monte.

▲ In 1966, the Mini finishes on positions one to three, but are all disqualified. A conspiracy. "Important members of the Monaco Automobile Club had already decided beforehand that a French national must win no matter what," recalls Mini driver Rauno Aaltonen. This disqualification was one of the biggest scandals in the history of motor racing.

Dwarf giant

___ When the British Motor Corporation unveils the Mini to an astonished public in the summer of 1959, it is far from clear just how much Sir Alec Issigonis' concept of a front-wheel-drive compact car will revolutionize the automobile world. The racing driver and motoring journalist Paul Frère is one of the first to put the compact front-driven pint-sized vehicle through its paces – and he's over the moon. The small car has a big career and its concept will be imitated quickly and often. For Mini-founder Sir Alec, the intention is not to race it – after all, the low ground clearance and the small ten-inch wheels make it unsuitable as a competition car.

Nevertheless, the favorable center of gravity, the wide track, the front-wheel drive, and its modern axle design and body stiffness more than offset the negatives. And when the sales department considers the publicity that the increasingly popular rallying scene generates, the running of three Mini 850 cars at the 1960 "Monte" is a done deal. From 1961, and under the direction of the new, ambitious sports boss Stuart Turner, the diminutive Mini nets its first class victories.

It doesn't take John Cooper long to become aware of the Mini's successes and he grabs the chance to outwit his opponent, Lotus boss Colin Chapman. Cooper asks Issigonis for one of his Minis – and thus the legendary Mini Cooper is born. The 997 cc and up to 85 hp Cooper engine is not new: it had already celebrated successes mounted in the Formula Junior single-seater. In the rally-Mini the power unit develops 70 hp. Moreover, Cooper reinforces the weak brakes (brake discs at

the front), and also revamps the transmission for racing.

The Cooper celebrates its debut in September 1961 and promptly wins the Coupe des Dames in 1962 (with Stirling Moss' sister Pat at the wheel). The largely unknown young rally driver Rauno Aaltonen stuns the rally establishment when he runs in second for a long time until the car is written off at the Col de Turini. In 1963, the 1000-cc Mini is followed by the Mini Cooper S with a short stroke, 1073-cc engine and 70 hp. The 635-kilogram lightweight production version reaches a speed of 160 km/h. The year 1964 heralds the 610-kilogram Mini Cooper S 1275 with a corresponding displacement and up to 95 hp.

Victories at the Rallye Monte Carlo are an integral part of the Mini myth. Three times the red front-wheel-drive dynamo with its white roof proves unbeatable: in 1964 with Hopkirk/Liddon, 1965 with Mäkinen/Easter, and in 1967 with Aaltonen/Liddon. Although 1966 is another good year for the Mini, the car is disqualified at the finish after questionable scrutineering.

Torturous rally outings serve as material tests for mass production

The officials justify their decision by announcing that the use of halogen lamps is forbidden. A key to Stuart Turner's success, incidentally, is the deployment of cars ahead of the rally contenders, to update ice notes.

Successes in circuit racing round off the Mini's impressive track record. Niki Lauda is arguably the most famous racing driver whose career began in a Mini Cooper. ___

What else?

In the lead-up to the final round of the Formula 1 World Championship, three drivers hold chances to clinch the title. Ultimately, second-place at the finale in Mexico is enough for the Ferrari pilot John Surtees to be crowned champion over Graham Hill and Jim Clark.

After brilliant performances in Formula 2, the Mainz-born Graz-resident Jochen Rindt makes his Formula 1 debut at the wheel of a Brabham-Climax.

Scotland's Jackie Stewart is on a winning streak in the Formula 3 team of Ken Tyrrell and grabs attention. He qualifies as a BRM works driver for the following season.

1965 | Alfa Romeo Giulia Sprint GTA

Spotlight on sport

↑ The GTA conquers its first European Touring Car Championship in 1966 and will defend it until 1972. The sideways slide on all four wheels of the Italian car becomes the preferred way of moving for the lightweight coupé. The photo shows the winning 1.6-liter GTA of Bianchi/Rolland at the six-hour race on the Nürburgring in 1967.

What else?

At the Schauinsland race as part of the European Hill Climb Championship, Ludovico Scarfiotti wins with a Ferrari Dino 246 P. The 220 hp of the 2.4-liter prototype make light work of the 530-kg car. The Ferrari race director at this time is Mauro Forghieri, who with Niki Lauda, will bring back the F1 world championship to Maranello in 1975.

◄ At the four-hour race at Monza as part of the 1966 European Championship, the glorious title hunt begins. The GTA ends the pursuit over the high-speed circuit on positions one through seven.

▼ Autodelta's extensive spare parts stock also has bulging fender flares made of GFRP.

___ In the mid-1960s, the signs at Alfa Romeo point to growth. The Giulia series boosts the marque with steadily increasing production figures, which warrant the move to a new workshop in Arese. In line with the new self-confidence, the Milanese make plans to build on the racing successes of their former factory cars. Since the mid-50s, the glamour of the sport has attracted private racers in lightweight Giulietta-coupés, above all, the SZ "Sprint Zagato" clothed in a Zagato body.

With the launching of the Giulia in 1962, the new sports sedans with their aluminum four-cylinder engines and double overhead camshafts prove themselves at touring car races. With the Giulia TI Super, even a sport version limited to 501 units is built as a homologation special, however it turns out to be too heavy. As a result, Alfa Romeo decides to develop a touring car intended primarily for racing, with a magnesium-aluminum-manganese-copper-zink alloy body based the Giulia Sprint GT, which was conceived by former Bertone designer Giorgetto Giugiaro and presented in 1963. Pure race technology is concealed under the lightweight skin: The proven aluminum four-cylinder inline engine now has dual ignition (as used for the first time in the A.L.F.A. Grand Prix car of 1914). In addition, it features large Weber dual carburetors, 6 x 14-inch magnesium rims and a rigid rear axle. The interior, too, is stripped down. To save weight, all insulation material is dispensed with. Using Plexiglas on the rear side windows sheds an extra 205 kilograms. All up, the GTA weighs in at only 745 kilograms, and with components from Car-

lo Chiti's factory race squad, Autodelta, it loses even more weight. Thus the car is dubbed the Giulia Sprint GTA, with the A standing for "Alleggerita", meaning "lightened".

In terms of price, at 2.995 million lire, the road-legal homologation GTA of 1966 is slightly more than half the price of a Ferrari 275 GTB. In 1968, the 115-hp, 1.6-liter Sprint GTA is followed by the GTA 1300 Junior, earmarked for the 1.3-liter displacement class. The GTA notches up titles at the European Touring Car Championship in 1966, 1967, and 1968, as well as 23 other titles (up to 1974) around the globe, bringing them home to Milan. Its smaller brother achieves another 31 championships between 1968 and 1975.

The GTA Junior, which undergoes an Autodelta makeover, develops up to 160 hp (instead of the standard 96 hp). This is good for a top speed of 210 km/h. The 220-hp GTA is given the suffix SA for "Sovralimentata" (1967) to indicate the oil-pressure-powered supercharger. The unfavorable turbo handicap factor, high fuel consumption, and its weight hamper the still-evolving technology. However, the GTA produced from 1968, with a displacement boost to two-liters and a power of 190 hp, is good for many victories and four titles – including the European Championships of 1970 and 1971.

GTA is synonymous with sportiness, dynamism and innovation

Henry's message to Enzo

___ Without Ferrari, the Ford GT40 would probably not have evolved. In the early 1960s, the race- and sports car manufacturer from Maranello is floundering financially in turbulent waters. A strong partner is needed to come to the rescue. The prestigious marque, famed for its sporting accomplishments, would fit perfectly into the portfolio of the mass producer from Detroit, as an image-promoting exercise. The strategists of the world's second-largest automotive group also recognize the marketing leverage of motorsport and, in 1963, announce that they will no longer comply with the American Automobile Manufacturers' Association safety resolution treaty. When the Americans are tipped off by the Ford subsidiary in Cologne and the diplomats in Milan that Ferrari is looking for a bride, the company auditors, engineers, accountants, and

If you can't buy Ferrari, then beat them

lawyers from the firm's headquarters in Dearborn begin to put together a detailed inventory and pen a comprehensive contract. Late in the negotiations, "il Commendatore" starts to have doubts about the marketing of the road-legal sports car under the name "Ford-Ferrari" and – especially when he hears that all race activities must be approved by Ford – he blows a gasket. On the spot, Enzo Ferrari tells the car tycoon Henry Ford he's pulling out. Thus, the partnership, or more accurately the takeover, fails. From 1969, Fiat takes up the role as partner.

Ford reputedly responds to Ferrari's rejection by saying: "Okay, we'll beat his ass." His battle cry is the start signal for one of the most expensive and extensive sports programmes in motor racing history. He gives the green light for the development of the mid-engine flounder, whose designation GT40 stands for "Grand Touring" and its low height of 40 inches. Indeed,

➤ The Ford GT40 wins the prestigious 24 Hours of Le Mans four times in succession between 1966 and 1969. From 1968, the V8 sports car carries the light-blue and orange livery of oil company Gulf – racing colours that will go on to acquire cult status. Gulf's motor racing tradition began in 1938, with Miller, at Indianapolis.

What else?

In Formula 1, a new regulation comes into effect – after many years of 1.5-liter engines. From now on, a 3-litre displacement is introduced. The capacity measurement used up until that time now represents the maximum for turbo- and super-charged engines. However, it's not until 1977 that Renault dares to build a turbocharged Formula 1 motor.

◄ Initially, the V8 boasts around 6,981 cc. The displacement for the 1968 season, however, is reduced to 4,942 cc in accordance with the regulations.

For the 1967 race, the aerodynamics of the flat 7-cylinder, low-slung 40-inch (ca. 1 meter) GT40 are revamped.

from 1966, Ford and his GT40 succeed in foiling Ferrari's domination in sports car racing.

The vehicle is designed in the USA, but developed, built, and unveiled to the press for the first time on April 1, 1964, in Heathrow, Great Britain. It's put through its paces in Italy, races for the first time in Germany at the 1,000-kilometer race at the Nürburgring, and notches up its maiden victory in February 1965 at Daytona. Over the course of its career, the GT40 secures wins at Sebring, Montlhéry, Silverstone, Spa, Reims, Hockenheim, and the list goes on. The most precious triumphs, however, are the GT40's victories at Le Mans between 1966 and 1969.

The opening act is a phenomenal triple victory for the Mk II, which differs from its Mk I (Mark I means first in the series) predecessor through the 427 big block V8 instead of the 289 small block engine. The name denotes its displacement in inches.

In metrics, the capacity of the large V8 – also mounted in the prototype-like Mk IV racing car from 1967 – is 6,997 cc, with the smaller unit at 4,736 cc. This boosts the performance from an initial 380 km/h (Mk I) to 485 (Mk II) and up to 500 km/h (Mk II B and Mk IV). The power output of the large-displacement engines is transferred to the road via a four-speed transmission, with the Mk 1 featuring a five-speed box. From 1968, the capacity for racing sports cars is capped at five liters; Ford responds with a V8 dubbed 302 with a displacement of 4,942 cc. Until 1970. Ultimately, Ferrari and then Porsche prepare to take on the five-liter class – and the Americans, after four straight wins, stay home.

Theory and practice

___ British Racing Motors was established immediately after the war. Former ERA initiator Raymond Mays, together with "Peter" Berthon, founded the race squad that would be active until the mid-1970s. In December 1949, the first BRM celebrated its debut. For the 1.5-liter formula in effect at that time, the vehicle was technically interesting, but proved unreliable due to its complexity. Even before the racer was fully ready for race action, a new regulation was introduced: From 1952, Formula 1 competed with Formula 2 cars, which meant pilots like Fangio and Moss could only demonstrate their prowess in races that followed Formula Libre rules.

BRM's first Grand Prix victory is celebrated in 1959. In the 1960s, the race squad enjoys a success streak: In 1962, BRM wins the constructors' title, and thanks to victories from Graham Hill and Jackie Stewart, the team continues to be at the top of its game over the following years – however, the combination of Jim Clark and Lotus is better.

At the third-to-last Formula 1 race held at Monza, the P83 makes its debut: a technically complex vehicle conceived on the drawing board of designer Tony Rudd, with whom BRM is eager to secure a top position. However, fitting the H16 as the load-bearing part of the monocoque proves to be too complex. Theoretically, the dark-green single-seater benefits from the power of 16 cylinders. In practice, however, the three-liter P83 at first delivers only 400 hp to the crankshaft. At its peak, this eventually reaches 420 hp. Still, to finish first, you first have to finish! And the first three races conclude with BRM retiring. Clark, too, driving a BRM-H16-powered Lotus 43, barely reaches the flag. Still, his arrival at the finish line at the Watkins Glen racetrack in America yields him a victory. This is partly the reason why Hill, who from 1962 wins every year with BRM, eventually switches to Lotus. In 1967, Lotus opts for the new Cosworth-8-cylinder engine, and with this opens a new and very successful chapter in Formula 1 history. However, the BRM P115, which makes its first appearance at the Nürburgring in 1967 with the identical H16-power plant, proves luckless. ___

The exhaust manifolds of the 400 hp 16-cylinder unit look like snakepits. Effectively, the H16 consists of two V8s with two crankshafts and no less than eight camshafts.

Innovations lend wings

**1967 & 1968
What else?**

Le Mans-winning Dan Gurney and Jo Siffert spray champagne over company owner Henry Ford II and race engineer Carroll Shelby, starting the champagne shower tradition that continues to this day.

Lotus paints its Formula 1 vehicles in the colors of the cigarette brand Gold Leaf. Sponsors now begin to push out the previously dominant national colors.

With a Porsche 911, the cornerstone for the track safety team of the ONS (Germany's highest national commission for motorsport) is laid. These racetrack safety teams with trained marshals and specially equipped vehicles quickly become mandatory.

➤ Chaparral mastermind Hall makes a name for himself with many aerodynamics concepts, from the "sucker car" to the Chaparral 2F of 1967 with its large, adjustable rear wing.

▼ By contrast, the 2D model from the 1966 and 1967 seasons, which is fielded at European races, looks conventional.

___ James Ellis Hall perfectly masters his dual role as a designer and driver. The Texan's designs attract attention, since he devotes a lot of energy to aerodynamics. The Chaparrals are distinctive in their innovative wings and spoilers, their ground effect as well as their lightweight materials – especially the mid-engine versions. Moreover, they also race with what seem like unsporty automatic gearboxes. Unlike the front-motor models, they are dubbed Chaparral 2 followed by letters in alphabetical order.

In 1962, planning starts for a mid-engine car, which makes its race debut in October 1963 at Riverside. For Hall, the Chaparral 2 represents the first genuine Chaparral, and indeed this machine mounted with a Chevy-V8 wins no less than 22 of 39 races. With the 2C from 1966, the pilots can adjust the angle of the large rear-wing by means of a pedal. This technology flows into Formula 1 in 1968. After a serious accident, however, it is prohibited from mid-1969.

The closed 2D from 1966, with its distinctive air intake box on the roof, is created specifically for the long-distance races of Le Mans, Daytona, Sebring and the Nürburgring. For the season, it is followed by the significantly more modern, smooth-surfaced

Jim Hall ist das US-Pendant zu F1-Genius und Lotus-Gründer Colin Chapman

2F with a movable brake and a stabilizing wing that's as wide as the car and towers two-meters above the rear. The 2F is the fastest in the field at seven of eight races. Like its predecessor, it wins wherever it reaches the checkered flag.

The large wing celebrates its premiere in 1966 in the 2E developed for the CanAm Series. For the 1968 season, it morphs into the 2G with 525 hp, with some aerodynamic details adopted from the 2F. With the narrow glass fiber body and voluptuous fender flares, the 2G appears as if it's about to burst with power. Compared to the opposition, the wing makes the difference here, too, and the Chaparral is the fastest car on the grid.

Next comes the 2H and – after the banning of wings – the ground-effect prototype 2J. In this design, fans extract air from under the vehicle and literally suction the car to the road. The "sucker car" proves so superior that it's banned at the end of the season. ___

1969 | Porsche 917

On top of the world

___ With the arrival of the Americans at Le Mans, with the Cobra and particularly the Ford GT40, engine volumes explode within a very short time. While three liters were previously good for victory, at times almost seven liters were necessary to bring home the laurels. Thus, the C.S.I. (forerunner of the FISA/FIA) sets the maximum displacement for sports cars at five liters for the 1968 season. When the homologation requirements for the 1969 season decrease from 50 to 25 vehicles, and news gets out that Ferrari will produce a small batch of five-liter racers, a fascinating arms race breaks out between Ferrari and Porsche.

In Stuttgart, the driving force behind the project is Ferdinand Piëch, grandson of Ferry Porsche, founder of the sports car make. Piëch is responsible for test and engine development, and is no longer content with the sports car brand going only for class wins; now he's determined that the cars from Zuffenhausen will play a major part in the overall victory. On the way to achieving this, he unleashes a flood of new prototypes (906, 910, 907, 908, 909), culminating in the brawny 917.

The go-ahead for the ambitious sports car project is given in July 1968. On the basis of the 908-eight-cylinder comes an air-cooled, twelve-cylinder 180° V motor with a spur gear in the middle of the crankshaft, four overhead camshafts driven by gear wheels, and a mechanical twelve-piston double row injection pump with a displacement of 4,494 cc. Although the maximum capacity is not utilized, this is more than offset by the advantage of sharing common parts with the 908 engine. The same applies to the initial suspension setup. The new race car

➤ In 1971, Porsche repeats its Le Mans win from the previous year. In its debut year of 1969, the still-aerodynamically-immature 4.5-liter vehicle retires after 15 hours. On top of this, that same year, the under-experienced private driver John Woolfe is killed in an accident in the first lap.

Pit stop at Le Mans. The pit lane is now separated from the start-finish straight by a guard rail, and the tradition of the Le Mans start, where drivers sprint to their racing cars, becomes a thing of the past in 1970.

unveiled at the Geneva Motor Show in 1969 is offered to prospective buyers for 140,000 Deutschmarks – as a comparison, the 911 T costs 19,970 DM. In April, the homologation hurdle is overcome, and in May, the 917 celebrates its race debut at Spa-Francorchamps. June marks the start of the sensation: The new 917 leads the field at Le Mans for a good 20 hours before the 92-centimeter flounder retires. Furthermore, it also has to be improved in terms of aerodynamics and handling – many drivers who get the chance to drive the 580 hp (at 8,000 rpm) race car, weighing 800 kg and capable of around 340 km/h, are filled with trepidation.

In 1970, a total of seven 917 with the new aerodynamics (five 917 short-tail, two long-tail) tackle the long-distance race at the Sarthe. And after twenty starts at Le Mans, Porsche makes it to the top of the world rankings and achieves the first outright Le Mans victory. This is the year when the images for the eponymous movie are shot, in which

Porsche puts all its cards on the 917 – and wins

Hollywood legend Steve McQueen drives a 917. The vehicle flying the Gulf colors is run by the semi-works team with John Wyer at the helm. For the 1971 season, Porsche boosts the capacity to 4,907 cc, which develops 600 hp. With this, the short 917 (4,140 mm) can reach 360 km/h, and the long version (4,780 mm) is even clocked doing 388 along the Mulsanne Straight.

All versions feature the tubular space frame with an extremely lightweight plastic body as well as individual wheel suspension, coil springs, internally ventilated disc brakes, and a 120-liter fuel tank. Most of the frames are made of aluminum, but to save weight, some are built with (fire hazardous) magnesium frames.

After winning the World Championship for Makes for the third time with the 917, Porsche finally decides to close this chapter at the end of 1971. Until then, however, five long-tail 917 (LH), two Spyders and 36 short-tail (KH) are built, which the company offers ready-to-race for 280,000 Deutschmarks. ___

What else?

Jacky Ickx is the first to lap the Nürburgring in under eight minutes. His time: 7:43.8, his car: a Brabham BT26A.

Cheating in the homologation scrutineering by members of the sport's governing body used to be common practice. But not at Porsche. When the FIA commission visits Porsche on March 20, 1969, to check the inventory, 25 of the 12-cylinder vehicles are lined up neatly in the courtyard. And although not all of them are 100% finished, the officials are impressed.

Of winged V8-dinosaurs

What else?

The astronaut Gary Gabelich achieves a speed of 1,009.526 km/h with the rocket-powered, 53,000 hp "Blue Flame" record car.

Jochen Rindt is posthumously awarded Formula One World Championship crown. Rindt died in an accident at the penultimate world championship round at Monza.

Although the movie *Le Mans* is not particularly successful, Steve McQueen produces an iconic film for motor racing enthusiasts.

The introduction of seatbelts marks the end of the traditional Le Mans start, where racing drivers sprint across the racetrack, leap into their cars, and take off. This procedure is the reason for ignition locks being positioned on the left.

➤ The "winged monsters" are the first homologation specials whose existence as road-going cars is solely due to motorsport homologation requirements.

____ The NASCAR Series is an American sanctum. Stock car races, which originate from beach races and moonshine runs, are mostly contested on oval circuits: huge amphitheaters designed for full-throttle action in front of well-packed grandstands. Established by Bill France in 1947, NASCAR stands for the National Association for Stock Car Auto Racing. The founder is regarded as the "Bernie Ecclestone" of the race series. Unlike in the CanAm or at Indianapolis with their purebred racers, NASCAR runs stock cars (i.e. production cars). Only at the end of the 1970s are genuine stock cars replaced by silhouette cars resembling their production origins.

At work under the colorfully painted bodies are strictly limited pushrod V8 engines, which still, to this day, feature carburetors. In 1970, the Dodge Charger Daytona and the Plymouth Road Runner Superbird dominate the oval racing scene. Booming under the hood is a standard 7.2-liter V8 with four-barrel carburetors and 375 hp: On request, however, are three dual carburetors (making 390 hp) or the 7-liter hemi engine.

The Road Runner belongs to the muscle car species. The Superbird – like its Dodge Charger Daytona twin – features a distinctive aero-kit, created in the Detroit design studio as a homologation special for racing. It consists of a massive, bow-shaped rear wing towering above the roof, and a tapered nose, which is fitted on the standard front. First, however, there are wind-tunnel tests, to simulate the slipstream conditions typically found in oval racing. In reality, the components generate 91 kg, or 272 kg of downforce (front/rear) and also optimize directional stability. The aero kit is complemented by air outlets on the side of the engine hood, and a reworked chassis. On the in-house test track, an identical Daytona is clocked at a phenomenal speed of 391 km/h!

Its race debut is celebrated in the late summer of 1969. Averaging over 320.94 km/h, the Charger Daytona becomes the fastest stock car ever. The Superbird's existence, incidentally, is down to Plymouth pilot and NASCAR legend Richard Petty. He is so impressed with the Dodge Charger Daytona that he asks for a Plymouth like the Daytona. When his request is denied, Petty switches to Ford. However, in the middle of the 1969 season, Plymouth lures him back. Despite his 18 victories, Petty doesn't clinch the 1970 title. Instead, it goes to the extended family: to the Daytona pilot Bobby Isaac (11 wins). And by the time Petty claims the title in 1971 and 1972, the head honchos at NASCAR have capped the engine capacity of the winged monsters to a maximum of five liters. ____

Early death and a long life

___ Lotus initially tackles the 1971 season with the starting numbers 2 and 3. It's only in the Monaco Grand Prix, the third race of the year, that the Lotus driven by Emerson Fittipaldi sports the number 1. The reason is the absence of the world champion, Lotus pilot Jochen Rindt, who was awarded the title posthumously in 1970 after his death in an accident at Monza, caused when one of the hollowed-out brake shafts broke.

The design of Rindt's racing machine, the Lotus 72, which had been run since the Jarama round in 1970, proves such a success that it keeps racing until 1975 with several modifications, represented by the letters B through F. The car is good for victories until 1974. All in all 20 wins, the drivers' title in 1970 (Rindt) and 1972 (Fittipaldi), as well as three constructors' world championship titles ('70, '72, '73) go to this delicate single-seater – the best car of the early seventies.

The Lotus 72 is ahead of its time and thus enjoys a long life

At the same time, Lotus trials other cars, for instance the 56B, at several Formula 1 rounds in 1971, or the Lotus 76 which emerges briefly in 1974 but is quickly replaced with the proven 72. The concept of an all-wheel-drive Formula 1 vehicle becomes a reality with the 56B, powered a Pratt & Whitney gas turbine, but it fails to make its mark – as do all four-wheel drive F1 vehicles. The downside of turbine-drive is the massive space the engine requires and the poor throttle response. The best the 56B can do is eighth place at the Monza Grand Prix in 1971, and second place in the non-championship round at Hockenheim.

The design precedent for the 56B is the Lotus 72. It's clear to see that this car's body is dictated by the wind-tunnel: a distinctive wedge shape with a

> The 1972 season brings a new sponsor. For Lotus, the color scheme changes from red-white-gold (Gold Leaf) to the characteristic black and gold (John Player Special) up to the end of 1986 (with the exception of 1979–81). The photo shows Emerson Fittipaldi at the high-speed Monza racetrack.

What else?

Marko/van Lennep set a record with their Porsche 917 at the 24 Hours of Le Mans with 5,335.313 km (average speed: 222.3 km/h), which will only be broken in 2010 (Audi R15, 5,410 km, Bernhard/Rockenfeller/Dumas). Both cars turn 397 laps, however, today the racetrack is longer due to the introduction of chicanes on the Mulsanne Straight.

◄ Emerson Fittipaldi's Lotus 72 at first features a rear spoiler installed directly above the rear axle.

A common sight in the early 1970s: a Lotus in the lead. Here, Ronnie Peterson heads the pack.

pointed, turbulence-reducing front, resulting in a better airflow over the rear wing. These aerodynamic tweaks alone contribute to a 15 km/h increase in maximum speed – a massive boost. With the gear ratio adapted to the high-speed Monza circuit, Rindt's Lotus 72 achieves a top speed of 328 km/h. The radiators migrate to the side pods, which redistribute the center of gravity to the rear. This style of design sets the direction for Formula 1. Ingenious, too, are the Naca cooling-air inlets, as well as the exhaust "chimneys" over the internal disc brakes. Their positioning reduces the unsprung masses and also averts heat from the tires, allowing the use of softer rubber compounds. Another new idea from Chapman is to turn the racing cars into moving advertising billboards. In 1969, the racers from Hethel no longer fly the traditional British Racing Green, but sport the red and gold paintwork of the cigarette brand Gold Leaf. This type of external financing quickly gains traction. From 1972, the Lotus con-

tenders turn up at races decked out in the black and gold "John Player Special" livery. This will remain in vogue until the mid-80s.

After Dunlop withdraws, 1971 heralds the first "tire war", with Goodyear and Firestone jostling hard for supremacy. At the Spanish Grand Prix, slicks emerge for the first time. Until then, non-tread rubber had only been used in karting and drag races. Gradually, Formula 1 turns to the slick suppliers. From 1972, extra-soft, short-lived qualifying tires appear on the scene. On the subject of transition: Problems occasionally crop up when Lotus switches from Firestone to Goodyear for the 1973 season, and uses tires that are not adapted to the design of the 72. But that chapter is short.

➤ Following the example of Yves Montand, James Garner (*Grand Prix*), and Steve McQueen, actor Alain Delon enjoys the role of racing driver. His partner, actress Mireille Darc, poses at his side.

Unique trinity

On the rally tracks, the Stratos sets the benchmark and notches up four straight championships. Its tamers are Munari, Waldegård, and Röhrl (photos). The road-going version (bottom photo), on the other hand, proves to be a slow seller. It is rumored that the last of the 502 units of the 50,000 DM two-seaters are sold with a 50% discount. Today, a Stratos starts at 100,000 Euros, with competition cars even fetching between 250,000 and 400,000 Euros.

What else?

A Porsche 914/6 appears at the racetracks for the first time sporting the orange Jägermeister livery. This paintwork will remain current until the DTM Opel Astra of 2000.

___ In 1972, the automobile world is still in order, naively so. The energy crisis and the call for more economical vehicles won't come for months. A hardline wedge from Turin appears on the competition stage. From 1973, the Stratos will be on a winning streak, racking up the World Rally Championship titles of 1974, 1975, and 1976, the European championships from 1976 to 1978, and will even stay at the top of the winners' lists in the early Group B era (1982). Sandro Munari, the most victorious and arguably the most famous Stratos driver, knows how to handle the mid-engine vehicle perfectly, with its short wheelbase making it rather skittish. Other big players to leave their names in the Stratos' rally history books are Bernard Darniche, Björn Waldegård, and Walter Röhrl.

The Stratos, on the other hand, writes automobile history. The short, wedge-shaped car is the first production sports car to be developed primarily for motorsport. Its futuristic design, conceived by Bertone's chief designer Marcello Gandini, fits the technical concept that revolutionizes rally sport. However, the 500 road-legal race cars produced are not exactly a commercial success. The last road versions will be sold for around 30,000 Deutschmarks in 1978. Nevertheless, the Stratos comes at an opportune time for Lancia: still laboring under the financial woes of the pre-Fiat era, this vehicle serves as an ingenious example for Group B vehicles.

Dallara welds the compact tubular space frame chassis in advance to take the fastest-possible way over the homologation hurdle of 400 units. The performance of the 192-hp production Stratos is already on a par with the Porsche turbo. In racing trim, the transversely-mounted engine, positioned directly behind the driver who is crammed into the cockpit compartment, puts out 280 hp, and with four-valve heads even develops 320 hp. The turbocharged Group 5 version, campaigned in circuit racing, produces 550 hp at 8,500 rpm and 1.4 bars of boost.

The V6 engine with its 65° cylinder angle comes from Ferrari. For homologation purposes (for the planned use of the engine in Formula 2), Ferrari, the parent company Fiat, and Lancia join forces and use the engine for the Dino models from Maranello (Ferrari) and Turin (Fiat) as well as the Stratos. Its displacement lies at 2,418 cc. While the bore and stroke of 92.5 to 60 mm remains unchanged for race outings, the compression ratio increases from 9:1 to 12:1. Three Weber dual carburetors are responsible for the fuel preparation. The compact sports car's unique futuristic shape, with a plastic body and cramped interior (the bulging doors have specially designed recesses for stowing helmets) is matched by its handling. The maximum speed of 230 km/h is mostly theoretical – in circuit racing it achieves closer to 300 km/h. This is due not only to the weight distribution of 63% at the rear axle, but also to the short 2.18-meter wheelbase, which turns even braking maneuvers into nerve-racking experiences. ___

The compact wedge is primarily designed for motorsport

New hue for white & blue

___ In the touring car Group 1 and 2 categories, the six-cylinder Ford Capri sets the tone, until BMW comes up with its own 3.0 CSL homologation special for racing based on the large coupé. The letter L for leicht (lightweight) in the model description reveals the approach of the Munich-based manufacturer. The CSL is created using the 3.0 CS as a baseline. Putting out 180 hp from a straight-six engine and with carburetors taking care of the fuel preparation, this version sheds more than 200 kilograms. Owners have to do without any sound insulation material and luxury accessories, but can appreciate Plexiglas windows as well as aluminum doors and hoods. The entry-level price for the basic model is a hefty 30,000 Deutschmarks. Homologation rules for Group 2 cars stipulate 1,000 vehicles, and this is accomplished with the 200 hp CSL with gasoline injection in late 1972 after the foundation of BMW Motorsport GmbH.

The sports version attracts attention. Its appearance is dominated by a distinctive front spoiler, air dams on the widened front fenders as well as (from the 3.5 CSL run from 1974) a bow-shaped spoiler above the trailing edge of the roof and a tall rear wing on the trunk lid. Thanks in part to these aerodynamically optimized components, the three-liter coupé turns into the most successful touring car of the 1970s. Behind the wheel of the impressive racer are drivers including Hans-Joachim Stuck, Niki Lauda, Ronnie Peterson, Dieter Quester, and Harald Ertl. Between 1973 and 1979, the vehicle notches up no less than six European Touring Car Championships. In addition, there are the prestigious high-profile outings in the American IMSA series. To avoid being mistaken for the "British Motor Works" across

the pond, emblazoned on the six-cylinder coupé driven by Stuck, Redman and Co is the brand logo "Bavarian Motor Works". However, there is no need to explain on home soil within the DRM (German Racing Championship).

The 3.0 CSL prepared by Alpina in 1973 to tackle the DRM division 1 produces 360 hp (7,500 rpm) from a 3,331 cc displacement. This accelerates the coupé to 100 km/h in 4.8 seconds; to 200 km/h in 15.7 seconds, and ultimately to 275 km/h. For this, the racing squad from the Allgäu asks for 140,000 Deutschmarks. Two years later, outputs of up to 440 hp are recorded with the now four-valve-head 3.5 CSL. The price increases to 150,000 DM. The small 2002, which the GS team and others field in Division 2, costs just half the price and is also good for

The spectacular rear wing is banned on German roads

victories. From 1977, the BMW 320 takes over from the 2002, and the BMW 635 follows in the tire-tracks of the CSL.

Probably the most well-known 3.0 CSL to line up at Le Mans in 1975 is that of art dealer and racing driver Hervé Poulain. His brightly colored paint job is the handiwork of US artist Alexander Calder, whose work of art represents the start of one of the most stunning collections of Munich one-offs – the BMW Art Cars. The most powerful 3.0 CSL can mobilize up to 950 hp (3,210 cc). Putting out a race-worthy 750 hp, it reaches 341 km/h – for instance at Le Mans or in the 1976 World Championship for Makes. ___

▲ The CSL feels as good on the Nürburgring-Nordschleife (top) as it does at Le Mans (center) or on the circuits in North America. It's not uncommon to see famous Formula 1 pilots at the wheel.

◄ At many DRM races, both the large and small divisions compete together: Porsche 911, Ford Capri RS and the CSL mix and mingle with the Ford Escort and BMW 2002.

Flat-out through the energy crisis

Martini, the vermouth specialist from Piedmont, begins its racing commitments in the late 1960s. Thanks to victories with the silver (later white) Martini-Porsche and successes in rallying with the Martini-Lancia, the distinctive color combination achieves cult status.

Porsche does its homework with the 2.1-liter 911 Carrera RSR Turbo, which leads to the creation of the 934, 935, and 936, as well as the road-legal 911 Turbo. The hunting grounds are major sports car races such as the 24 Hours of Le Mans (left) and the 1,000-km race at the Nürburgring (below).

___ In 1972, when Porsche boss Fuhrmann sees how unsuccessful his 911 S is in its fight against the Ford Capri RS and BMW 2800 CS, he springs into action. At race pace, Porsche creates the 911 derivatives Carrera RS 2.7 and Carrera RSR, producing at first 300 hp (2.8 liters), and later 330 hp (3.0 liters). In racing trim the emphasis is on performance, lightweight, and aerodynamics. This puts the Stuttgart manufacturer back on track for victories, and at the same level as the racing-designed six-cylinder coupés from Cologne and Munich.

Moreover, despite the energy crisis, the 911 Turbo, which is intended for road use, is in the pipeline. Motor racing successes appear to be an effective way of freeing turbo technology from the image of disreputable tuning. In fact, the technology is old, with the first turbo patent dating back to 1905. Problems in the implementation of the technology in automobiles led to engineers opting for superchargers for decades. The technicians at Porsche and charger manufacturer KKK still manage to find solutions to the as yet unresolved problems: Groundbreaking bypass technology improves the drivability and throttle response, and gives control back to the driver to call up the desired engine power by means of a throttle pedal.

The road-legal sports car, which stands on the starting blocks, fits the sporting plans perfectly. In Stuttgart, the focus is on the 934 (Group 4, GT vehicles, 400 cars in 24 months) and the 935

Norbert Singer is the technical mastermind behind the turbo racer

(Group 5, special production cars with standard silhouettes) as well as the open Group 6 prototype 936 – the code designation is a combination of the internal "turbo" digits (930) and the new race classes that come into effect from 1975. Along the way, there is still a great deal to do – for the road and the race car. Lubrication, bearings, seals and more prove challenging. The high temperatures require new materials and welding techniques. Once again, the racing division shows they're more than up to the task of finding quick solutions.

The Porsche 911 Carrera RSR Turbo is created as a "work tool". Recognizable by the massive rear wing, the voluptuous fender flares (the rear axle of the car is two meters wide!) and air inlets instead of rear side windows, the new race car conceals pure brawn under the hood: the Turbo produces 500 hp from just 2,142 cc (the turbo handicap factor is 1.4) at 7,600 rpm and is capable of 300 km/h. One hundred km/h is achieved after just 3.2 seconds, with the RSR Turbo reaching 200 in 8.8 seconds. The engine output is transmitted to the spool rear axle via a five-speed gearbox. The body is made of sheet steel, but is finished with plastic parts. Concealed behind the wide slicks is individual suspension with coil springs (replacing the standard torsion bars) and internally ventilated disc brakes. The 120-liter fuel tank is mounted behind the driver. All up, the 911 Carrera RSR Turbo tips the scales at 750 kilograms. ___

The wedge from Milan

___ In 1975, the time is ripe for the wedge-shaped sports car prototype (in accordance with Group 6 regulations), from the workshops of Alfa Romeo. Eight years after the Tipo 33 series of mostly eight-cylinder, two- and three-liter sports cars are defeated by the larger-capacity vehicles from the manufacturers from Stuttgart and Modena, which are entangled in an arms race, the 1975 world championship crown goes to Milan.

Alfa Romeo had already set the course for the 1973 season with the introduction of the new 12-cylinder. At the Targa Florio debut, victory slips through the fingers of the de Adamich/Stommelen duo. However, in their hands, the car turns into a winner. At Monza, virtually on Alfa Romeo's doorstep, the first victory for the still flat-bodied "33" is achieved. The impression of a distinctive wedge-shape is enhanced

The 12-cylinder races in Formula 1 and proves unbeatable in sports car racing

by the small 13-inch wheels. Fitted at the front axle are the small format 9.0/20.0x13"; at the rear are the whopping 14.0/24.0x13". Under the fiberglass body is a steel tubular space frame with reinforcing aluminum sheets. The sides of the 670-kg light-weight Spider house the safety tanks.

The Tipo 33TT12, now with an imposing air intake scoop, which ducts the air into two large filters, celebrates a masterful debut. At the 1974 season-opening round at Monza, three red wedged-racers stand on the first three grid rows (each sharing a row with a Matra) and cross the finish line in positions 1, 2, and 3. For this season, Bernie Ecclestone, the team boss of the Brabham Formula 1 racing squad, opts for the 500 hp (at 11,000 rpm) 3-liter, 4-valve, 12-cylinder with its four camshafts driven by gears

➤ WKRT stands for the Willi Kauhsen Racing Team. WKRT takes over from the Alfa-works team operations squad, Autodelta, for the 1975 running of prototypes in the World Championship for Makes.

What else?

BMW initiates the series of art cars, which are still legendary today. With the 3.0 CSL sporting Alexander Calder's design, the first objet d'art races at Le Mans.

Niki Lauda breaks the seven-minute barrier in 6:58.6 at the Nürburgring with his Ferrari 312T.

◄ The wedge-shaped body line of the Tipo 33TT12 sets the trend for production car styling. Small front wheels allow a flat front design.

The road to success is long. The first Tipo 33 appears in 1967 and is at best good for class wins. Double victory at the 1971 Targa Florio is a moment of glory.

at the rear (instead of chains at the front of the V8). Like the Maranello motors, the Alfa engine is flat and powerful. Brabham engineer Gordon Murray immediately gets to work on a matching vehicle.

In the 1974 season, Alfa is defeated each time by a Matra, at the Nürburgring, in Imola, and at the Österreichring. Watkins Glen is written off as a retirement. Outings in the World Championship for Makes end for the time being. At the end of the season, it's enough for third overall behind Matra and Gulf. In 1975, the sports car prototype from Milan is the one to beat. Thanks to exemplary teamwork by Autodelta and team leader Willi Kauhsen, who consistently manage to put a great car on the track and find a perfect setup for each racetrack, Alfa pilots Merzario, Laffite, Bell, Mass, Pescarolo, Stommelen, Ickx, and Andretti dominate with seven wins from eight races. Alfa Romeo wins the 1975 World Championship for Makes convincingly from Porsche,

Alpine, and Chevron. Arturo Merzario is crowned champion ahead of his teammate Derek Bell.

The 33TT12 is further developed into the 33SC12 and ultimately produces up to 640 hp, thanks to turbocharging. After a gap year, Alfa Romeo will return in 1977 and win eight world championship rounds and the World Sports Car Championship – the Makes World Championship, however, is reserved for Group 5 entries. Over the following years, the silhouette of the red wedge will influence designers, especially in terms of the contours of production sedans.

Renaissance in red

The single-seater, freed of its thin FRP skin, reveals the fragility of the monocoque designs of this era. The characteristic helmet belongs to Niki Lauda's teammate Clay Regazzoni.

In 1975, Niki Lauda is crowned F1-champion with the 312 T. At the wheel of the 312 T2, he's the man to beat in 1976 until a serious accident at the Nürburgring halts his charge. Nevertheless, he misses out on successfully defending his title by a mere one point. In 1977, the title again goes to the pilot of the 312 T2.

The 312 T of 1975 is distinguished by its huge airbox. Here, Lauda tackles the Karussell corner at the Nürburgring.

___ The 312 T2 is the first Ferrari since 1965 to tackle a new Formula 1 season sporting the starting number 1. Claiming the world championship the previous year, Niki Lauda ended Scuderia's eleven-year drought. The type designation expresses the technical details: three-liter capacity and twelve cylinders as well as a transversely mounted gearbox (T for transversal). The 2 distinguishes the vehicle as the successor to the 1975 car, adapted to the 1976 regulations.

The chassis is given the designation Tipo 629. The front and rear wheels are mounted on double wishbones, with inboard springs over telescopic shock absorbers fitted at the front. Thirteen-inch wheels are still used today in F1. The wheelbase of the 4.32-meter single-seater comes to 2,560 mm. Its weight: 592 kilograms. The engine, which is used until 1981, is supplied by a 200-liter fuel tank. This flat V12 with a 180°-cylinder angle mobilizes 500 hp at 12,200 rpm. Power is transmitted to the rear wheels via a five-speed gearbox, with the rear wing and rear axle fixed to the box. The special features of the gearbox design are that it needs less space, and it's positioned in front of the rear axle, which proves favorable for the center of gravity. The volume of the combustion chambers, each with 249 cc, adds up to a displacement of 2,992 cc. The Ferrari engines are regarded as the powerhouses

Niki Lauda is a magician and the successful Ferrari 312 T is his wand

of Formula 1 cars of this era. Only with the so-called "wing cars" of the late 1970s to early 1980s will the design of the 180°-V12 turn into a disadvantage, as they take up too much space. However, the 312 T2 still brings home seven victories between 1976 and 1978, and the constructors' title in 1976 and 1977. However, it's not only the wins that make Lauda and the 312 T2 famous: On the Nürburgring, the fastest man (1975 pole-setting time of 6 minutes and 58.6 seconds – a record that still stands) is involved in an accident that he only narrowly escapes alive. He still carries the burn scars.

Over the course of 31 world championship rounds, the Ferrari is manned by such greats as Niki Lauda, Clay Regazzoni, Carlos Reutemann, and Gilles Villeneuve. In 1976 Lauda narrowly misses out on defending his title after missing several races and retiring in the rain chaos at Fuji, just one point shy of James Hunt. However, in 1977, he retaliates, reclaims the title – and withdraws from racing before the end of the season. The T-models designed by Mauro Forghieri yield 27 victories and 19 pole positions. ___

Young and wild

___ The German Racing Championship (DRM) proves to be a favorite with the crowds thanks to its cutthroat duels between the large BMW coupés, Porsche, and Ford Capri racers in the big division, as well as the smaller BMW and Ford Escort contenders in the small division. Races are contested at the Nürburgring, Salzburgring and Norisring, Hockenheim and Zolder, as well as the airfields of Wunstorf, Mainz-Finthen, Kassel-Calden, and Diepholz. Divided into two divisions – up to two and four liters taking into account the 1.4 turbo handicap factor, the packed DRM grids offer spectators breathtaking race action between 1972 and 1981 (from 1982 to 1985, the IDRM is eligible for Group C sports cars).

Group 5 regulations come into effect in 1977, and the new BMW 320 follows in the footsteps of both the popular small division BMW 2002 and the BMW

BMW motorsport shines in white with blue, purple and red

3.0 and 3.5 CSL contesting the big division. The introduction of these new regulations heralds a certain visual change. The silhouette still resembles that of the production counterpart, but the flares and spoilers grow significantly. The 320 turns into a popular car to take racing, after all, the car with the kidney-grill and blue and white propeller emblem makes up the lion's share of the touring car grids. Under the hood sits a 1,998-cc four-cylinder normally aspirated power unit with a compression ratio of 11.2:1. The engine produces 298 hp at 9,250 rpm. This corresponds to the remarkable power output of around 150 hp per liter. With a total weight of 765 kilograms, the power-to-weight ratio equals about 2.5 kilos per horsepower. The vehicle is shod with voluptuously-sized tires; 10.0/23.5-16" at the front and 12.5/25.0-16" at the rear, positioned under

As usual, things heat up at the Norisring. The BMW Junior Team is new to the action, and they give the veterans such a shakeup that the BMW race director, Jochen Neerpasch, is finally compelled to rein in his hotspurs.

What else?

Renault fields the RS 01 in Formula 1 featuring a turbo for the first time. The 1.5-liter V6 produces 500 hp. To achieve this output, the normally aspirated competition needs a three-liter displacement.

The last Targa Florio is contested on May 15. The event hasn't been part of the World Sports Car Championship since 1974.

Voluptuous fender flares and a spoiler at the front and rear are part of the Group 5 program. The BMW 320 follows in the footsteps of its predecessor, the BMW 2002, and continues to fight for honors against the Ford Escort.

With its spectacular cars and races, the DRM proves extremely popular with fans and is a very successful predecessor of the DTM.

the large-format fender flares made of composite plastic. Thanks to the favorable power-to-weight ratio and high grip level, the 120,000-Deutschmark BMW 320 accelerates from standstill to 100 km/h in 4.4 seconds, to 180 km/h in 10 seconds, and to 200 in 12.2 seconds.

Like the 02, the 320 are again prepared and run by reputable tuners such as Alpina, Faltz, and Schnitzer. Moreover, the BMW motorsport department also campaigns a pack of untamed 320 racers – distinguishable by the typical BMW motorsport colors. Behind the three-spoke leather steering wheels sit members of the newly founded BMW Junior team. With Eddie Cheever, Marc Surer, and Manfred Winkelhock, the youth development program initiated by BMW race director Jochen Neerpasch provides the stepping stone into Formula 1. And they give plenty of fodder for discussion: whether it's because of resounding victories, brutal crashes

(Eddie Cheever writes off the first Junior-320 before the start of the maiden season-opening race) or with their boisterous behavior on the racetracks. After the opposition complains bitterly about their behavior at the Norisring, Neerpasch grounds his three juniors for the next race. As an amusing contrast, seasoned specialist Hans-Joachim Stuck turns up in his orange Jägermeister Faltz BMW 320 emblazoned with the lettering "BMW Senior Team".

From 1978, the performance-boosting turbocharger is also run in the small division and is successfully run alongside the normally-aspirated vehicles. As an example, the Schnitzer-BMW 320 Turbo mobilizes 410 hp from 1,426 cc – with the vehicle weighing virtually the same.

Wings against flying

___ In the second half of the seventies, the British Lotus team under Colin Chapman can look back on six constructors' world championship titles, and is one of the most successful squads in Formula 1. But their most-recent titles date back to 1972 and 1973 and were courtesy of Emerson Fittipaldi, Ronnie Peterson, and the Lotus 72. After those two successful seasons, Lotus is thrown back to the midfield.

It's high time for another stroke of genius – and it comes. In 1977, the racing squad unveils the Lotus 78, the first "wing car". With this car, Lotus lays the foundation for a new vehicle philosophy and is rewarded with second place in the constructors' classification. It makes sense to perfect the concept and strengthen the advantage over the competition. The Lotus 79 for the 1978 season becomes the blueprint for the wing-car era. It is the brainchild of Colin Chapman, Martin Ogilvie, and Geoff Aldridge. "The Lotus 78 was definitely a great car," says Lotus pilot Mario Andretti at the start of the season, "but the 79 will KO the competition." And he's right: he wins round one and follows up with seven more victories with the black-and-gold Lotus 79. He wins the world championship convincingly, ahead of his teammate Ronnie Peterson.

The chassis, engine, and gearbox – aluminum monocoque, Cosworth-V8, and Hewland unit – are standard Formula 1. New is the aerodynamics, in which the side pods of the vehicle are shaped like inverted aerofoils. The underside is sealed off on the side by sliding side "skirts". This layout creates negative pressure under the vehicle, which by far eclipses the downforce generated purely by front

Colin Chapman brings wing profiles and ground effect to motor racing

and rear spoilers. To maximize the surface needed for ground effect, the rear suspension moves close to the gearbox, the exhaust migrates away from rear diffuser, and the fuel tanks, previously housed in the side pods, now sit between the driver and the engine – where they are still positioned in Formula 1 today. Thanks to this design, a new era begins in which Formula 1 cars can practically be driven upside down under the ceiling. The aerodynamic downforce ensures that the cars actually seem to stick to the road. Hence, it's no surprise that the competition is keen to quickly match Lotus' competitive advantage.

The first wing cars of the rivals appear on the scene in 1978, and the following year they're standard amongst all racing teams. The high cornering speeds soon take their toll – pilots start to complain of losing consciousness briefly due to several g of lateral acceleration. The death of Patrick Depaillier in 1980 in an accident on the ultra-fast Ostkurve of Hockenheim is attributed to this. And thus, the movable skirts are banned, the ground clearance is raised and, ultimately, the underbodies are straightened out and diffuser areas minimized. However, the emergence of wing cars has put a spotlight on the significance of aerodynamics in racing. ___

▲ The Lotus pilots win eight of sixteen races in the 1978 season and hand Lotus the last of seven constructors' titles for the time being. The podium ceremonies of those years are far from the professional standard seen today. The Lotus 79 celebrates its race debut at the 1979 Belgium Grand Prix in Zolder (bottom photo). Andretti immediately wins.

◄ Big hairstyles and sideburns are in fashion in the 1970s, as demonstrated by Italian-American Mario Andretti.

From win to win

Porsche provides just one 935 customer version based on the earlier factory car (photo left). The Kremer brothers' team from Cologne continues to develop the vehicle. They turn a rough diamond into their 935 K3 jewel, and with this, Klaus Ludwig dominates the DRM in 1979, and wins in the American IMSA series as well as at Le Mans (bottom center).

◄ Pit stop for the Kremer team 935 with tire changes at the DRM race at Belgium's Zolder racetrack in 1979. This was the most successful squad in the DRM that year.

What else?

Not long after Christmas, participants head off on the 10,000-kilometer rally from Paris to Dakar for the first time.

The BMW M1 races as part of the ProCar series as a Formula 1 curtain-raiser. For Le Mans, BMW commissions Andy Warhol to paint its Group 5 mid-engine sports car.

____ In 1976, the World Championship for Makes is run for the first time with so-called Group 5 production cars (silhouette), and the 935 emerges on the scene. Its technology is now perfected thanks to the development work done on the 911 Carrera RSR Turbo. As a consequence, the vehicle is successful from day one. After the factory manages to win the World Championship for Makes and Sports Cars with the 935 and 936 flying the Martini colors, Porsche offers a version to its customers. The vehicle quickly becomes extremely popular and thus the 935 makes up the lion's share of the grids.

In 1977, Porsche demonstrates the possibilities of its in-house developments with the small 1.4-liter 935 dubbed "Baby" and the 935-78 "Moby Dick". "Moby Dick" represents the pinnacle of what Porsche has put on the racetracks based on the 911. The vehicle features a fiberglass body glued to the aluminum frame, with a load-bearing roll cage and with six centimeters taken off the lower part of the body. Mounted under the long rear section is a 3.2-liter air-cooled six-cylinder engine with water-cooled four-valve cylinder heads and two turbochargers. The power unit puts out 750 hp at 8,200 rpm and propels the 1,080-kilogram flounder to 366 km/h along the Mulsanne Straight of Le Mans (without chicanes at this stage). With this, project leader Norbert Singer has taken full advantage of the rules. Afterwards, the factory halts development work and passes the expertise on to private teams. Parallel to the factory missions, the 935 is fielded by many customer squads.

Amongst the more well-known teams, such as

the Gelo Team of Georg Loos, Dick Barbour Racing, Max Moritz Porsche, and the Kremer brothers' squad, Porsche Kremer stands out thanks to its own development work. With the 935 K3, Kremer puts its own small production run on its wheels for the 1979 season. And there's no way around this contender: Klaus Ludwig wins the 24 Hours of Le Mans as well as the German Racing Championship (DRM) after clinching ten wins and a second place from eleven races!

On the engine side, the K3 motor is a match for the factory engine in the 935-78: It, too, features a bi-turbo 3.2-liter six-cylinder engine mobilizing 740 hp. In practice – after a tweak to the boost pressure – it is even capable of developing 800 hp. The five-speed gearbox is also standard with a spool replacing the differential. Visually, however, the vehicle is less extreme. Its proportions look more like those of the production 911, and the aerodynamically perfected shape, thanks to the plastic specialist Eckehard Zimmermann ("dp"), impresses with its functional simplicity. Another functional feature is its stiffer roll cage, which makes the rear cross member superfluous and shortens the time taken to change the engine, if necessary.

In June 1981, shortly before the new Group C regulations come into effect, Kremer turns up at the racetrack with another trump card: the K4. The extreme K4 with its lightweight 65-kg frame, three-piece Kevlar body and a downforce-generating underbody, is sold for 400,000 Deutschmarks, predominantly in the United States.

The 750 hp 935 K3 continues winning into the Group C era

Rolling lab with laurels

___ In 1979, a bunch of French adventurers, desert lovers, and motorsport enthusiasts organize a rally that will become the most grueling race in the world. The rally takes several weeks and demands mammoth performances and hardships.

At Volkswagen and Audi, a small group congregates around developer Roland Gumpert, who recognizes the opportunity such a sporting adventure offers. On the one hand, the race from Paris to Dakar, which is open to vehicles of all kinds, allows them to put the performance capabilities of VW's new all-terrain vehicle to the test. On the other hand, the stresses placed on man and materials offer an opportunity to contribute technical development work: keyword quattro.

With the sheet-steel off-road body resting on a ladder-type frame, the Iltis (German for polecat), with its enormous ride height, certainly doesn't look like it belongs to the racing vehicles species. However, for the swift trans-Sahara journey, transverse

A factory entry in a field of adventurous privateers

leaf springs and drum brakes are sufficient. Thanks to permanent all-wheel drive, a ventilated waterproof clutch and a centrifuge for the dry air filter to separate out sand particles, as well as its extraordinary robustness, it is the perfect competition vehicle.

With twin carburetors and classic tuning measures, the 1.7-liter four-cylinder power unit is boosted to 110 hp. At work under the hood of the Gumpert-Iltis is a 160 hp five-cylinder motor.

Even big leaps over dune crests, or a roll, can't hurt the Iltis. And when a catapulted stone totally destroys a prop shaft, the VW continues with just its front-wheel drive, through the sand to the finish. Ultimately, the 10,000-kilometer event concludes with a double victory for Volkswagen and positions four and nine. A good 25 years after this success, VW again tackles the "Dakar" challenge. ___

▲ The rally outing of the Iltis serves Volkswagen and Audi as a means to sell all-terrain vehicles to the French Army and to test the power train for the Audi quattro, which will be unveiled at the 1980 Geneva Motor Show. But the Dakar-Iltis is also a rolling laboratory for car suppliers. INA Schaeffler, for instance, uses it to test its dustproof throttle valve bearings.

Start of the carbon-fiber era

1980 & 1981 What else?

With the Alfasud Trophy, run since 1975, Alfa Romeo establishes a one-make cup that soon becomes a shining example for other manufacturers. The races, run with identical cars, guarantee gripping duels. In 1980, eventual Formula 1 pilot Gerhard Berger contests his first Alfasud Trophy season.

Walter Röhrl is crowned WRC champion in 1980 with Fiat, and signs on with Mercedes. After Mercedes abandons its rally plans, he competes successfully in the 1981 German Rally Championship, with a Porsche 924 Carrera GTS.

___ At the season-opening round at Long Beach, it's obvious that the McLaren MP4 represents a totally new generation of race car. While the boxy competitors and predecessors display sharp edges, the new matt-black single-seater from Woking (GB) gleams in its harmoniously shaped simplicity. And now this new type of chassis constitutes just five components.

The secret is carbon fiber. The black filaments are spun out of carbon and have already been tried and tested in the aerospace industry. The material is extremely expensive and not easy to process. However, it offers unbeatable advantages in terms of weight and stability, and thus the triumphal march of this material proves unstoppable.

The mastermind behind the ground-breaking construction technique is Britain's John Barnard, who replaces Colin Chapman as Formula 1's technical whizz. Hercules, an American specialist company, supplies the fibers and mats, which are then glued, forming chassis structures. Their customer base includes companies such as NASA. Initially, there is still the concern that, in the event of an accident,

Thanks to McLaren, carbon fiber becomes the most important chassis material

the new race cars would break and splinter like icicles. Regular McLaren pilot Andrea de Cesaris – better known for his accidents than for his results – very quickly dispels these concerns. In fact, the introduction of carbon fiber signifies another major step forward in terms of safety. As well as the accident-prone Italian, Irishman John Watson also takes the wheel of the single-seater (which is painted in the traditional Marlboro colors), and achieves a maiden victory at the MP4's seventh outing at his home race in Silverstone. It's the first McLaren win since 1977.

In September 1981, double world champion Niki Lauda turns the first test laps at McLaren and shortly afterwards announces he's coming out of retirement. Ron Dennis is the reason for the upheaval at McLaren. With his engineer Barnard, he has been working for three-and-a-half months in secret.___

➤ McLaren pilots John Watson (photo) and Andrea de Cesaris are the first to enjoy the considerably safer and faster McLaren-Ford MP4 with a carbon-fiber monocoque. For Niki Lauda, the new technology is a good argument for his Formula 1 comeback.

Wins, deaths, and a long life

___ Porsche hits the nail on the head with the Porsche 956, built to comply with the Group C regulations from 1982 (closed sports cars where the minimum 1.1-meter height, 800-kg weight, tank volume, vehicle and tire width are prescribed, but not a homologation figure). On its very first attempt, the new racer wins the 24 Hours of Le Mans.

Concealed under the wind-tunnel-perfected fiberglass body is an aluminum chassis in a monocoque design. The aerodynamically-engineered underbody generates downforce-conducive ground effect, which allows cornering g-forces of 2.5 g, 2.5 times the force of gravity, and deceleration forces of over 2 g. At work behind the two mandatory seats and the fuel reservoir is an evolution of the traditional flat-six engine. With an initial capacity of 2.65 liters, the unit later grows to 3.2 liters, with the performance also tracking upwards from 620 to more than 670 hp. This makes the Group C cars more powerful than the normally aspirated Formula 1 racers of that time. The 962, developed for the North American IMSA series (for safety reasons with the foot pedals now behind the front axle), features a power unit with a 2.86-liter displacement, two valves and one turbocharger. The 962C, earmarked for the FIA world championship, is powered by an efficient four-valve 2,650-cc engine with two turbochargers and a water-cooled cylinder head.

Another technical innovation is the Porsche double clutch transmission (PDK), which is now mounted

➤ The aerodynamically designed underbody generates a decent portion of downforce. At 321.4 km/h, the downforce equals the weight of the Group C flounder, meaning that at this speed, the long-tail 956 can literally be driven upside down on the ceiling – as this model in the Porsche Museum impressively illustrates.

The factory cars, decked out in the Rothmans colors from 1982 to 1987, serve as the benchmark for the many private teams who also put their trust in the flounder. The photo shows the Le Mans-winning car of 1987 in which Derek Bell, Hans-Joachim Stuck, and Al Holbert share driving duties.

in the factory cars. Volkswagen will eventually develop this experimental unit for use in series production as the DSG (Direct Shift Gearbox). In addition to the factory cars, the 956 and 962 are hot favorites amongst customers. At first, the 956 comes with a price tag of 630,000 Deutschmarks. Just three years later, in 1985, Porsche charges 796,000 DM for the 962.

Visually, the 962 is recognizable by its lower front overhang and longer wheelbase. Both the 956 and the 962 are available as a long- and short-tail. The drag-reducing long-tail version with less down-force is fielded exclusively at high-speed circuits like Le Mans, and underlines its strengths on the 6-km Mulsanne Straight with top speeds close to 400 km/h, at the same time proving economic at a time when Group C limits overall fuel consumption. Le Mans becomes the hunting ground of the

Group C cars win
sprints and marathons

modern flounder: From the time of its debut in 1982 until 1987, the 956/962 wins six times in succession. In 1994, another success is notched up by the 962 GTLM, which is now based on Jochen Dauer's road-homologated race-car derivative.

The Group C Porsche marathon-sprinter clinches one win after the other – whether in the FIA World Endurance Championship, at national race series such as the "sport auto Supercup" or the American IMSA series. Manned by such greats as Jacky Ickx, Derek Bell, Hans-Joachim Stuck, Jochen Mass, Stefan Bellof, Manfred Winkelhock, Klaus Ludwig, and Keke Rosberg, the 956/962 continues to net victories and titles. But every light has its shadow: racing driver aces Stefan Bellof, Manfred Winkelhock, and Jo Gartner are fatally injured in the 956/962; Kris Nissen survives a crash but is seriously injured.

What else?

Gilles Villeneuve and Riccardo Paletti lose their lives, and a serious accident ends the F1 career of Didier Pironi.

Arguments erupt between the world federation FISA and the constructors' association FOCA, which results in most of the FOCA-affiliated teams boycotting the San Marino Grand Prix. Only 14 cars start.

At work under the aerodynamic rear is a partly air-, partly water-cooled six-cylinder boxer engine with twin turbocharging (left). In 1987, Porsche will experiment with a double clutch transmission (PDK) and thus contribute to a technology that, from 2003, flows into production cars.

Well loaded

What else?

Stefan Bellof breaks the 200 km/h barrier in training for the 1,000-kilometre race at the Nürburgring, with a lap time of 6.11.13 minutes. Afterwards, Bellof writes off his Porsche 956 at Pflanzgarten.

▲ Bernie Ecclestone's race team and the creative technician Gordon Murray establish pit stop tactics that still provide drama in Formula 1 today.

➤ Brabham-BMW reaps laurels that turbo pioneer Renault would very much liked to have harvested. Nelson Piquet becomes the first to win the world championship in a car powered by a turbo engine.

___ In qualifying, the turbocharged power units, with a displacement of just 1.5-liters, produce 1,400 hp. At the pinnacle of their development, the vehicles manage to put out 1,000 hp even in race trim. This makes the turbos the most powerful Grand Prix cars in motorsport history.

The pioneer of turbocharged engines comes from France: in 1977, Renault turns up with the first turbo in Formula 1. To get the output of the turbocharged units on a par with the 500-hp three-liter normally aspirated engines, FIA prescribes a displacement multiplication factor of 1:2.

Thus, the engine capacity limit is set at 1.5 liters. But now, more compact engines with six or just four cylinders are enough and this frees up space and saves weight. Room is now needed for the turbines. The downsides are the delayed response (turbo lag) and the increased need for cooling.

With the Renault RS10, the first turbo wins a Grand Prix in 1979. In 1980, Ferrari also uses the new engine technology, with Hart fielding a turbo in 1981, and BMW following suit in 1982. The four-cylinder baseline engine comes from the BMW 1500 sedan, which at this time can only be found in collectors' garages and scrap yards. In 1983, BMW discloses its performance at between 700 and 800 hp. Unlike the normally aspirated engines, an exact value cannot be specified as the performance can

BMW uses dated engines for the Formula 1 four-cylinder unit

be tweaked with a twist of the boost pressure controller. However, such a maneuver comes at the expense of durability and is therefore only short-term.

The Brabham-BMW BT52 is undoubtedly an icon of the turbo age. The slender, simple Brabham BMW becomes the first turbo world champion. The arrow shape initiated by Brabham's engineer Gordon Murray emerges after the ban on wing cars is announced at the beginning of the season. The large side pods disappear, and Murray moves the radiator toward the rear axle to achieve a streamlined shape.

The year 1983 not only yields the first turbo champion with BMW, it also marks the end of an era for normally aspirated engines: The last car powered by a normally aspirated unit to win a Grand Prix – until the end of the turbo-engine ban in late 1988 – is the Tyrrell piloted by Michele Alboreto. Brabham initiates a new tactic in the second half of 1982, whereby they start the race with half a tank of fuel, build up an advantage and then make a pit stop halfway through the race to refuel and change tires. In 1983, almost all teams copy this tactic (although refuelling during the race is banned between 1984 and 1993). Once tire changes are reintroduced, pit stops again add to the suspense. ___

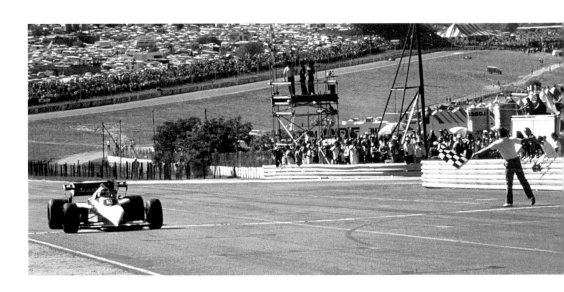

Dream assignment

__ When it comes to turbo expertise, Porsche is top of the list thanks to experience gained in racing and production. Hence, the Arabian owner of Techniques d'Avant Garde, Mansour Ojjeh, bankrolls the McLaren racing team into the turbo era with decent cash injections. Engineers from Porsche's think tank at Weissach are contracted to develop a new Formula 1 power plant and thus help the sports car producer make a comeback to Formula 1 after a 20-year absence. The engineers start with the proverbial blank sheet of paper – a dream assignment. The only conditions are that the engine has to be suitable to use in a wing car, and it has to eclipse all previous F1 motors in terms of performance and consumption.

Porsche perfectly fulfils the customer order with two title wins

McLaren plays in the premier league of Formula 1. Generous sponsorship funding, first-class drivers and cutting-edge technology – such as carbon fiber that flows into automotive sport from the aerospace industry – turn McLaren into a figurehead. And by choosing a new engine partner, the team under Ron Dennis has struck a good deal. Using the code name PO1, a 150-kg 1.5-liter V6 is conceived, with the cylinder banks positioned at a 60° angle – to assist the aerodynamics – mobilizing 850 hp at 11,000 revs per minute with a 2.5-bar boost pressure. Ultimately, the power unit will develop a good 900 hp, and even reach 1,000 hp in qualifying.

The engine runs for the first time at the end of 1983, in the converted MP4/1E, but experiences teething problems. However, the McLaren MP4/2 is ready just in time for the start of the 1984 season, and dominates with virtually no serious threat. Niki Lauda and Alain Prost win 12 of the 16 world cham-

➤ With the V6 Turbo manufactured on behalf of a customer, Porsche rounds off its motorsport successes. At the same time, the Stuttgart marque notches up one victory after another with the 956/962.

What else?

In the Group C, fuel consumption formulas regulate the performance level. Fuel is limited to 2,210 liters, divided between a maximum of 25 pit stops over 24 hours.

◄ Niki Lauda (here at Hockenheim) wins five rounds in 1984; his teammate Alain Prost scores seven. At the end of the season, the Austrian pips the Frenchman at the post by half a point and pockets his third world championship title.

In 1985, the Frenchman launches a counterattack, and with five victories, takes home the first of four world championships.

pionship races, 4 of them double victories. And although Lauda's five wins are two wins less than his teammate Prost's, In the end the Austrian enjoys a half-point advantage and is crowned world champion. Logically, McLaren takes the constructors' title home to Woking.

A year later, Prost wins five times in the MP4/2B (without winglets) and secures the world championship honors he narrowly missed out on the previous year. Niki Lauda climbs to the top of the podium just once before he hangs up his racing helmet for good. And McLaren is richer by another constructors' title. In 1986, the dominance of the PO1 begins to wane. Nevertheless, Prost claims four victories with the McLaren MP4/2C and defends his title. However, his new teammate, Keke Rosberg, comes away empty-handed and the constructors' title goes to the Williams team campaigning the new Honda engine. With this, the days of the TAG Turbo are numbered. After another season with the MP4/3-

TAG, the relay baton goes to the Honda-V6-Turbo, which McLaren will adopt in 1988.

With the perfect optimization of the engine and turbo technology in the PO1, a major leap is made in terms of engine electronics. And the TAG crew also makes a name for itself in this field. Ultimately, a course is set for a new era of electronics. Telemetry becomes a magic word. It represents the collation of a large amount of onboard data which is transmitted via radio to the pits. From there, the engineers can directly adjust the engine control of the vehicle's electronic system and also influence such performance parameters as boost pressure and mixture preparation.

The long
and short of it

___ "With this, even a trained monkey could win," Walter Röhrl initially grumbles about the Audi quattro. Despite his complaints, the best rally driver of his time finds his way into the quattro cockpit. By the time the rangy redhead from Regensburg joins the Audi squad, Hannu Mikkola, Michèle Mouton, and Stig Blomqvist have demonstrated the superiority of all-wheel drive technology to the rally world. In 1979, the first 300 hp rally-quattro emerges, and the following year, the all-wheel-drive production car celebrates its much acclaimed premiere. After the quattro debut other manufacturers adopt the technology for their models. From the 1981 season, Audi impressively underlines the advantages of all-wheel drive with rally successes.

The 1981 models mobilize a stable 310 to 340 hp and identical torque values from the turbocharged five-cylinder inline engine. A front grille modified from the standard model creates space for the intercooler, which becomes necessary due to the use of larger KKK turbochargers. The reservoir for the dry sump lubrication is fitted in the trunk with the oil cooler above. Interestingly, the new differential technology features a locking front, mid, and rear differential. The center-differential is replaced with a rigid driveshaft for gravel, snow and ice – for more controlled slides. In 1982, the World Manufacturers Championship goes to Ingolstadt. In 1983, Röhrl, driving for Lancia, snatches the trophy from the Ingolstadt marque, however, Audi and Blomqvist are crowned champions the following year. Toward the end of the sea-

The S1 storms through forests and fields with up to 530 hp

son, the "short" quattro Sport celebrates its debut. This car is Audi's answer to the new Group B mid-engine vehicles, like the Peugeot 205 turbo 16. Compared to the "long" quattro, the wheelbase of the quattro Sport is shortened by 30 centimeters. Wide fender flares (for large-format tires) and a large scoop on the hood (for the new four-valve cylinder head) are features of the rough-diamond contender. In rally trim the technical specs include: 400 hp at 7,500 rpm, 460 Nm at 5,500 rpm and 1,100 kg.

It takes until the end of the 1984 season for Blomqvist to score a win. The big breakthrough, however, is not achieved by the "shorty". Hence Audi launches the next evolutionary stage – the quattro Sport S1. The vehicle can be identified by its wild spoiler package and its boxy fenders. For improved weight distribution, the engine radiator is mounted next to fans, with the alternator and battery stowed in the luggage compartment. New in the car is the PDK double clutch transmission, facilitating ultra-quick gear shifting without interruption in the flow of power. This is a Porsche invention which finds a first-class production successor with the Volkswagen DSG. The 2.2-liter power unit develops 476 hp and 480 Nm. Thanks to three differentials, the S1 catapults from zero to 100 in just 3.1 seconds. The S1 contests the last third of the 1985 WRC season but claims only one victory. However, glory comes in the USA, where it conquers the Pikes Peak summit in the legendary "Race to the Clouds", winning three times straight until 1987. ___

▲ At its 1981 premiere, the quattro is homologated for Group 4. The reorganization of Groups A, B, and C stipulates the production of 200 specials and allows the debut of the "shorty", the Sport quattro (center). For the 1985 season, the S1 represents the wildest car in the Group B era (bottom). In the WRC, the S1 yields just one victory. Walter Röhrl puts in an inspired drive to win the Pikes Peak Hill Climb.

What else?

Christian Danner is the first European champion in the maiden 2002 European Formula 3000 Championship. Nick Heidfeld and Juan Pablo Montoya go down as all-time greats, with seven victories each.

Porsche's most
expensive PR giveaway

Porsche tackles the Paris-Dakar rally three years running. After the start of the 911-lookalike type 953 in 1984, the crew from Stuttgart fields the Group B homologated 959 (1985 and 1986). They score two victories.

1986 sees the most fully developed Porsche compete, resulting in a double victory for Metge/Lemoyne ahead of Ickx/Brasseur. And the "dogs-body" crew Kussmaul/Unger driving the "chase car" even manages to clinch sixth overall. The dress rehearsal takes place in 1984 at the Pharaoh's Rally (photo bottom).

___ When the time comes for Porsche to develop the "Group B turbo with all-wheel drive", according to insiders like Porsche turbo engineer Heinz Dorsch, the developers are given free rein. The intention of the technological showpiece is to underline the expertise of the company. Thus, the Group B homologation special (200 cars are required), dubbed the 959 at its market launch, is developed using only the best of the best: Composite materials, a race-proven air- and water-cooled flat-six engine, and electronically controlled all-wheel drive.

The first all-wheel-drive prototypes are already under development in 1981. At the end of 1983, it's time for Porsche to broach the all-wheel subject with the public. Three 4WD 911 equipped with near-production 3.2-liter normally aspirated Carrera engines are quickly created in the race department. They still lack technical subtleties such as electronic torque distribution and are sent into the desert to see how they perform. The three promptly win the Paris-Dakar rally.

It doesn't get much better than this. And after the successful premiere in 1984, Porsche sends three 959 lookalikes mounted with the 959 drive train but powered by normally aspirated Carrera engines to the Sahara in 1985. However, the chance to win is dashed by maladies and accidents. In 1986, the production-ready 959 finally turns up for duty. In preparation for the Dakar, it wins the Egyptian Pharaoh's Rally ... and in 1986 goes on to clinch a double victory at the Dakar. René Metge wins ahead of Jacky Ickx. Project leader Roland Kussmaul, driving a modified 959 as the swift service car and spare parts transporter, finishes in sixth place.

All-wheel drive is put to the hardest of tests at the Dakar

The 959 power unit with a 2.85-cc displacement is derived from the 956/962 and in the production car develops 450 hp. Out of consideration for the poor fuel quality in Africa, the engine output of the rally-959 is reduced to 380 hp. Like the first Dakar-911, the 959 is fitted with a double wishbone suspension all round. However, the 959 features reinforced suspension mounting points. Added to this are electronically controlled power distribution and a speed-dependent ride-control system. The rally car also features a higher ride height and two fuel tanks with a total capacity of 270 liters. Fuel consumption lies between 20 (liaison section) and 30 liters (special stage), notleast due to the reduced top speed. While the production 959 achieves a speed of 315 km/h, the engineers calculate the speed of the Dakar-959 at 200 km/h, with Ickx ultimately setting a top speed at the rally with 235 km/h.

Since the immense development costs for the limited edition showpiece (292 units) is far in excess of the 420,000 Deutschmark selling price, it earns itself a name as the "most expensive PR giveaway in Porsche history". Ultimately, however, Porsche's customers then and now benefit from the development work put into the 959. The drive technology of the all-wheel drive 911 models such as the Carrera 4 (starting with the 964) and turbo (starting with the 993) had previously proven itself under the toughest conditions imaginable in desert racing.

Steady course to success

___ When the motorsport team returns from the debut of the successor to the winning 635 CSi-coupés (including the 1986 European Championship) at the season-opener of the new World Touring Car Championship in Monza, it brings two messages for the BMW Executive Board – one good, one bad. The good news is that the new racer from Munich has immediately locked out the first seven places at the highest-ranking race. The bad news is that they were all disqualified. The reason: the trunk hood of the new M3 is made of Kevlar instead of the same material as the production 3-series that rolls off the assembly line. And the thickness of the metal also comes under intense scrutiny for non-compliance with the regulations.

With the M3, the Motorsport GmbH defines new standards

However, with the homologation of the BMW M3, these problems are resolved and BMW turns up with a very hot iron in the fire. To clear the homologation hurdle, FIA requires 5,000 vehicles to be produced within a year. The responsibility for this falls to the BMW subsidiary, the Motorsport GmbH, with the M3 – after the mid-engine and racing M1 – representing the second car of the fledgling affiliate. Despite the turbulent start to the season, the M3 still wins in its premiere year, claiming the World Touring Car Championship, the European Championship, the DTM, and six other series titles. Added to these is a victory at the Corsica Rally as a round of the WRC.

With the M3, a manufacturer once again shows it has the courage to develop an extravagant touring

➤ The 10,000 rpm four-valve four-cylinder brawny-sounding engine isn't just good for gripping touring car race action on the Nordschleife – the passage "Pflanzgarten" is always good for kicking up the heels.

What else?

Al Unser Snr. triumphs at the Indy500 at the age of 47 years and 360 days, making him the oldest winner. The four-time victor has also set a record with 644 leading laps.

◀ Large wheels, an adjustable rear spoiler and increased capacity are only some of the measures that keep the BMW M3 on the winning road in the DTM between 1987 and 1992.

In compliance with Group A rules, the production (red vehicle) and race version show very clear parallels.

car for racing without recoiling from the resulting costs. The legendary GTA is a good example of this. Visually, the M3 looks a lot like the then-current 3-series (E30). However, the muscular boxed wheel flares, a voluminous front spoiler lip, the section of the rear window modified for aerodynamic efficiency, the roof panel and trunk lid as well as a large rear wing are a clear indication of what the M3 is intended for. And hidden under the lightweight body is pure racing technology, starting with the four-valve four-cylinder M1 engine initially with a 2.3-litre displacement through to its powerful brake system and dogleg sports transmission (first gear down to the left) and sporty features such as limited slip differential and oil cooling.

For the 1988 season, a throttle-valve slide replaces the butterflies. Thanks to the larger intake valves, the performance increases from 295 to 300 hp (at 8,000 rpm). This is enough to again keep the opposition at bay in the European Touring Car Championship and in ten other championships. In

1989, the engineers take another step (320 hp at 8,500 rpm), which can be heard loud and clear by spectators at the racetracks: The husky sound of the four-cylinder racer at full revs is unmistakable. On top of winning the DTM title against a pack of Ford Sierra Cosworth and Mercedes-Benz 190E 2.3-16 come another 15 national and international titles – from the Italian to the European Hill Climb Championship for production cars. In keeping with the "evo trend" in Group A, in 1990 the 2.5-liter M3 Sport Evolution emerges with adjustable spoilers. In the DTM, for instance, the M3 continues its winning streak until the end of the Group A era (Class 1 is introduced in the DTM from 1993). And in the hands of amateurs, the sports sedan, prepared to comply with Group A and near-production Group N regulations, will continue to be raced successfully for a long time to come.

Edgy champion

___ In 1979, when Lancia came up with an answer to the Giorgetto Giugiaro-designed Volkswagen Golf, the Turin-based company had no idea of the Lancia Delta's sporting potential. The Stratos' career was coming to an end on the rally tracks of the world, and the 037 was still a twinkle in the designer's eyes. Sports car racing was center stage. Fielded in this category was the 1979-debuting Beta Montecarlo in Group-5 trim, with which Lancia scored the 1980 and 1981 World Championship for Makes.

Lancia returned to rallying for the 1982 season with a Beta Montecarlo derivative, the low-slung Group B Rallye 037, which continued the Stratos' success streak by winning the manufacturers' title of the World Rally Championship. As the successor to the 037, the Delta slid into the rallying scene. The Delta S4 was a true Group B monster, developing 480 hp thanks to a supercharger and twin-turbochargers. It had permanent all-wheel drive and a tubular space frame chassis, and made generous use of carbon fiber. In 1986, the S4 won 15 rallies, representing not only the pinnacle of performance

in rallying, but also the end of the Group B era after the fatal accident of works driver Henri Toivonen. From 1987, the WRC is run with Group A vehicles. The Lancia Delta HF 4WD steps into the void and snatches the crown, followed by the Integrale, which becomes the yardstick in its various evolutionary stages in the WRC, until 1992.

With the Integrale, the wider track of the production car is optimized for rallying, with the factory fitting bigger fender flares. The turbocharged two-liter four-cylinder in the Integrale receives a power boost in 1989, from 280 to 295 hp. Abarth, who is responsible for the engine of the 1992-WRC-winning Delta Integrale 16V Evoluzione, specifies the output at 300 hp – the maximum for Group A. One of its secrets of success is the all-wheel drive with its three differentials. ___

⬆ After the end of the breathtaking Group B rally monsters, near-production Group A vehicles also know how to deliver an action-packed show, with the Lancia Delta Integrale playing the lead role.

⬇ The workplace of double WRC champions, Juha Kankkunen and Miki Biasion.

With the touch of a finger

1988
What else?

Roger Dorchy achieves a record speed of 405 km/h on the Mulsanne Straight with a world championship-Peugeot.

___ The special thing about the Ferrari 640 is that the pilot no longer needs to take a hand off the steering wheel to change gears. For the 1989 season, Ferrari turns up for the first time with an automated, conventional seven-speed gearbox. Gear shifting is done by means of shift paddles positioned on the steering wheel, which emit electronic impulses.

After teething troubles are fixed and control problems are solved, this technology quickly yields success. Thanks to its use in Formula 1, the innovation is adopted by other race series and in the manufacturing of production cars. The first standard car to feature the "F1 gearbox", the Ferrari F355 F1, is followed by other sports cars, coupés and sports sedans, through to the extremely fuel-efficient Volkswagen Lupo 3L. In motorsport, regulations are quickly introduced to put a stop to its use in the various racing categories. In Formula 1, it remains state-of-the-art.

Nigel Mansell joins forces with Ferrari's regular driver Gerhard Berger. Mansell makes a perfect start

Mansell is the first F1 pilot to keep his hands on the steering wheel while shifting gears

to the season by winning the opening round at his maiden race with Ferrari. Both Ferraristi score a win each and a number of podium results. In terms of the world title, however, technical hiccups hamper them and Ferrari from achieving better results. The race director is Cesare Fiorio, the successful ex-Lancia sports boss.

Also new in the 1989 season are the engines. After the banning of all-powerful turbo engines, normally aspirated motors are reintroduced. To avoid going from one extreme to the other, the displacement is capped at 3.5 liters. From initial revs of 11,000 to 12,800 rpm, the engines prove capable of almost 600 hp. At this stage, the number of cylinders is still open – in favor of the eight-cylinder unit is its weight, dimensions, and fuel consumption, with power and revs advocating for the twelve cylinder. Thus, the path that Renault and Honda follow with a ten-cylinder unit proves to be the right direction. Only the racing squad from Maranello remains true to Ferrari's traditional twelve cylinder.

___

➤ A pyrotechnic display from the underbody is part of the F1 show of this time.

▼ Nigel Mansell begins the 1989 Formula 1 season with a victory (photo). By the end of the year, the squad from Maranello will have claimed three wins.

Grand four-wheel results

Hans-Joachim Stuck wins the car's premiere in the DTM with what are still Audi's traditional racing colors (left). In 1991 the Ingolstadters commemorate their own Silver Arrow past (right). Frank Biela defends the DTM title. The dominance of this powerful all-wheel-drive car seals the fate of the "classless DTM society."

◄ The 1990 season finale becomes a show of power. Stuck wins both races, flanked each time by teammates Frank Jelinski and Walter Röhrl.

___ Audi demonstrates the prowess of its quattro technology at rallies, where treacherous surfaces bring its benefits into high relief. After withdrawing from rally sports in the late 1980s, the Ingolstadt company enters new territory without further ado. The new order of the day: circuits, which showcase the qualities of all-wheel drive on smooth surfaces. Following appearances in the Trans-Am (1988) and IMSA (1989) series in the USA, Audi enters the popular DTM (German Touring Car Championship).

In 1990 Audi comes up with a real heavyweight. At 1,220 or 1,300 kilograms, the V8 weighs a quarter of a tonne more than BMW's M3. Its 3.6-liter engine generates 416 hp and 380 Nm of torque, and a six-speed transmission sends the power to all four wheels. That gives it the edge not only on straight stretches but also when accelerating out of curves. The car has a peak speed of 300 km/h and is the field's quickest sprinter from 0 to 100 km/h, needing just 4.6 seconds. Lightweight four-piston rigid calipers are used to decelerate its three-piece 18-inch wheels.

Two experienced drivers sit at its power-assisted steering wheel: Hans-Joachim Stuck and Walter Röhrl. Stuck, the son of former Auto Union Silver Arrow driver Hans Stuck, drives the V8 from the very start of the season. Rally legend Röhrl joins him as of the race on the Norisring. For the season finale a third member joins the team: Frank Jelinski. With spectacular conditions for the season finale in Hockenheim (five drivers have a chance to win the title),

Introduced on rally terrain, the quattro also proves itself on asphalt

Audi posts two triple victories and Hans-Joachim "Strietzel" Stuck wins the championship. The ease with which Audi mows down the competition causes some consternation in the background, and gives BMW and Mercedes another 60-kilogram advantage.

Audi revs up even more for the 1991 season. Alongside the sms racing team led by Nuremberg native Konrad Schmidt, Audi Center Reutlingen (AZR) enters the V8 Evo with an evolved aerodynamic package and an officially confirmed output of 442 hp (at 9,300 rpm). In addition to Stuck and Röhrl (at the Hockenheim finale), sms also has promising young driver Hubert Haupt. Jelinski and Biela drive for Audi Center Reutlingen. The Audi teams have to do without the new racing ABS used by the competition. But they do have water-cooled brakes – like in the rally Audis. Also new are radial tires and 19-inch wheels. Stuck and Biela win four races each, and Biela takes the title.

In 1992 Audi and its sterling team drive under a new color – silver. But they cannot repeat the success of previous years. Following extended disagreements about weight classes, fuel reductions, and higher handicap weights, as well as protests by competitors about the new V8 engine with a 180° crankshaft, the Ingolstadters leave the DTM in the middle of the season. Audi (along with BMW) moves on to the worldwide Super Touring car series with Class 2 cars. ___

The Silver Arrows

___ A booming sound like an offshore racing boat draws all eyes to the dark-blue flounders zooming across Nuremberg's Norisring in the 1987 Supercup series. The Group C sports cars from Switzerland regularly appear at German events as part of this series. Under a synthetic shell reinforced with carbon and aramid, their five-liter Mercedes V8 engines with two turbochargers pound out 720 to around 800 hp (at 0.7 to 1.2 bar of boost pressure).

The car's predecessor, the first Sauber-Mercedes with the designation C8, achieves notoriety at its premiere in Le Mans with a spectacular airborne number on the Hunadières straight. John Nielsen survives the flight of more than 20 meters un-scathed. His car does not. Undeterred, team director Peter Sauber prepares the ground for Mercedes' return to racing and for his team's future in Formula One. About a year after this accident, Henri Pescarolo and Mike Thackwell win the 1,000-kilometer race on the Nürburgring in the C8. In 1987 the C9 acquires a stiffer aluminum mono-coque. The car's backbone weighs 48 kilograms, including the suspension mounts. The C9 enters 33 races by 1990, winning 18 of them. It starts in dark blue, then switches to silver. In 1988 the Sauber squad becomes the Mercedes factory team, and the decision makers in Stuttgart finally give the green light to return to racing, which they left after the 1955 tragedy in Le Mans. In 1988 the still blue "Silver Arrows" wear advertisements for Mercedes subsidiary AEG and the slogan "powered by Mercedes-Benz." Starting in 1989 the 902-kilogram and 1.07-meter flat cars shine in the traditional silver. Mercedes' 1989 victory in Le Mans is pure gold.

Experienced drivers like Jochen Mass and Jean-Louis Schlesser sit at the wheel, along with protégés Michael Schumacher and Karl Wendlinger. In April of 1989 the C11 makes its debut in Monza and promptly wins. Schumacher drives for the first time at the next race in Silverstone. He and Mass will win the season finale in Mexico. The new Silver Arrows win additional races and are rewarded with world championship titles in 1989 and 1990. While the C11's drive system is tried and true, its chassis is now made of carbon fiber.

The "Silver Arrows" successes and duels with Jaguar help sports car racing enter a renaissance. And that is accompanied by new competitors like Peugeot. In 1991 Sauber-Mercedes gears up with the new 755-kilogram C291. Its aerodynamically optimized chassis now contains a V12 naturally aspirated engine with 650 hp at 13,000 rpm. In 1991 Schumacher wins the last race with Silver Arrow sports cars at the Autopolis in Japan, breaking a string of failures by the still experimental and not quite mature racers. Sauber and Mercedes will join forces in Formula One in 1993. ___

Mercedes uses old hands and hungry newcomers

The Sauber-Mercedes C9 takes its first laurels in dark blue – with financial backing from Kouros and from AEG (above). These successes enable Mercedes-Benz to celebrate its comeback to international racing, and open the door to the color silver's return to the sports car scene (left). The C11 kicks off an extraordinary development program. Its successor is the C291 (bottom photo).

Mercedes races with old hands like Jochen Mass and Jean-Louis Schlesser as well as talented and ambitious young drivers like Michael Schumacher and Karl Wendlinger. Both the company and the junior drivers use these contests as a spring-board to Formula One.

Of wins and automation

___ The Williams-Renault posts ten victories to dominate the 1992 season. And Nigel Mansell finally succeeds in winning the world championship title that has slipped through his fingers a few times in the past. The FW14B is based on the previous year's FW14 model, albeit with improvements to the failure-prone semi-automatic transmission and the brakes.

The FW14B's outstanding rigid chassis, efficient aerodynamics, and high-powered, reliable engine all function harmoniously together. In addition, years of development work have enabled Williams to perfect the active suspension. The system goes through 12,000 kilometers of testing in preparation for the racing season, largely at the hands of Riccardo Patrese and test driver Damon Hill. It maintains constant clearance between the

F1 drivers are assisted by sophisticated computer-controlled systems

underside of the car and the surface of the road, enabling a quantum leap in aerodynamic efficiency. The electronic set-up also works perfectly over the entire racing distance – regardless of the level of fuel in the car. Uneven spots on the driving surface are simply ironed out. Assisted by traction control based on variable displacement, Mansell can make spirited use of the accelerator. Spinning wheels when exiting curves are now a thing of the past.

Active suspension and the particular type of handling it demands are not every driver's cup of tea. But they are made to order for the crusty Englishman. This complex system is made possible by continuous telemetric analysis of the sensor data. Motion values on the high, center, and lateral axes are registered and countersteering commands issued in just four milliseconds to the elec-

▶ A new era in Formula One requires computers and large teams. Here, Riccardo Patrese waits at the wheel for a qualifying session.

What else?

Defending champion Audi unexpectedly announces that it will be leaving the DTM. This follows disagreements about the use of a non-homologized crankshaft.

◀ Nigel Mansell wins the 1992 title in the Williams. The following year Alain Prost (photo) takes the wheel and his fourth title, and then the Schumacher and Brawn era begins.

Computers have long since replaced drawing boards and are crucial to the development of modern Formula One racers.

tro-hydraulic suspension control via internal push-rod kinematics.

The constant ride height causes head designer Patrick Head and aerodynamics expert Adrian Newey to devote greater attention to the lower half of the car. Of note on the FW14B are the air-guidance profiles on the sides of the front wing that extend back to the front axle, which send air past the front tires into the side pods with minimal resistance. The airstream also hits the underbody more favorably thanks to the slightly elevated front. And the laterally mounted semi-automatic seven-speed transmission enables the engineers to further elevate the rear diffuser with its air flow components. This promotes downforce and thereby enhances the handling properties.

Renault's engine assembly is also first-class. A team led by Bernard Dudot and Jean-Jacques His produces the engines for Williams. A Renault RS3B 3.5-liter 72° V10 with an estimated output of 680 hp and 13,500 rpm is used for the first half of

the season. Starting with the race in Hungary, a 67° RS4 gives drivers an additional 1,000 rpm. The high rpm levels are made possible by Renault's first use of a pneumatic valve control system, which renders classic valve springs obsolete. In Belgium Renault also experiments with variable induction pipes, which will sharply limit experimentation with special fuels by mid-season. Renault's partner Elf has created no fewer than 75 different blends, giving the engines a clear edge in performance over conventional products. They are said to enable a good 50 more horsepower ...

Days of thunder, part one

___ A small Italian knocks the master from its throne, and that on the Nürburgring Nordschleife, the home turf of the main actors in the DTM (German Touring Car Championship). Just a few laps in a rental car on the Eifel region's world-famous circuit give Nicola Larini and his Alfa Romeo 155 V6 TI a first-row starting position, despite the fact that he has only rudimentary knowledge of its more than 25 kilometers. He needs eight minutes and a good 46 seconds for a lap of the narrow tradition-laden circuit next to the modern Grand Prix course. The roar of his 11,500-rpm six-cylinder engine accompanies the two exciting door-to-door races that the pros provide in the world's most demanding touring car series. Larini and the Alfa Corse factory team end up winning both races, as well as the 1993 DTM championship with victories in Zolder (Belgium),

on the Nürburgring GP course, Wunstorf, Nuremberg, Diepholz, and Singen. Larini's teammate Alessandro Nannini, a former Formula One driver, wins the two final races in Hockenheim. The all-wheel-drive car prepared by Alfa Corse in the town of Settimo Milanese, wins twelve of twenty races.

Nannini and Larini build on their successes the following year. Brand colleagues Kris Nissen and Stefano Modena also put in a good showing. They share the coveted points, so do not end up winning the title. But with 13 wins in 24 races, the further developed Alfa 155 V6 TI is also the most successful racer in 1994's first-class field. In 1995 and 1996, Christian Danner, Nicola Larini, and Michael Bartels add five victories and "Sandro" Nannini, Gabriele Tarquini, and Nicola Larini add nine to the DTM and ITC tallies.

➤ Christian Danner is part of Alfa Romeo's factory driver quartet from the start. The car's three-liter V6 engine generates 420 and then 450 hp at up to 12,000 rpm and is good for a range of around 500 kilometers until requiring an overhaul of around 30,000 marks.

◄ Nicola Larini and his Alfa Corse racer with starting number 8 immediately dominate the 1993 season. The car enjoys cult status today and is well represented in racing games.

➤ Alfa Romeo's engineers first work for Ferrari's F1 team and position the V6 low in the car. The top-heavy tendency of the Class-1 racer is a disadvantage of the all-wheel drive.

What else?

Fiat launches the Trofeo 500, a one-make rally cup that becomes popular in many countries. The car is the "Cinquecento" powered up by Abarth.

The touring car regulations governing the DTM's fascinating high-tech racers are called Class 1. They allow naturally aspirated engines with a maximum of 12,000 rpm and 2.5 liters of displacement, and all-wheel drive. Their silhouettes correspond to those of production cars, but there is room below the wheel hubs for a lot of aerodynamic fun and games. Sweeping wheelhouse extensions and spoilers on the rear lid are customary. Additional technical liberties are taken in the four racing seasons from 1993 to 1996, which turn the racers ever more into thoroughbred prototypes – far removed from classic racing touring cars. The DTM (and the ITC, its sister series held in Europe in 1995 and then worldwide) mutates into a silhouette series and heads straight into financial exodus.

In developing the Alfa 155 V6 TI, Alfa Corse benefits from the lengthy and successful series expertise of its sister company Lancia. The car's intelligent all-wheel drive is a direct descendant of that in the record-setting, title-winning Delta Integrale. The predecessor of the 155 V6 TI, the Alfa 155 GTA that enters the Italian touring car series (CIVT) in 1992 is also still powered by the turbocharged Integrale four-cylinder engine. The DTM racer's now extensive carbon shell contains a classic Alfa V6 drive system mounted low in the chassis. Its 420 to 460 hp are transmitted by a six-speed gearbox to 18- and then 19-inch wheels. The "Nano's" sequential transmission becomes standard and is ultimately also controlled by toggle switches on the steering wheel. ___

> **Each victory is rewarded by a serpent devouring a Mercedes star**

Schumi's first shenanigans

___ Two and a half years after his Formula One debut, Michael Schumacher wins his first world championship title with Benetton. With eight wins (out of the twelve races that counted for him), Schumacher and Benetton-Ford are the team of the year. But this is a season of both light and darkness. Ayrton Senna suffers a fatal accident in Imola, and a number of incidents suggest that Schumacher might be fudging and Benetton might not only be brilliant. The season is marked by debate about the prohibition on electronic driver and traction assistance systems. All active suspension, anti-lock, and anti-slip systems, fully automatic and programmable transmissions, electronic fly-by-wire gas-pedal control, and telemetric interventions are no longer permitted. Electronic developments in the engine sector are still allowed. The Hockenheim race produces

**The F1 pushes the limits –
and Benetton exceeds a few**

the "refueling scandal" when a fire in the pit lane leads to the revelation that the Benetton team has been illegally manipulating the fueling system. Schumacher is disqualified and given a two-race ban for ignoring a black flag in England. In Spa-Francorchamps the Benetton's bottom board is found to lie outside the requisite tolerances. And most controversial of all, a questionable collision between title contenders Schumacher and Damon Hill mars the season's final race in Australia.

But there is no doubt about the extraordinary driving skills of the young German who lays the foundation for his unparalleled collection of titles in 1994. The Benetton B194 is a fine brainchild of Ross Brawn and Rory Byrne, whom Schumacher will follow to Ferrari. The previous year's model was already considered the best car in the field. But even

▲ Kerpen native Michael Schumacher wins his first Formula One title and becomes one of racing's greats. Team director Flavio Briatore and technical experts David Byrne and Ross Brawn are some of the brains behind his success.

▼ A Ford Zetec R V8 3.5-liter engine resides in the rear of the Benetton. Displacement will be limited to three liters the following year in order to reduce power.

What else?

Roland Ratzenberger and Ayrton Senna die in accidents in Formula One. No fatal accidents have occurred since, thanks to significantly improved safety features.

Michael Schumacher (right, front) and Ayrton Senna (in a Williams-Renault with starting number 2) dominate the top tier of racing until the tragic death of the Brazilian driver in Imola. The season features exciting races, disqualifications, and a duel for the title between Schumacher and Damon Hill (in a Williams-Renault with starting number 0).

a genius of Schumacher's caliber is unable to make up for its 80-hp deficit. One key to the B194's success is its reliability. Another is surely the superb racing team led by Flavio Briatore and Tom Walkinshaw. Schumacher's role in Benetton's success is clear when he is sidelined by the ban and his teammates can only take the B194 to the middle of the field. Schumacher has three different teammates for the 1994 season: JJ Lehto, Jos Verstappen, and Johnny Herbert.

The B194 is made at a model factory of nearly clinical qualities in the English town of Enstone, which Benetton starts operating in 1992. The car's most striking feature is its high nose, which helps make its central axis horizontal. This is an aerodynamic coup that ever more teams will copy in seasons to come. Newly constructed by Cosworth, the Zetec R V8 engine containing pneumatically controlled valves and engine electronics from Ford is located at the rear of the carbon dugout. The cylinder banks display a 75° angle, and the final displacement is 3.5 liters. It generates about 750 hp

with around 14,500 rpm, which is 1,000 more than its predecessor. The six-speed, semi-automatic transmission is mounted laterally behind the engine and controlled by toggle switches. In keeping with the regulations, the B194 initially weighs 505 kilos, and then 515 starting with the race in Canada.

Michael Schumacher is the last champion to use the Ford-Cosworth engine

Schumacher's title is a step ahead of Benetton boss Briatore's plans. The 1994 season was initially viewed as a chance to develop expertise, and Benetton has a contract for 1995 to use Renault engines, which are considered the gold standard.

———

From the road to the winners' platform

___ The sports-car sector booms in the 1990s. After Enzo Ferrari's death in 1988, his cars become valuable collector's items regardless of their vintage. Eyeing a share of the pie, manufacturers produce a large number of new and fabulous models. McLaren ends up putting the ultimate sports car on the road – faster, more powerful, and offering more driving pleasure than any car before. No matter the cost! The idea is born in 1988.

Gordon Murray proceeds to design a streamlined, well-proportioned car body with a centrally placed driver's seat and therefore space for a total of three people. Like in Formula One, the car is made of carbon fiber, and costs 1.4 million marks in 1994. A four-valve V12 engine from BMW Motorsport with variable camshaft control (VANOS), a 6.1-liter displacement, and 627 hp is installed behind the passenger seats. Presented in connection with the 1992 Monaco Grand Prix, this road-going sports car sprints from 0 to 100 km/h in 3.2 seconds and has a peak speed of more than 360 km/h. It is not intended to be entered in races. But Ray Bellm and Thomas Bscher, who are both racing drivers and business managers, see the matter differently. A pharmaceutical executive and a banker who later heads Bugatti, they convince Ron Dennis to let the McLaren F1 race

and receive the necessary support. Murray adapts the F1's engine to meet the air restrictor requirements, gives it another approximately 15 hp, cuts the weight, and adds the requisite safety features and details. Tipping the scales at 1,100 kilograms, the F1 GTR enters the BPR sports car racing series, which will become the FIA GT World Cup in 1997. The car immediately wins ten races and the title, as well as Le Mans.

BMW and Bigazzi enter the F1 GTR in races the following year. Le Mans is won by Manuel Reuter, Alexander Wurz, and Davy Jones in an open Joest Porsche LMP, but the F1 GTR wins nine races in the BPR and four in the Japanese GT championship as well as both titles. The Porsche 911 GT1 is the first serious new competitor, and other makers are working full speed ahead on road-homologized thoroughbred GT1 racing cars for the 1997 season. The air is getting thinner for the McLaren F1.

McLaren responds with the long-tail version of the F1 GTR, which has around 680 hp. But the sports-car racing scene is moving toward pure-blooded GT1 cars and LMP prototypes. A total of 107 McLaren F1s are made from 1993 to 1997, 28 of them as GTR racing models. ___

▲ The McLaren enters the BPR series and then promptly conquers Le Mans, taking four of the top five places. The winning car is driven by Yannick Dalmas, JJ Lehto, and Masanori Sekiya.

◄ The McLaren is the world's fastest road car of its time. With a carbon-fiber body and enormously healthy genes, it also has first-class racing qualities.

> Juan-Pablo Montoya achieves what Michael Andretti has not managed to do. Based on a CART title and a series of spectacular maneuvers, the Colombian driver vaults to Formula One and proves his skills there as well, emulating his equally successful teammate and predecessor Alessandro Zanardi (photo).

Frontrunner in the USA

___ Corkscrew Corner is one of the most famous curves in the world. A long uphill straight on the track in Laguna Seca is followed by a downhill left-right-left combination. The entrance to this passage is not visible from the cockpit. With a daring maneuver in the last round of the final race of the American IndyCar World Series founded in 1979, Alessandro Zanardi overtakes leader Bryan Herta – on the outside! And wins the race. The Italian driver has just performed one of the greatest passing maneuvers in the history of racing.

Reynard is one of the biggest chassis makers for the U.S. counterpart to Formula One. Founded in 1973 and named for Adrian Reynard, it produces monoposti for various series until going bankrupt in 2001 (after which the BAR F1 racing team moves into its building and Zytek takes over its chassis production). But Reynard is also active in Formula One. In 1996 half of the starting field in the IndyCar series drives with Reynard chassis. Regulations stipulate a number of identical parts, which benefits budgets and makes opportunities more equitable. In the mid-

1990s the engines come from Ford, Toyota, Mercedes, and also Honda. The Reynard 961-Honda wins eight of the 16 CART races in 1996. And Reynard chassis win the championship seven times in a row from 1995 to 2001.

In 1996 the Honda V8 engine with a 2.65-liter displacement and 720 to 800 hp wins 11 races. The Honda assembly with nearly 900 hp used by Ganassi-Reynard is considered the benchmark to this day. The car's tank is limited to a volume of 132 liters, making refueling a necessity for races that are up to 500 miles long. In combination with a seven-speed transmission, the cars can hit speeds well in excess of 350 km/h.

The CART (Championship Auto Racing Teams, Inc.) racing series flourishes during these years in the USA, Canada, Brazil, and Australia. But a dispute over naming rights between CART and the owner of Indianapolis Motor Speedway leads to a break between the CART series and the IRL (Indy Racing League) – newly founded in 1996 – whose jewel is the Indianapolis 500 race with IRL cars.

The Ganassi team dominates CART racing for years

What else?

In 1995 the DTM gets an international sibling, the ITC (International Touring Car Championship). The following year, the DTM name temporarily disappears from view. Because the high-tech racing cars become too expensive, the end of the racing season also means curtains for the Class 1 cars. The top level of touring car racing will now be run exclusively with Class 2 cars, which are known as Super Touring cars.

A virtually prefab serial winner

___ Tommi Mäkinen becomes something like the "Fangio" of rally racing with various Lancer Evolution models, winning four successive WRC titles from 1996 to 1999. The first title in 1996 is with the Evo III. Each year brings another level, up to the Evo VI of 1999. The Evo IV of 1997 features a new basic chassis, which stays in action until the premiere of the Mitsubishi WRC in 2002. Until then, the Mitsubishi team relies on the homologized Group A Lancer. In 1997 the competitors start developing World Rally Cars, which the regulations have made easier to homologize (20 cars suffice); Mitsubishi, on the other hand, does not need to do so. The Lancer Evo enjoys such popularity in amateur racing and as a road car that it effortlessly surmounts the homologation hurdle of 2,500 cars

The Evo is so popular that Mitsubishi doesn't have to develop a WRC car

for Group A classification – for each level of the Evolution. That makes Tommi Mäkinen and Richard Burns' vehicles the last Group A factory cars in the WRC. The Lancer Evo's technical specifications include a four-cylinder turbocharged engine with charge-air cooling, two overhead camshafts, 1,995 cc of displacement with a bore/stroke ratio of 85 to 88 millimeters, and compression of 8.5:1. With engine output limited by the regulations to 300 hp although an additional ten percent are surmised, modifications benefit primarily the torque levels and handling properties. The Evo III (440 Nm) gains 80 Nm on its way to becoming the Evo VI (520 Nm). All-wheel drive is standard, as is a sequential six-speed transmission starting with the Evo IV. Regulations stipulate a minimum weight of 1,230 kilograms, which can rise to 1,350 de-

➤ Tommi Mäkinen takes his fourth WEC title in a row in 1999 with the Evo VI (here at the rally in Spain). Mitsubishi also dominates marathon racing with the Pajero, and racks up a series of Dakar victories.

What else?

The Mitsubishi Lancer is also predestined to win production-based Group N world championship titles.

Jacques Villeneuve becomes the F1 world champion. The finale can hardly be more dramatic: Villeneuve, Michael Schumacher and Heinz-Harald Frentzen have exactly the same top qualifying time. Schumacher loses his chance for the title by intentional ramming Villeneuve.

◄ The IV is the 1997 version of the Lancer. While Mitsubishi continues to concentrate on Group A cars, competitors produce new World Rally Cars (WRC). Mäkinen still ends up winning.

Mäkinen and Burns (after
winning two seasons with
the Evo IV) race through
the woods with the Evo V
in 1998.

pending on the rally. The diameter of the eight-inch wheels can vary from 15 inches for gravel to 18 inches for asphalt. They have water-cooled and internally ventilated brake discs the size of pizzas and rigid calipers whose braking power is distributed from the pedal via balance bars. Three differential gears enable slip-free distribution of the propulsive power. The chassis of these four-door sedans contain McPherson front and multi-link rear axles. The springs and adjustable stabilizers are also adapted to the purpose at hand.

Even though not obvious at first glance, these internal modifications have an enormous effect. For the Evo IV, the engine position next to the new multi-link rear axle is rotated by 180 degrees. The intelligent all-wheel-drive control system is superb, with electromagnetic control of the front and middle differentials. A classic laminated differential is also used. In Mäkinen's hands the Evo IV is nearly invin-

cible in 1997 and early 1998. It wins six rallies and takes second and third place two times each.

When the Evo V premieres in the 1998 season, it continues its predecessor's string of successes to post five wins and two third-place finishes. It also wins the WRC title. Recognizable by its new spoilers, the Evo V has an impressive track width adjusted for the WRC. Its suspension geometry has been reworked, and it also features newly programmed differential control. For the Mitsubishi Lancer Evo VI used in 1999 and early 2000, the engineers focus once again on enhancing the all-wheel drive and suspension systems. The car wins five WRC races and places fourth overall.

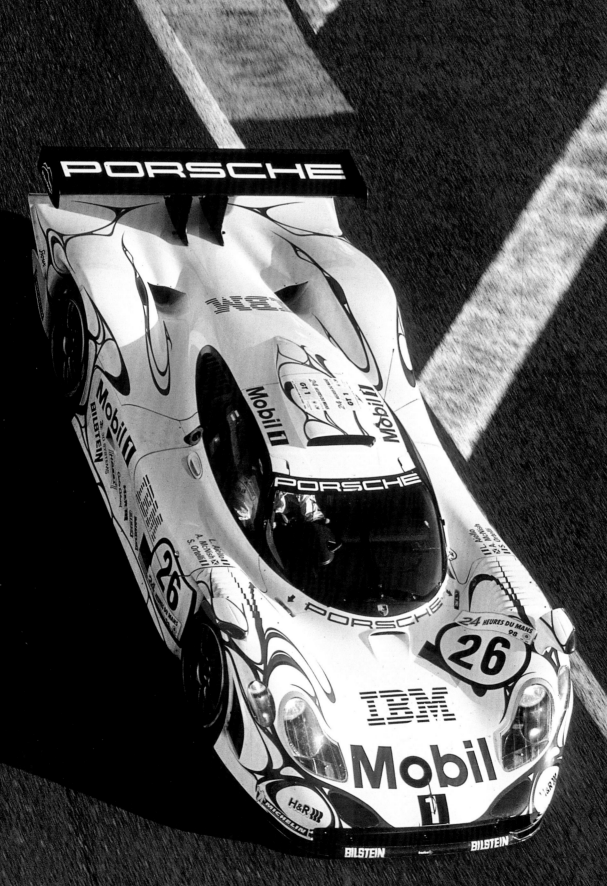

Birthday win in Le Mans

___ The popularity of the privately organized BPR Endurance GT Series, which seems to arise of its own accord, gains the series official status as the FIA GT Championship in 1997. Because contenders such as Porsche as well as Nissan, Toyota, and Mercedes-Benz lack the uncompromising sports cars like the McLaren BMW needed for this program, and because the regulations require the existence of GT1 homologation vehicles, these manufacturers quickly come up with such vehicles, for a maximum price of 1.5 million marks plus tax.

Porsche wins the race leading up to the race, and enters an early 911 GT1 in Le Mans in 1996. The two new "production sports cars" land on the podium, albeit below the Joest Porsche WSC prototype. But the reigning powers in the GT category – the Ferrari F40 and the McLaren BMW F1 GTR – continue to exercise control, including at the three remaining BPR races.

In 1997 McLaren gives its long-tailed F1 an even more uncompromising edge. Also entering the field is the racing version of the Mercedes CLK-GTR. Panoz, too, poses a major threat. Porsche's most obvious modifications for Le Mans consist of aligning the visuals more closely to those of the 996. McLaren and Mercedes then divide up the wins in the FIA GT series.

While Weissach is making a good two dozen cars of the first 544-hp GT1 series – complete with the 911's standard sheet-metal firewall, a steel cage, and carbon add-on parts – the Porsche motorsport department produces a thoroughbred racing car for the 1998 season with a street-legal model to serve as a fig leaf. Like its competitors, the 911 GT1 1998 now has a carbon-fiber monocoque with Kevlar/carbon composite add-on parts. It is the first "carbon Porsche." Meticulous attention to detail makes the car an impressive 100 kilos lighter than its predecessor as well as considerably stiffer and more aerodynamic. Its dimensions are barely compatible with the narrow passageways at freeway construction sites: length x width x height of 4.89 x 1.99 x 1.14 meters. A 100-liter tank is located between the passenger compartment and the engine. The engine matches that of the preceding 911 GT1. Its specifications are also familiar: a flat-six with a 3.2-liter displacement and two KKK turbochargers. But the engine block directly descended from the 993 turbo is now water-cooled. The four-valve cylinder heads have been around now for over a decade. With its air intake limited by restrictors, the engine is good for 550 horsepower.

A sequential six-speed transmission passes the output and torque (630 Nm at 4,250 rpm) to the rear wheels via twin wishbones. The

The 911 GT1 gets a street-legal fig leaf

brakes feature four carbon discs the size of pizzas (380 mm) held mercilessly in place by rigid calipers with eight pistons each for the front wheels and six for the rear. Besides the street-legal version there will be five racing cars, two of which will give Porsche a double victory in Le Mans. ___

▲ The 1996 Porsche 911 GT1 (above) resembles the 911 model of the 993 series still in production. The car's visuals and aerodynamics are adapted to the newly introduced 996 series version in 1997 (center). Following these GT1 models with clear though remote relations to the standard production vehicle, Porsche produces a thoroughbred racing car for the 1998 season.

◄ After two victories by Joest's open Walkinshaw Porsche, Stuttgart succeeds in winning with its closed GT1. Open cars dominate thereafter, with BMW in 1999 and the Audi R8 as of 2000.

The spice of ice

▲ Adapted specially for the popular sport of ice racing in France, these compact sports cars have short wheelbases, all-wheel steering and drive, short gear ratios, and narrow spikes to enable them to sprint on slick surfaces.

◄ It's important to "position" the cars well in advance of each curve in order to emerge from the drift and start sprinting down the next straight as soon as possible.

What else?

For the first time, Zakspeed enters the Chrysler Viper GTS-R in the 24-hour race on the Nürburgring. Over the next few years, this ten-cylinder GT2 sports car from America will dominate numerous endurance contests and the 24-hour race on the Nordschleife.

___ Aside from events like the "Monte" or Rally Sweden, ice races tend to be an ideal recreational activity for race-car drivers who can't wait for the next season to start. These spectacular contests, which are generally individual events as opposed to series, have long traditions. In fact, the first date back to before the war. In France, motorsport enthusiasts from various disciplines begin racing older cars with spike-studded tires on ice in the early 1970s. But the big names and brands only start entering the fray when French rallycross driver Max Mamers responds to the low level of interest in his own sport by launching a new series with the help of powerful sponsors, namely, the Trophée Andros.

The cars initially consist of decommissioned WEC racers, modified stock cars, and seriously upgraded compacts. Spectators at winter sport sites like Val-Thorens, Isola 2000, and Serre-Chevalier admire Group B dinosaurs like the Peugeot 205 Turbo 16, Lancia Delta S4, and Rover Metro 6R4, stock cars like the Mercedes 190E 2.3-16 and BMW M3, and the all-wheel Citroën AX. When Group B monsters are banned in the mid-1980s, the Trophée Andros and rallycross become the last realms of action for these breathtaking rally racers. But specially designed prototypes – compact, agile, and powerful – quickly end up calling the shots on the narrow ice tracks that wind between walls of snow. The wheelbases and overhangs of BMW 3-series cars and the like are promptly shortened, and all-wheel drive and steering become essential.

Attracted by the popularity of this spectacular

Opel manages to tame Formula One stars like Jean Alesi

series that regularly features rally greats, touring car aces, and Formula One stars battling on slick surfaces, Opel France joins the action in the winter of 1993-1994. In late 1998, it produces a car for the new season in the form of the Astra (G), which follows in the footsteps of the title-winning Opel Astra V6 (F) and Tigra. The synthetic body of this thoroughbred racing prototype conceals a tubular space frame and V6 engine that starts with a 3.3-liter displacement and 420 hp. It also has a sequential transmission, all-wheel drive, four-wheel steering, and the obligatory spikes for contests on ice. Ten-time ice-racing champion Yvan Muller takes no fewer than four titles with the Astra V6 4x4 in the winters from 1998 to 2002.

Opel maintains an entire series of sports versions of the Astra. The top models are the Astra V8 coupe for the DTM and its sister version prepared for the 24-hour race on the Nürburgring. Also present are a six-cylinder mid-engine prototype for the Trophée Andros, a rally vehicle based on the two-liter kit-car regulations, and homologized Group N versions of the Astra and Astra OPC for amateur racing. ___

Days of thunder, part two

___ The DTM (Deutsche Tourenwagen Meisterschaft, or German Touring Car Championship) is the scene of legendary racing battles in the mid-1990s, so the touring car fan community is understandably disappointed when the series is discontinued after the 1996 season. Seeds for the plan of reviving this popular German spectacle start germinating in highly tuned racers whose basic form resembles those of their production siblings parked along the tracks. In 2000, the day finally arrives when the DTM (now known as the Deutsche Tourenwagen Masters, or German Touring Car Masters) is reborn. Opel, Mercedes, and the ABT-Audi team are the actors on this newly created stage.

For reasons of cost control the new DTM regulations require conformity in as many parts as possible. These include tires (Dunlop), wheel size (18 inches), brakes (AP six-piston calipers with carbon-fiber discs), transmission (sequential six-speed from X-trac), drive type and train (rear-wheel with uniform differential), along with a safety cell that shifts the driver's position well towards the center of the car. The same applies to the general aerodynamic characteristics (width, height, and rear wing). Engine control (Bosch) and the basic layout of the eight-cylinder power plants are also harmonized to level out the playing field. Two 28-millimeter air restrictors limit the four-liter, four-valve V8 assembly's power development to around 7,500 rpm and 450 horsepower.

Many reasons promote technical conformity at the new DTM

The car's roar is even more impressive than that of the earlier four- and six-cylinder DTM racers that bore the star. Without sophisticated electronics, semi-automatic transmissions, and hydraulically controlled differentials, and therefore without the extremely high technical development and maintenance requirements of the earlier DTM Class I cars and the technologically highly sophisticated Super

➤ Three brands enter the new DTM: Mercedes-Benz, Opel, and ABT-Audi battle for the honors with technically similar V8 racing cars. The visuals of the CLK, Astra coupe, and TT bodies now closely resemble those of production cars.

◄ Mercedes factory driver Bernd Schneider wins the title in 2000, following his Class 1 DTM and ITC titles in 1995. He will take further DTM titles in 2001, 2003, and 2006.

▼ Spectacular displays of
sparks are part of the
new DTM, where experi-
enced touring car pros
like Klaus Ludwig (photo)
face everyone from young
drivers to former Formula
One racers.

Tourers, the DTM racers of the 2000 generation put
on a fabulous show – and that is the point.

The drivers need not exercise any restraint. In
conjunction with a classic racing suspension (front
and rear twin wishbones), the cars' abundant power
(500 Nm at 5,000 rpm) and immense deceleration
afford drivers an unadulterated racing experience.
The new DTM racers therefore meet with more ready
approval than vehicles like the subjectively less dynamic front-wheel drive cars of the Super Tourer
era.

The new CLK DTM cars are developed and entered
by AMG. Upon being acquired by Mercedes, AMG
is restructured into the company's own tuning subsidiary and rebranded as HWA (Hans Werner
Aufrecht). Once again, the technical mind behind
the new model is Gerhard Unger, who has previously
devised DTM racers based on the Mercedes 190 and

C class as well as the CLK GTR for Le Mans and the
FIA GT Championship. The CLK has a longer wheelbase in comparison with competitors from Rüsselsheim and Kempten based on the Opel Astra
Coupé and the Audi TT. This turns out to be a defi-
nite advantage, because its superior handling even
manages to compensate for the extra ten horsepower of the Opel assembly. In each of its two years
of action, the CLK DTM takes eight wins and the
title. Bernd Schneider – the DTM winner in 2000
and 2001 – is also the first champion to successfully
defend his DTM title. In 2002 the DTM switches back
to four-door sedan visuals, but retains its proven
technical features largely as before. ___

2001 Audi R8

Ascent to Olympus

___ Following its success in rally sports, Audi also
cleans up in the touring car sector, from the IMSA
series and the DTM to the various Super Tourer
championships. So the engineers in Ingolstadt start
thinking about new challenges, and quickly hatch
plans for a new field of action – the 24 Hours of Le
Mans.

In 1999 the Audi Sport team led by Dr. Wolfgang
Ullrich produces a sports car prototype for Le Mans.
Known as the R8R (R for roadster), it debuts as an
open-top car in accordance with LMP regulations.
But the team quickly follows that with a closed-top
R8C (C for coupe) on account of the LMGTP regulations for closed GT racing cars that offer additional
liberties (such as larger air restrictors and higher
charge pressure for 30 more horsepower and a car
body that is 15 centimeters longer and therefore
more aerodynamic), but only require thinner tires
and manual transmission instead of a steering
wheel toggle and shift hydraulics. The first appearance in Le Mans is essentially a warm-up. After
24 hours the Joest team's R8Rs take third and
fourth place, just a few laps behind the victorious
BMW V12 LMR and runner-up Toyota GT One. However, the coupes entered by Audi UK do not finish
the race, on account of long repair breaks due to
differential damage.

➤ The Audi R8 wins the
24 Hours of Le Mans five
times. The sports car also
posts more wins in the
ALMS (American Le Mans
Series) than any other
open prototype.

◄ If a team manages to win three times in a row, the ACO challenge trophy remains in its hands – which is what Audi achieves in 2002. Although the races from 2000 to 2002 are very different, the silver-red R8 driven by Tom Kristensen, Frank Biela, and Emanuele Pirro always comes out in front.

➤ The R8 is a favorite customer racing car as well. Supported by Audi North America, the ADT Champion team also benefits from ex-Formula One pros Johnny Herbert and JJ Lehto.

Thanks to the experience thereby gained, it's not hard to decide that the next R8 should be open and authentic – in other words, uncomplicated. The design, which had previously sought to reflect the production cars, now focuses resolutely on the purpose at hand. Form follows function. So Formula One quality of the nose should come as no surprise. It rises fluidly toward the rear, surrounds the cockpit, reaches its climax above the biturbo-V8 engine, and tapers off high between the two wheel arches with their equally streamlined cladding. One key to success is the fuel-stratified injection system (FSI), which – for a 90-liter tank volume – enables stints of a lap or two longer than the competition and therefore reduces the number of fueling stops. As a side benefit, the hot-running, highly compressed turbo engines are also better at starting up after the stops.

The company works feverishly on the approximately 100-bar injection system and its auxiliary components. The car takes over the R8R's 3.6-liter, 610-horsepower V8 engine, which transmits 700 Nm of torque (at 5,750 rpm) to the rear axle with a limited-slip differential via a carbon clutch and sequential six-speed gearbox.

The new R8 is a major coup. It immediately starts winning and racks up five victories at the 24 Hours of Le Mans. With success in other contests like the American and European Le Mans Series (ALMS and ELMS), it remains the benchmark for years. With 63 wins in 80 races, it is the most successful sports car prototype of all time – even today.

Due not least of all to this series of wins, Audi takes its rightful place amongst the most renowned automotive Olympians. And that at a time when image claims might seem to have been staked for decades.

With 63 wins in 80 races, the R8 is the most successful prototype

What else?

NASCAR legend Dale Earnhardt dies in a crash at the Daytona 500. To this day, fans still raise three fingers during round three in memory of the seven-time champion.

Jutta Kleinschmidt is the first woman to win the Dakar Rally. She pilots a Mitsubishi Pajero Evo with Andreas Schulz as co-driver.

◄ The flat hood covers a V8 engine whose thirst is stilled by fuel-stratified injection. Racing serves as a stress trial for production car development.

Rhapsody in red

The first five years of the new millennium are the era of Ferrari and Michael Schumacher. They take six manufacturers' and five drivers' titles in a row. In Schumacher's shadow, teammates Eddie Irvine and Rubens Barrichello also win the occasional race.

Michael Schumacher's outstanding driving skills, which also benefit from painstaking and uncompromising test work, produce a string of victories and titles.

What else?

Laurent Aiello, the Super Touring Car champion of 1997, wins another touring car title in Germany in 2002. Instead of a two-liter STW Peugeot 406, he now drives a DTM ABT-Audi TT-R.

___ Michael Schumacher becomes the world champion for the fifth time in 2002, equaling the record set by Juan-Manuel Fangio. After winning titles with Benetton in 1994 and 1995, the German driver switches to Ferrari in 1996. Even with a number of car failures, he finishes his first season for the "Reds" with third place in the drivers' championship. It will take four more years and two runner-up titles until he again claims top honors for himself in 2000. For its part, following a 16-year hiatus Ferrari has been winning the manufacturers' title since 1999, when "Schumi" had to settle for fifth place on account of an accident. But now in 2000, Ferrari and Schumacher kick off an unrivaled series of victories that will give Ferrari five more consecutive manufacturers' titles and Schumacher five in a row as well. In 2006 the best race-car driver of all time will fight his way through to the final race but ultimately have to concede defeat.

Of the eleven Ferrari F1 racers driven by "MSC" in his active career, the F2002 is one of the most successful. Of Ferrari's 15 victories in the championship's 17 races, eleven are posted by Schumacher and four by his teammate and runner-up, Rubens Barrichello, although the first of Schumacher's eleven is the season's premiere in the previous year's F2001. However, the F2002 also posts three triumphs in the first four races of the 2003 season, which yields a grand total of 18 victories. The tabloids promptly christen the F2002 the "Red Goddess." The F2004, in which Schumacher clinches the championship with six races to go, will be similarly successful, posting 15 wins in a single season.

Scuderia's secret lies in consistency and determination

The secret of success lies in the consistency and determination that general manager Jean Todt impresses upon the team – known for its Italian nonchalance – right from the start of his tenure. A former rally world champion (as co-driver) and racing director for Peugeot (WRC, Paris-Dakar, and Le Mans championship titles), Todt enjoys the full support of Ferrari chairman Luca di Montezemolo and can recruit the successful Benetton trio of Schumacher, Ross Brawn (technical director), and Rory Byrne (head designer). An outstanding driver, superb team leadership, and a racing car without weaknesses are the pillars of the company's success. Ferrari has learned from its mistakes in the 1996 season and instituted the most efficient quality control systems for years now. The result is the most reliable car in the field.

The most expensive race of the year in terms of development work is always Monza. On this high-speed track – much of it at full speed – ground is gained primarily on the long straights. Specially developed high-speed aerodynamics that take the entire vehicle into account are therefore crucial. Costs have to cover not only the personnel and wind tunnels but also the components and spare parts, which head straight to the museum after each race. That easily adds up to more than half a million euros.

Following in its own footsteps

____ Touring car racing has always been the main motorsport activity of Alfa Romeo. Even the A.L.F.A. 24 HP for the Targa Florio would be considered a touring car by today's standards. But the Giulia Sprint GTA, Alfetta GTV, Alfa 75 Turbo, and Alfa 155 – touring car icons that also win European titles – are even more striking and memorable examples.

Class 1 stands for the technically advanced path that the DTM and ITC take from 1993 to 1996. That leaves space below for Class 2: four-cylinder, two-liter touring cars that look much more like production cars. The two-liter vehicles are therefore rightfully designated "Super Touring cars." Championships governed by the same worldwide regulations pop up in Europe, Asia, and South America for these racing sedans. The first Class 2 season, which is in 1993, features an international showdown at which touring car aces from the different national series fight it out at the season finale. For 2000, the FIA announces a European cup for Super Touring cars (Euro STC), which is then upgraded to full status as a European championship in 2002. There from the start, Alfa Romeo is virtually predestined to win with the 156. The red sedans take four titles from 2000 to 2003.

While the two-liter Alfa transmits power to the 19-inch front wheels at the limit of 8,500 rpm and 315 hp as stipulated by Super Turismo regulations, "Super 2000" rules now require 17-inch wheels with uniform tires. With 270 horsepower (at 8,450 rpm), the 1,055-kilo Alfa 156 Super 2000 is the most powerful car in the field.

The two successive 50-kilometer sprints are the key to success for the European championship, and the range of participating brands ensure exciting action. As if that were not enough, the first six finishers of the first race have to start the second heat in reverse order from the first three rows. Added weights for the highest places and different weight distributions balance out design-based competitive advantages amongst front, rear, and all-wheel drive systems. In 2005 the European championship becomes the world championship. Alfa Romeo focuses on two-liter racing touring cars and becomes the dominant force in the FIA series. The Alfa 156 is an eminently deserving successor to the Giulia GTA, Alfetta GTV6, and Alfa 155 models. ____

▲ Alfa Romeo focuses on two-liter racing touring cars and becomes the dominant force in the FIA series. The Alfa 156 is an eminently deserving successor to the Giulia GTA, Alfetta GTV6, and Alfa 155 models.

◄ When the cars arrive for servicing at the pit, the choreography always impresses fans and rivals.

➤ In addition to its racing and off-road abilities, the Race Touareg is designed to be exceptionally robust and low-maintenance. After all, the rally takes more than two weeks and each day is as challenging as a Grand Prix. The cars are dismantled and thoroughly checked in improvised shelters every evening.

Racing over rough terrain

___ In the late autumn of 2003, a year after introducing the production SUV of the same name, Volkswagen presents a Touareg for the desert – the Race Touareg. This is a thoroughbred off-road racer. The only parallel to its production sibling lies in the fact that its engine is based on the five-cylinder TDI. Mounted low behind the front axle, the two-and-a-half-liter diesel engine starts off generating 231 or 260 horsepower. The Race Touareg 2 presented in the late summer of 2005 then generates around 285 hp. The usable rpm range of 1,800 to 4,500 is quite large for a race car, and a sequential six-speed gearbox transmits the power. The lightweight body has been optimized to enhance driving dynamics and visibility. The RT2's flat, sharply descending front enables drivers like Kleinschmidt, de Villiers, and Sainz to maneuver more easily in camel grass or at the foot of sand dunes than is possible in the 2004 or 2005 models of the first production series.

The tightly designed carbon body contains a 300-kilogram tubular space frame made of high-strength aerospace steel. The tank, which regulations require to enable a range of 800 kilometers, is located in front of the rear axle in such a way that it hardly affects the car's center of gravity as its diesel fuel levels diminish. An electronic system calculates the remaining range based on previous fuel consumption rates, allowing drivers to utilize the remaining fuel – and therefore adjust the speed – more advantageously. When entering towns, Kleinschmidt, Sainz, and their colleagues can set the correct speed at the touch of a button, like in Formula One.

But it takes a while before the Race Touareg is immortalized as a "Dakar" champion. Overall victories only come after the contest is moved from Africa to South America. The many spectators in 2009 and 2010 witness two commanding appearances of the Race Touareg 2, followed by Volkswagen's third consecutive win with the 310-hp Race Touareg 3 in 2011. ___

Drivers and team reap the rewards of dedication

What else?

After receiving the rookie title in 2003, Sebastian Vettel takes the Formula BMW ADAC title with 18 wins in 20 races, thereby qualifying for the Formula Three Euro Series and for test drives with BMW Williams F1.

Farewell to the V10s

___ As fate would have it, the team led by ex-Benetton manager and former Schumacher boss Flavio Briatore ends Ferrari's streak of six consecutive manufacturers' and five drivers' titles. Renault and the young Spaniard Fernando Alonso put in a commanding performance to become the world champions. They post seven victories in 2005 – or eight, including the season opener by Alonso's teammate Giancarlo Fisichella, who then suffers bad luck and fades from view alongside the impressively composed Spaniard.

This season is the last summer for the three-liter, ten-cylinder engines with a good 900 hp and more than 19,000 rpm. Next year the international federation wants to lower curve speeds again and limit engines to two and a half liters of displacement and eight cylinders. For this 2005 season, it has already required higher noses and limited the size of the rear wing. New tires designed for the duration of races that last a maximum of two hours plus restrictions on replacing engines initially help to reduce speeds in curves. But they do not discourage competition. On the contrary, the Renault factory crew that grew out of the Benetton team puts the new regulations superbly into practice and sets the season's benchmark.

Aerodynamic efficiency, impeccable interplay between chassis and tires, the right balance, and smoothly programmed traction controls pose challenges to hosts of engineers not only on the racing and test courses but also at their home development centers. Far more wind tunnel time goes into making fine adjustments to these racers than to production cars. Renault makes the most of it all. The R25's power plant, a 2,998-cc, 72°-V10 known as the RS54, has around 30 fewer horsepower than the Mercedes-Ilmor FO-110R in the McLaren MP4-20, but more than compensates for

▶ The 2005 season will mark the end of the three-liter V10 engines that apply around 900 hp to their crankshafts.

◀ Fernando Alonso knocks F1 legend Michael Schumacher from his pedestal in 2005. He will successfully defend the title in 2006 – and Schumacher will temporarily withdraw from Formula One.

▶ The modern Formula One features sophisticated aerodynamics and highly developed cars.

that with exemplary reliability. Scoring points in 17 of 19 races, Alonso is ultimately much more productive than rivals Kimi Räikkönen and Michael Schumacher.

Compared to its rivals, the R25 is considerably more back-heavy. That enhances grip, but leads to disproportionate wear on the rear tires. However, adjustments to the weight distribution and traction control plus four successive engine evolutions optimize this situation. Detailed regulations lay the basic requirements for the carbon-fiber monoposto: weight (including driver and on-board camera) of 605 kilograms, dimensions (length/width/height) of 4.8 x 1.8 x 0.95 meters, front track width of 1.45 and rear of 1.4 meters. The wheelbase is 3.1 meters. Also made of carbon fiber, the A-frame arms and

Proven adage: to finish first, you first have to finish

suspension elements with a relay mechanism in the form of a pushrod system are the usual Formula One standard.

So although the Renault R25 does not offer sensational innovations, it is brilliant – at least in the hands of the Spaniard. It is an instrument that performs as reliably as clockwork. And that confirms the old adage that in order "to finish first, you first have to finish!". The Renault only comes under pressure when the somewhat faster McLaren manages to improve its own reliability. But by then the season is already coming to a close.

Acid test passed

After BMW wins the 24-hour race on the Nürburgring with a diesel for the first time in 1998, Audi brings a CI engine to Le Mans. The victorious direct-injection diesel then serves as an ambassador for more efficient engine technology in America, where diesel drives traditionally face resistance.

◄ Alan McNish (right) and Tom Kristensen (left) are two of Audi's emissaries to the New World. Here, they drive 650-hp diesel cars at Laguna Seca in California.

___ In keeping with the brand's motto of "Vorsprung durch Technik," the R10 TDI follows in the footsteps of the extraordinarily successful Audi R8 racing sports car. Extraordinarily well, in fact. The silver flounder starts by winning the 12 Hours of Sebring, which is considered a dress rehearsal for Le Mans. And then the team from Ingolstadt makes history again when the car wins the classic endurance race in France – a first for a diesel-powered race car.

Following technology like all-wheel drive ("quattro") and fuel-stratified injection ("FSI"), Audi draws attention to diesel technology with its first racing car to use this type of drive. The company has been preparing the ground since 1989 with innovations in its production cars. Thus far diesels have only rarely appeared in motorsport, and have not been seen at all in highly developed and sophisticated racing cars until the premiere of the R10 TDI. Lower fuel consumption and high torque levels are the traditional strengths of these turbocharged, direct-injection, compressed-ignition systems, which also make them suitable for arduous endurance contests. For the drivers, diesel engines mean longer stints, even greater care with the accelerator, and unusually low levels of background noise – which makes them partially dependent on visual signals from the steering wheel when choosing the right shifting points at 5,000 rpm. The 5.5-liter aluminum V12 TDI generates 650 hp, and an even more impressive 1,100 Nm of torque.

The central component of the R10 TDI is its high-safety carbon-fiber cell, which essentially consists of the seat pan with rollover units and attachment points for the engine and front-wheel suspension. For its part, the rear-wheel suspension is articulated with the flanged gearbox-engine assembly – as is usual for racing cars since the advent of monocoque construction. In addition to the underfloor, the carbon-fiber body components have been enhanced a great number of times vis-à-vis those of the R8.

As usual, the silver factory cars are entered in Le Mans and the American Le Mans Series by the experienced Joest team. For Le Mans, the two Audis have the victorious Sebring team of Tom Kristensen/Allan McNish/Dindo Capello (start number 7 with yellow rollover protection) and the trio of Emanuele Pirro/Frank Biela/Marco Werner (start number 8, red). This time Danish native Kristensen, who has posted a record-setting string of wins in Le Mans, does not end up in first but rather in third place, even though his car starts at the pole. The lap time of 3:30.466 minutes means an average of 233.482 km/h – including the two Hunaudières chicanes driven since 1990. But in 2006, the laurels are taken by the trio in the silver-and-red car.

Never change a good thing: The team members all know each other from the R8 days

The Audi R10 TDI continues its success with a comeback in the American Le Mans Series (ALMS). The diesel racer remains unbeaten throughout the season and gives Audi an early title in the ALMS. A made-to-order triumph. All the more so given the company's trailblazing efforts, which are promptly emulated in 2007 by Peugeot. ___

The flying classroom

___ Nico Rosberg, Lewis Hamilton, Nelson Piquet (Junior), and Timo Glock are a few of the top drivers whose record in the GP2 series qualifies them for greater challenges and who go on to careers in Formula One. Held in conjunction with the European Formula One program, the GP2 is guaranteed to draw the attention of F1 team managers and recruiters. In 2005 it becomes the highest league below the top tier of racing, taking the place of the Formula 3000, which has played that role for two decades. In the mid-1980s Formula 3000 replaced what was known by the logical name of Formula Two, which then experienced a somewhat lukewarm revival in 2009. But back to the GP2: uniform technology is used in its cars – as is otherwise the case for one-make cups. The carbon monocoque comes from Dallara, and the four-liter V8 that now generates 600 horsepower is from Renault. Shifting is done with toggle switches on

Renault adds a GP2 monoposto to its Formula mosaic

the steering wheel, and the slick uniform tires are from Bridgestone – as is the 100,000-Euro prize money. Complex electronics are prohibited, but the teams still encounter a number of technical hiccoughs. These are quickly dealt with, and the GP2 develops into a successful series. Launched in 2008, the GP2 Asia is an extremely successful offshoot that draws large numbers of spectators.

The Dallara name has long been a major player in the manufacture of sports and racing cars. Giampaolo Dallara starts working for Ferrari in 1959, switches to Maserati in 1961, and then to Lamborghini in 1963. In 1968 he joins De Tomaso as technical director, and Alejandro de Tomaso requests that he develop a Formula racing car. The first Dallara construction enters Formula One in 1970, and De Tomaso F1 cars also become the basis on which Frank Williams builds his team.

➤ Timo Glock enjoys systematic support from the Post Speed Academy and success in the GP2, which help him gain a place on Toyota's Formula One team in 2008.

◄ Glock is the third title winner to qualify for Formula One with a Dallara Renault GP2. The launch of the GP2 lends a clearer structure to motorsport. The earlier feeder level for the top tier of racing was variously called the Formula Two, the Formula 3000, and the Formula Three.

What else?

The year 2007 marks the last season in which the Champ Car and IndyCar series have to compete for spectators. A unified U.S. monoposto racing series will start up again in 2008. Sébastien Bourdais leaves at the end of the 2007 season after winning his fourth Champ Car title in Formula One.

Dallara starts his own business in 1972. His commissions include working with Cesare Fiorio on the Lancia Stratos, developing a Fiat X1/9 Sport, and helping Williams construct the 1974 Formula One Iso. That is followed by jobs with former employer Lamborghini and with the Martini-Lancia racing team, a leading player on into the Group C era with its LC2 and LC3 models in the 1983 and 1984 seasons.

In the late 1970s Dallara meets the Austrian Canadian Walter Wolf. Active with his own team in Formula One at that time, Wolf also starts supporting young talent in Formula Three. In 1979 the Wolf WR7 makes waves as the first "honeycomb" aluminum composite construction, and becomes a model for the entire industry. Dallara is designing and building Formula Three cars at this time. With numerous commissions for different Formula classes, the workshop in Varano de Lelegari near Parma has been building a strong reputation in high-level

racing and its order books are consequently well-filled. Dallara creations also enter Formula One under the Scuderia Italia logo from 1988 to 1992.

Now the largest manufacturer of Formula Three racing cars, the Dallara name becomes linked with countless future driving greats whose early international successes are achieved with Dallara F3 constructions. The central Italian workshop also supplies cars for the Indy Racing League (IRL) in the USA, as well as the standard chassis for the IndyCar series.

Dallara is also Audi's first choice when it comes to developing the R8 sports car for Le Mans, and it makes the carbon chassis for the open Audi that enters Le Mans for the first time in 1998. The decision is quickly justified by the car's success. ___

The lion and the Green Hell

The 911 GT3 RSR, which now has a price tag of 380,000 Euros, is a fixture not only on the Nordschleife but also in GT series like the ALMS. The photo on the left shows the cockpit, the one on the right a GT3 R Hybrid with flywheel energy storage. The KERS version makes an impressive showing in the 2010 edition of the 24-hour race on the Nürburgring.

◄ The Manthey Porsche wins for the fourth time in a row in 2009. Summerlike track conditions and strong competitors, including the factory-supervised ABT Audi R8 GT3 R, produce a new distance record.

▼ Voluminous fender extensions and spoilers make it easy to distinguish between the GT3 RSR and the GT3 Cup.

___ There are all kinds of names for 911 racers: R, ST, Carrera RS and RSR, RSR Turbo, 934, 935, "Baby" and "Moby Dick," SC and SC RS, Carrera Clubsport, Carrera 4x4, 959 and 961 IMSA GTX, Carrera 2 Cup, Turbo S GT Le Mans, Turbo IMSA, Carrera Cup and Carrera Cup RSR, GT2 and GT2 Evolution, GT1, GT3 Clubsport, GT3 Cup, GT3 Supercup, GT3 R, GT3 RS, GT3 Rally and GT3 RSR, and various other designations that incorporate displacement and year of origin. What all these cars share is a love of competition, ever since the first of their kind entered the "Monte" back in 1965 (and took second place!).

The 911 has also always felt at home on the Nordschleife of the Nürburgring. Six-cylinder sports cars have traditionally made up the lion's share of the starting fields at 24-hour and other endurance races. Germany's most popular racing event with nearly a quarter of a million spectators, the 24-hour contest on the Nürburgring currently has the world's largest starting field – with more than 180 cars. Although the regulations are constantly being modified, the GT3 RSR wins in May of 2009 for the fourth time in a row. The first 24-hour drives on the "Ring" date back to before the Second World War. One inspiration for the race that has been held annually since 1970 would have to be the Marathon de la Route, which in turn grew out of the Liège-Sofia-Liège rally. But a growing number of cars and higher levels of traffic sent the event to the circuit in the Eifel region at the end of the 1960s.

Even though appearances can be deceiving, some of the RSR's victories in the "Green Hell" hang by a thread. Top-notch competitors like the Dodge Viper and the Audi R8 LMS GT3 have long since turned the endurance race into a 24-hour sprint. And the fact that it is held on the world's most challenging track with a large field of racers of different speeds plus frequently volatile weather conditions makes it extraordinarily exciting. But the 911 is a safe bet. Certainly in the Eifel. And all the more so when entered by the Manthey team with factory support.

Of the different 911 racing versions in the late 2000s, the GT3 RSR is the sharpest draw. The true grandchild of the Carrera RSR 3.0, which starred in endurance races and the DRM in the 1970s, it currently has a 3.8-liter displacement that will exceed 4.0 liters in 2009, with differing air intake and mass restrictions depending on the regulations. The naturally aspirated engine block comes from the GT1, which gave Porsche another victory in Le Mans in 1998. A favorite around the world, the GT3 RSR is enhanced on a continuous basis. Benefits of the 2009 version include a weight-optimized braking system and streamlined cable harness. The louvers, which are openings in the front hood, indicate an optional air-conditioning system – an extra comfort feature now required for safety reasons at many GT races. ___

The Porsche 911 has always been eager to race

From Zero to Hero

___ Formula One faces big changes for the 2009 season. The FIA has ordered comprehensive alterations. Environmentally friendly hybrid technology is returning to the top tier of racing. Still an option in 2009, KERS becomes mandatory in 2010. KERS stands for Kinetic Energy Recovery System, which means that braking energy stored in an intermediate system can be deployed at the press of a button. This gives drivers of KERS-equipped cars an additional 81 hp (60 kW) for 6.7 seconds of every lap. It is useful for the start, for overtaking, and for preventing other cars from overtaking.

Brawn acquires Honda bankruptcy assets and posts win after win

New aerodynamic regulations curtail the proliferation of bizarre wings. An overhaul committee has reworked the aerodynamic package to make the cars less vulnerable to the dirty air thrown up by those in front. This increases the importance of the slipstream and makes it easier once again to turn outbraking maneuvers into passing attempts. The result is a gigantic front spoiler extending the width of the entire vehicle with flaps that can be adjusted from the cockpit, and a seemingly long-legged rear wing that is only 75 centimeters wide. After ten years of grooved tires, slicks – which enhance the mechanical grip – have now returned to Formula One. All the fins, flaps, barge boards, chimneys, and other ubiquitous supplementary wings are now prohibited. This is intended to lower costs, which is the FIA's second major concern given that the world is going through a bank-triggered recession. It looks like belts will be tightened not only amongst the manufacturers but also by the sponsors.

Honda is an early casualty of the recession in the automotive sector. The Japanese take the occasion to cut jobs, close factories, and withdraw from Formula One. The 700-member team led by ex-Ferrari mastermind Ross Brawn, who came to Honda in 2008, is about to disband. Because liquidating

➤ The flat rear of the Brawn BGP 001 contains a 2.4-liter Mercedes V8. Traction control is prohibited as of 2009. Engine speed is now limited to 18,000 rpm, and each vehicle is limited to a maximum of eight engines per season.

◄ Before the season starts, Brawn considers calling the team Tyrrell again because the Honda crew derives from BAR (British American Racing), and the BAT tobacco giant (British American Tobacco) built that team in 1998 from the celebrated group led by Ken Tyrrell. In 2010 Brawn GP is acquired by Mercedes-Benz and becomes Mercedes GP.

What else?

After the Dakar Rally is hastily canceled due to a terrorist threat, this most iconic of marathon rallies finds a new home in South America. It will now be held on the plains and heights of Argentina and Chile.

the well-equipped factory in Brackley will incur high costs for Honda, Brawn – with the help of F1 power broker Bernie Ecclestone – ultimately gets the nod to acquire the team for a symbolic sum as part of a management buy-out and thereby go into action. That ensures that 20 cars will continue to start in Formula One. But the Brawn GP name is new. The streamlined car opts to do without KERS. And despite the monoposto's lackluster colors, it attracts attention right from the start. The last team to start test drives before the season, Brawn leaves everyone else in the dust. That pattern holds in the races themselves. At first the competitors ascribe this to an aerodynamic trick. The double-decker diffuser ensures better downforce and considerable contro-

Double-decker diffusers offer sophisticated aerodynamics

versy. But even when the other teams retrofit their own cars with these diffusers, Jenson Button and Rubens Barrichello do not budge from the front of the pack. The BGP 001 is an excellent example of a harmonious, homogeneously conceived racing car from front to back. Early in the 2008 season Brawn begins working on the 2009 model. He and his engineers use three Honda wind tunnels and Brawn's own expertise, which gave Benetton and Ferrari no fewer than 14 world championship titles plus the Group C Jaguar XJR in the late 1980s as the successor to the overpowering Porsche 956/962 of the time.

The never satisfied

___ Camille Jenatzy's record-setting electric vehicle from the year 1899, christened the "Red Devil" and "La Jamais Contente," resonates 111 years later in the name of a Venturi that zooms across the Utah Salt Flats. Like its namesake, this car too has an electric drive.

The cigar-shaped racer is the product of close cooperation between Ohio State University and Venturi, a French manufacturer of limited-production vehicles. Founded in 1985, Venturi makes a name for itself with mid-engine cars that also enter the BPR GT series. With the "Jamais Contente," the company sets records while putting the world's fastest electric car into action, stoking the already lively debate on the future of automotive powertrains.

The swift "Volt Cigar" sets a world record of 515 km/h

The dress rehearsal for the "Buckeye Bullet," as the car is also called given the input from Ohio, takes place in September of 2009. The fuel-cell drive under its smooth shell, which will be replaced a year later by lithium-ion batteries, propels the car to an FIA record for fuel-cell powered electric vehicles of 487 km/h.

Another attempt takes place in August 2010 on the vast salt flats of Bonneville, which have drawn high-speed vehicles for decades. The flat car, which is 11 meters long, barely a meter wide, and weighs 1,950 kilos, is required to race one kilometer each in opposite directions. The judges measure an average speed of 495 km/h, and an official top speed of 515 km/h. With this new record confirmed by the FIA, the Venturi becomes an ambassador for electromobility. Its 400-kilogram battery pack drives a three-phase induction engine with 800 hp or around 590 kW. As is the case for record-setting cars powered by combustion or jet engines as well as vehicles designed for drag racing, two braking parachutes provide deceleration at the end of the stretch.

➤ The Venturi Buckeye Bullet makes a name for itself in Europe as the "Jamais Contente". The car's reference to Jenatzy's record-setting electric vehicle of 1899 is no coincidence.

What else?

Formula One enjoys one of its most exciting seasons. Following 19 races with five different winners, any one of a quintet might still end up winning the title. Finally Sebastian Vettel (Red Bull), Fernando Alonso (Ferrari), and Red Bull teammate Mark Webber battle it out at the finale in Abu Dhabi. Vettel becomes the youngest F1 champion of all time. Also of note are the founding of Mercedes GP, the new Mercedes-Benz factory team, and the comeback by Michael Schumacher.

◄ The Bonneville Salt Flats serve as the scene of the action once again. The salt pan has drawn record-seeking drivers for decades.

With ever more debate on how to lower CO_2 levels and with the resulting objectives for modern automotive engineering, alternative drive concepts and environmental factors start playing major roles in racing as well.

An early example comes from the Group C era in the mid-1980s, when turbocharged sports car prototypes are subject to strict regulations. U.S. race-car maker Panoz produces a hybrid car for Le Mans in the late 1990s, although it does not pan out. When Formula One introduces the Kinetic Energy Recovery System (KERS) in 2009, the time is nearly ripe for modern hybrid engineering. Although the energy storage systems disappear briefly in 2010, they enjoy a comeback in the 2011 Formula One. Porsche causes a stir with the GT3 Hybrid on the Nürburgring in 2010. Its flywheel stores braking energy that drivers can use shortly thereafter when needed for acceleration. And Volkswagen's Scirocco Cup launched in 2009 also takes environmental aspects into account. The creators of this exciting series determine that the cars should run on CNG – which leads to an 80 percent drop in CO_2 emissions.

▼ Roger Schroer clocks an average of 495 km/h, and a high speed of 515 km/h.

The older, the bolder

___ Audi and Mercedes-Benz are two pillars of the DTM. The series' extensively optimized, carbon-fiber cars with silhouettes made to resemble their road-going counterparts are so expensive, along with the associated teams of engineers and technicians, that the decision makers start thinking about reducing costs and effort to more acceptable levels while also further developing the series. The 2011 season therefore becomes a swan song for racing cars like the Audi A4 DTM, which conceals its technical sophistication under unremarkable attire. The good 460-hp, 4-liter V8 engine and numerous shared components in the drivetrain and chassis, all concealed under a tight corset, lead to concerted efforts in the field of aerodynamics. Spectators can spot some results in the form of winglets, flaps, and other reflectors below a line running through the center of the wheels. Completely hidden but incomparably more efficient are the air channels that run through the car. What used to be cooling-air inlets have long been developed into cutting-edge aerodynamic shafts that control the flow of air through the car and provide maximum down-force at ideal points. These include inside the rear wheel-houses and the back of the floor, which now serves as a diffuser.

It's hard to spot the sophisticated aerodynamics and aerated body

While teams like ABT, Rosberg, and Phoenix enter these vehicles in races and handle the associated logistics, the cars themselves come from Audi Sport in Ingolstadt, or as of 2015 in Neuburg an der Donau. A host of engineers and specialists arrives to support the teams and also help coordinate the races. Potential discrepancies due to different years

What else?

New regulations for the WRC reduce displacement to 1.6 liters. The all-wheel-drive racers continue to have 300 hp but their torque levels drop from around 700 to 400 Nm.

Ernst Moser's Phoenix team often displays a sixth sense that boosts drivers to masterful tactical performances. The "used cars" also have a weight advantage of 25 kilos. Although still standard in the DTM at the time, the fuel stop will be eliminated in 2012 in the wake of multiple accidents involving fuel cans not being removed quickly enough from cars during the extremely brief pit stops.

of construction are theoretically compensated for by weight. New cars therefore tip the scales at 1,050 kilograms, while model year or used cars weigh 25 kilos less – including the weight of the driver. In the 2011 season, the Korean tire manufacturer Hankook joins Dunlop, which has previously been the sole supplier. And technical parameters are joined by psychological factors. Martin Tomczyk is shifted from a new car to a chassis built back in 2008, which is now entered by the Eifel-based Phoenix team instead of ABT with its track record of producing champions. Phoenix's manager Ernst Moser and his team have a burning desire to prove they can win, and a tenacious competitor in Tomczyk with his downgraded car. Mercedes' top driver Bruno Spengler announces early on that he will be switching to DTM returnee BMW at the end of the season. And the HWA crew has no wish to hand starting number one to their rivals from Munich as a dowry. Tomczyk and his Schaeffler Audi work well with the new tires and use the weight advantage to their benefit. Promptly nicknamed the "Caipirinha Express," the Schaeffler Audi becomes a contender for the title. Tomczyk, Phoenix, Audi, and Schaeffler do in fact end up winning the DTM championship. The quartet

accomplishes this in unprecedented form, gaining points in all ten races, winning three of them, climbing the podium eight times, and never finishing lower than fifth. This is Schaeffler's first title under its umbrella brand name and with a completely branded car – the technology group was previously active in various racing disciplines as a co-sponsor under its INA, LuK, and FAG product names.

The dynamically aerated Audi A4 DTM with the visuals of the A4 model known internally as the "B8" wins three DTM championships in the four years from 2008 to 2011. The close of the 2011 season also ends the era of four-door racing touring cars. In 2012 the DTM will switch to two-door coupes.

———

Full Pull

___ "Full pull" is the tractor-pulling community's designation for an unbroken schlepp over a distance of 100 meters. At first one might think this should not be a problem for behemoths with a double rear axle and up to 8,000 hp. But these special tractors, which compete in different displacement and power classes, strain with all their might to pull a sled fitted with a metal plate and loaded with a weight of up to 24 metric tons. The farther they go, the more the plate wedges into the ground and hinders their progression. That makes this racing discipline an ideal stage to demonstrate the abilities of clutches and bearings.

The Le Coiffeur team supported by Schaeffler enters the 2.5-metric ton class with a vehicle whose 4,000-hp, 36.7-liter engine comes from Rolls-Royce and is usually found in airplanes. The vehicle sees action over a period of seven years. Continuous modifications keep it up to date and successful. Led by founder Frank Bartholomé, its team ends up taking one European and five German titles. ___

◀ Powerful forces on the materials make tractor pulling an ideal test lab for components like clutches. A single season will put the same strain on the parts as 10,000 hours of use under normal conditions. The season is short, and a race runs a maximum of 100 meters ...

▶ The pit stop remains a major dramatic element of the DTM. As in Formula One, it now features two different tire compounds. Drivers have to use both in the course of the race, creating tactical opportunities for them and their teams.

Of milliseconds, millibar, and millimeters

The powertrain for DTM racing cars – a four-liter V8 configuration with a sequential six-speed transmission – has been a familiar presence since the year 2000. But at the beginning of the 2012 season, the participating manufacturers, ITR organization, and DMSB regulatory body agree on a new chassis. Making the cockpit out of carbon and shifting the driver's position back toward the center of the car are designed to further increase safety. When BMW joins the field, there are now three instead of two manufacturers.

The DTM remains a tight affair. Less so in literal terms, because the drivers sit in the middle of the cars in stiff and safety-enhancing space frames. But on the track, everything comes down to fractions of a second. In the qualifying sessions for the starting positions, the 22 drivers almost always post times within a second of each other, or within less than half a second on short stretches like the Norisring. So tiny mistakes and minute changes to adjustable parameters like the suspension and tire pressure can make the difference between a champ and a chump, or a hero and a zero.

The engineers therefore devote major attention to the details, at least where permitted. A number of small add-on parts start appearing below an imaginary line running through the wheel centers to guide airflow around the car body as efficiently as possible. Even the outside mirrors are further developed into aerodynamic components that generate downforce.

All DTM racers have a driver safety cell close to the center of the car

An adjustable rear wing is introduced in the 2013 season. Known as the Drag Reduction System (DRS), it is based onFormula One. On designated parts of the tracks and within defined windows of time, namely, at a maximum distance of two seconds from the car in front, the wing tilts down 15 degrees, which boosts the peak speed of the now 480-hp cars by as much as 7 km/h and therefore makes overtaking easier in this highly perfected and balanced racing series. Another new development is the introduction of a second tire compound, which leads to different race strategies and therefore creates additional excitement.

Through-flow systems for the car body are prohibited, but BMW develops a "blown diffuser" for the M3 DTM, following the example of tech genius Adrian Newey's work for Red Bull in Formula One during the Vettel era. It is promptly banned in the DTM, which still offers spectacular races but is plagued by an increasing number of regulatory controversies and technical restrictions. But fans are pleased that the DTM starts holding two races per weekend, as it used to do back in the golden days of the 1980s and 1990s.

As of the 2013 season, the silhouettes are taken from mid-sized coupes in standard series production at Audi, Mercedes, and – in 2014 – BMW.

The field is well balanced, which means an impressive level of competition, with a dozen and a half drivers often posting qualifying times within a second of each other.

➤ Schaeffler's commitment to the DTM is also part of its branding process. Its name covers established products including INA, LuK, and FAG, and the company will also be listed on the stock market under Schaeffler in 2015. The photo shows Mike Rockenfeller's RS5 in the 2017 season.

Top of the pack in the world's toughest race

___ The Baja 1000 runs through Mexico's Baja California. Desert, salt lakes, gravel, dust, scrubland, cacti, impassable coastal areas, and ranges of hills without any discernable tracks – these are the conditions facing around 250 contestants every November. They enter motorcycles, ATVs, and every conceivable four-wheel vehicle in a quest to master the challenges of maintaining the fastest uninterrupted pace. Some teams switch drivers at service stops they determine themselves, but this is not required. The fastest complete the torturous course, which can extend more than 1,800 kilometers in what can be sizzling daytime and freezing nighttime temperatures, in well under a day. Their Trophy Trucks are the top category of vehicles in the field, whose opposite end includes elderly Volkswagen Beetles that scrabble across the desert with

At 2.2 tonnes the AGM X6 is a lightweight compared to some three-tonne Trophy Trucks

air-cooled flat-four engines. The leaders of the pack simply have to have V8 power plants with enormous displacement (7.4 liters) and serious output (more than 800 hp), most of which come from specialty workshops that usually supply the drive systems for NASCAR. An extremely robust four-speed transmission shifts the gears. And a torque converter handles the transfer of power between the engine and the gearbox. This is where Schaeffler comes in. The company also provides bearings, timing chains, material design, and damage assessment. Extreme stress on rough terrain poses the ultimate endurance test for all the components in use.

As is the case for the X6 built up by All German Motorsports, which tackles the terrain with rally icon and Schaeffler representative Armin Schwarz

➤ The All German Motorsports team from Escondido in southern California earns its keep in part by selling and servicing cars from German makers. That is the origin of the idea to use the silhouette of the BMW X6. The vehicle sticks out in the field of Trophy Trucks, whose designs are based on American pickups.

◄ Schaeffler engineers from Germany and the USA help prepare the off-road racers. In addition to robust bearings, special expertise is needed to analyze materials and to design engine, powertrain, and torque converter components. Torque levels generated by the NASCAR V8 engines are so high that Trophy Trucks use torque converters instead of the usual clutches.

at the controls, the wheeled behemoths can be more than two and a half meters high. They also have a push bar mounted on the front, which they use to shove the vehicle before them in order to signal their intention to pass in the clouds of dust that severely limit visibility. But sometimes they have to cover more than 100 miles before the car in front makes an error that finally allows an overtaking maneuver. Precisely because of all the dust and flying debris, the vehicles do not have windshields. These would break. Instead, the drivers and co-drivers wear armored helmets and visor systems that contain breathing tubes for dust-free air. Driving a Trophy Truck can resemble speed boating at times. The 39-inch wheels enable acceleration from 0 to 100 km/h in less than seven seconds. Peak speeds of up to 230 km/h are possible on straight stretches of terrain. Wheels and robust construction

aside, the trucks' spring systems with meter-long paths can gobble up obstacles the height of two beer crates as if they simply were not there.

SCORE stands for Southern California Off-Road Racing. Usually consisting of five races, its World Desert Championship culminates in the legendary Baja 1000. Participants in what may well be the toughest race in the world have included Hollywood actor and amateur racing driver Steve McQueen.

———

Space travel is nothing in comparison

___ Porsche CEO Matthias Müller, racing director Fritz Enzinger, and Porsche shareholder and Supervisory Board chairman Wolfgang Porsche hug each other with tears in their eyes. It is shortly after 4pm on a Sunday in the middle of June, in western France, and the 83rd edition of the classic endurance race in Le Mans has just finished. After a 16-year hiatus and an attempt the year before, Porsche wins the 24-hour race.

The foundation was laid two and a half years earlier. Following many years of focusing on customer racing, one-make cups, and smaller classic contests, Porsche's development center in Weissach and its racing center in Flacht start preparing for the company's return to the top category (LMP1) of the World Endurance Championship (WEC), which includes the 24 Hours of Le Mans.

A special feature of its LMP1 racers consists of hybrid technology. That means combining a combustion engine with an electric drive, which includes energy recovery and coasting capacities. The cars have not only all-wheel drive but also a breathtaking overall output of more than 1,000 hp. In short, they are the technically most sophisticated racing cars in history. Depending on their technical systems and energy storage capacities, LMP1 racers can enter different megajoule classes that allow different amounts of energy, i.e., fuel and supplementary

➤ The fin and openings on the fenders are required for safety reasons. They prevent the prototypes from taking off the ground, as used to be seen with Group C and GT1 sports cars. The photo shows the 2017 aerodynamic version of the 919 Hybrid.

◄ For Schaeffler the sophisticated WEC racers are pioneers in the hybrid technology that the company is developing and producing for road-going vehicles.

electrical power, per lap. Porsche selects the 8MJ category, which allows less fuel but more electrical energy than the lower MJ categories. This amount of energy, however, corresponds to about one tank of fuel over the length of the race. The resulting focus on the electrical energy boosts technical development to such an extent that the Porsche 919 Hybrid uses about 30 percent less than the previous year's cars for an average speed of 250 km/h on the Le Mans circuit (most of which consists of what are normally public roads).

The rule-makers base their expertise on the fact that Audi, Porsche, and Toyota, each of which has a different powertrain and energy storage philosophy for the LMP1, are now battling for fractions of a second in their quest for victory. Audi is entering a four-liter six-cylinder diesel engine, Toyota is starting with a 3.7-liter V8 (which will become a 2.4-liter

More investment has gone into high-tech LMP1 hybrids than any other racing cars

V6 in 2016), and Porsche is focusing on modern downsizing with four cylinders and two liters of displacement. The latter's 500-hp assembly is so compact it looks more like an ornament than a combustion engine. The car also has two energy recovery systems. On the front axle, braking energy is fed to the battery for the electric motor, which also generates around 500 hp. And behind the driver, who is seated beneath a small dome, a turbocharger provides a second source of power. It not only forces induction air by means of exhaust gas into the combustion chambers, but also recovers energy by converting heat into kinetic and then electrical energy.

The vehicles, which of course are made of carbon fiber, resemble UFOs more than cars. Because of the unprecedented challenges involved in operating them, each is driven by a team of three drivers, both

for six-hour races and in Le Mans. The drivers have to master the complex art of accommodating continuous fine adjustments to the parameters and adapting their styles to regulation-based tactics in order to use and recover energy as efficiently as possible while reaching the maximum speeds allowed by the perfect racing strategy. They are supported by three dozen engineers who monitor the races on banks of computer screens.

Computers, which are also members of the team, constantly adjust the strategies and send drivers essentially remote-controlled signals for the most efficient modes of motion. Amidst the hectic rush of the race, this is the only way to determine and

ensure the best possible speed for each individual lap while simultaneously making sure that the maximum allowable amount of energy is recovered and also deployed. Occasional rapid-fire pit stops are absolutely necessary, but now seem peripheral. ___

The 2015 winning team of Hülkenberg/Bamber/Tandy clocked 395 laps to cover a distance of 5,382.82 kilometers. The seven-speed transmission shifted gears 25,293 times. Over the course of 24 hours, the car made 30 pit stops to refuel.

The 2016 version is on the left, the car that premiered in 2014 on the right.

➤ In 2017 the Formula Student's combustion and electric cars will be joined by a third category for driverless vehicles. All of the students who engage in these contests are closely observed by industry representatives, who make up no fewer than 2,500 of the 6,000 visitors to the German event in Hockenheim.

Testing trumps studying

What else?

At the end of the 2016 season, Bernard Charles "Bernie" Ecclestone leaves Formula One stage at the age of 86. The sale of Formula One to the Liberty Media corporation is the major event in the background. Ecclestone ran Formula One for more than 40 years, turning a repair shop-based series into a profitable enterprise for many participants. Following Ecclestone's tenure as "supreme leader," the F1 will be run by the triumvirate of Chase Carey, Ross Brawn, and Sean Bratches.

___ The races themselves in worldwide Formula Student series are of comparatively less importance than the work leading up to them. The focus is on designing and constructing single-seater cars that can be powered by either fuel or electricity. The contests run for several days and are held around the world in the form of national events that also welcome participants from abroad. The 2016 event in Germany, for example, attracted 3,600 students in 113 teams from 28 countries. They compete in eight categories for a total of 1,000 points. In addition to five dynamic disciplines (acceleration, skid pad, autocross, endurance, and efficiency) there are three static categories (engineering design, cost and manufacturing, and business plan).

Relatively unencumbered by regulations, the Formula Student racing series is an ideal opportunity for up-and-coming automotive engineers to acquire racing experience alongside their regular studies. That makes them valuable future employees of automotive and technology companies, who swell the ranks of sponsors and regularly send several thousand representatives to the events.

Initially the object of ridicule, electric cars have now achieved the same status as combustion vehicles in the Formula Student due to a shift in emphasis toward electromobility. The winning team in 2016, KA RaceIng from the Karlsruhe Institute of Technology (KIT), enters cars in both categories.

The KIT 16E weighs 180 kilos and accelerates from 0 to 100 km/h in 2.5 seconds – as fast as its counterparts in Formula One. With a track width of 1.20 meters and wheelbase of one and a half meters, its compact dimensions take some getting used to. The final gear ratio limits the speed to 116 km/h, but no more is needed because the races are held on a small pegged-out course at the Hockenheim paddock. The young engineers have developed the electric drive themselves, as well as the gearbox, suspension, monocoque, electronic systems, and other components. The KIT team's combustion car weighs ten kilos more than its electric sibling, and needs 0.8 seconds more for the sprint up to 100 km/h. Regulations limit combustion engine displacement to 610 cc, and electric drives to a maximum of 85 kW. ___

Dawn of a new era

In the 2016-2017 season the uniform chassis supplied by Spark and produced by Dallara are given a disc-shaped front spoiler. That serves the visuals more than the aerodynamics, which are less important on winding urban courses. ABT-Schaeffler driver Lucas di Grassi posts two impressive come-from-behind wins in Hong Kong and Mexico along with a final spurt in the championship to take the title.

The two wings at the side of the cockpit have no aerodynamic function. The streamlined cladding covers side-impact protection systems. Protective elements are also integrated into the design of the front wing and behind the rear wheels. The Dallara Formula E chassis is extremely robust in general, and the cars are able to keep running even after minor collisions.

___ The first Formula racing series for electric cars, initiated by Alejandro Agag and supported by Jean Todt, starts with a bang in mid-2014. The new series promptly polarizes the traditional racing world. And wins a place for itself not only in urban centers but also in the hearts of new fans.

The Formula E season runs from the autumn of one year to the summer of the next. Performance figures from the first season are hardly appealing to racing fans. With 150 kW or around 203 hp for a weight of 896 or 888 kilograms (second season) and a peak speed limited to 225 km/h, the cars are at about the level of the Formula Ford. The grooved uniform tires and non-downforce-generating aerodynamic components encourage no little skepticism. But teams with Formula One experience and leading suppliers and car makers quickly become involved. Names like Prost, Senna, Piquet, and Villeneuve cause fans to sit up and listen. The drivers come both from the GP and the WEC. It soon becomes evident that these races on urban circuits are exciting to watch and the cars are challenging to handle. Drivers have two cars each, and 56 kWh of energy at their disposal – about as much as the average two-person household in Germany would use in six days. At the obligatory pit stop, they switch to the other car.

The shooting star Formula E becomes established in record time

The first season's field is composed of uniform cars manufactured by Spark. The carbon monocoque comes from the Dallara racing car maker, the electric drive is from McLaren (borrowed from the P1 super sports car), the battery is from Williams, and the five-speed transmission from Hewland. With cost trajectories and development options in mind, the rule-makers provide a clear road map with expanding development windows. This means that teams are free to develop their own powertrains as of the second season in 2015-16. The Schaeffler technology company – a sponsor of various racing series for years and the ABT team's exclusive technology partner – develops a new powertrain. Right from the start, the Schaeffler MGU01 is one of the best. Lucas di Grassi posts three wins with it and is a contender for the title down to the last race. The powertrain features not only lightweight construction but also better performance figures than the previous model. After all, the 175 kW for the races and 200 kW for the qualifying sessions allowed for the second season are based on the same 32-kWh batteries of the first.

The Formula E therefore becomes a development center and test lab for electromobility, which is quickly coming to the attention of the population at large. For the series' third season, in 2016-17, the

powertrain is optimized again. Audi, whose racing and production-car technology derives from joint efforts with drivetrain specialist Schaeffler, joins the team. Plans call for a new uniform battery by the fifth season, which would eliminate the need to switch cars in the middle of the race. Recovery and peak energy will be raised (from 100) to 150 and 250 kW, respectively. New ideas like FanBoost attract interest. This enables fans to give their favorite drivers a one-time boost of 100 kilojoules per race via Facebook and other social media platforms, which can help overtake a rival. And the Formula E succeeds in something the other racing series may never manage – the return to city centers. Its zero-emission monopostos compete in London's Hyde Park, around the Dôme des Invalides below the Eiffel Tower in Paris, on Red Square in Moscow, and on Alexanderplatz in Berlin. ____

The 2015-2016 season is the second in the new FIA Formula E. Following the uniform technology of the first year, the powertrains may now branch out. The drive system from Schaeffler and Compact Dynamics already wins in its second race, in Kuala Lumpur.

The Formula E gives development engineers opportunities akin to those in the early days of racing. ABT-Schaeffler's electric powertrain and three-speed transmission should be viewed in this light. The electric motor is located below the spring-and-shock-absorber assembly on the rear axle.

A completely new approach

___ The Roborace championship will open racing to driverless cars. Ever more driver assistance systems are accepted and appreciated on the roads. The step from cruise control with vehicle-interval radar and lane-departure warning systems to fully automated driving is now easily conceivable, and will soon be made. But do races with automated cars still qualify as a sport? They would certainly lack the duels between drivers. But their cars would remain a battleground for engineers, and – as is always the case in motorsport – the object by which to achieve the greatest possible technical advances within the framework defined by the regulations. "In that respect we're certainly talking about racing," says technology fan and Schaeffler Formula E driver Lucas di Grassi.

Like in the early days of racing, the Roborace series will also serve to accelerate technical development. The Roborace organization has already come up with two development vehicles on its way to producing a racing car. Known as DevBots, they are full of sensors and electronic control units. Their chassis are based on LMP2 prototypes, which still have a cabin for a driver – or rather a safety operator. The Roboracer conceived by former Volkswagen Advanced Designer Daniel Simon no longer reserves space for an occupant. Simon is well versed in science fiction, and has also designed cars for Hollywood productions including *Tron: Legacy*, and *Oblivion*. By contrast, Roborace is already a reality. The

FIA has become involved in stipulating its length (4.8 meters) and weight (1,000 kilograms). The car's futuristic carbon shell contains four 300-kW electric drives and a 540-kWh battery that accelerates it to over 320 km/h. In theory, Roboracers can compete on the tight urban circuits already used for the FIA Formula E world championship.

The car's impressive figures include its number of light sensors (five), radar systems (two), ultrasound sensors (18), and optical speed sensors (two), along with a GNSS positioning system and six AI cameras. Artificial intelligence enables it to use the data it acquires to learn more. Two PX2 "brains" from NVIDIA are said to be able to perform 24,000,000,000,000,000 (24 trillion) operations a second.

But as would be expected for a research environment, Roborace is considered more of an open platform than a racing series. It is intended to accelerate the development of software and other systems for driverless cars. Highly publicized successes could also gradually persuade the public that a hands-off approach to steering could well be a good thing. That will make Roborace an interesting arena for car makers and suppliers who want to see more of this type of engineering. And that is no different from the early days of racing history in general (see the beginning of this book). There was no shortage of skepticism and resistance to new technology back then, either. ___

The Roboracer's design is from Daniel Simon, a former Volkswagen employee who works on future-oriented projects and has also designed cars for Hollywood productions.

The story comes full circle: Roborace is viewed with the same skepticism that automobiles and racing encountered at the beginning of the last century. One response back then was the Red Flag Act in the United Kingdom, which required a person to walk in front of road vehicles and wave a red flag to warn pedestrians.

Law and order

___ With the ever-advancing proliferation of the automobile, a growing range of different models on offer and the perpetual progress of the motorsport milieu, the need for new regulations is as constant as progress itself. The automobile associations are almost as old as the automobile itself. They promptly assume control of the sporting world as well. For the races of the Gordon Bennett Cup, for example, the rules stipulate that both the drivers and the vehicles be selected by the respective national associations. And these remain the rule-makers and governing sports bodies for the proper organization and execution of all manner of motorsport events to this day.

It is the motorsport highlights of the national scenes that give rise to the Formula 1 World Championship. Road races become more seldom and develop into the illustrious major events such as the Mille Miglia, Targa Florio and the Carrera Panamericana. Others, such as the famous, or perhaps infamous, Liège-Sofia-Liège race, shift to race circuits and become events such as the Marathon de la Route held on the Nordschleife of the Nurburgring, or the 24-hour race of today. These races primarily involve touring cars and GT vehicles. Another endurance classic, the 24-hour race at Spa-Francorchamps in Belgium, comes to host both touring cars and – most recently – purebred sports cars and GT racing machines. The granddaddy of all endurance races, the "24 Heures du Mans," by contrast, is regarded as the ultimate test for ultra-fast sports cars and prototypes – not to mention their drivers, of course. In the pre-war era, the race serves as a sort of demonstration drive for the still relatively young invention, the automobile, with organizers insisting on a minimum of four seats to underscore the relation to series automobiles. In doing so, they essentially restrict the event to touring cars.

After the war, the rule-makers adopt a more expansive approach. The advance of assembly-line production and spread of the self-supporting body design are among the reasons for the ever-increasing classification into Grand Prix, sports car and touring car races. In an effort to delimit the different automobile forms, models and types and ensure equal chances through the restriction of permitted tuning measures, the automobile sport associations – first and foremost the international CSI (Commission Sportif International), and later the FISA, or FIA, as it is known today (Federation International de L'Automobile) – create the necessary framework for fair competition. The result is regulations for formula race cars, sports car prototypes, GT cars and touring cars. Like the cars themselves, the regulations are subject to constant transformation. In order to limit excesses and circumscribe the model ranges of the manufacturers, growing developments in the motorsport scene and gains in expertise of individual teams, the rules are updated every five to six years. But the basic classes remain in place for a very long time.

Until the early 1980s, the world of motorsport is divided into two categories: Category B includes the thoroughbred race cars. And Category A encompasses homologated production cars used for racing purposes. Each of the categories, in turn, is subdivided into various groups, and the groups into numerous displacement classes.

ategory A of homologated series production vehicles – cars, in other words, that have been approved for racing by the automobile association after fulfilling the quantitative stipulations – encompasses the Groups 1 through 5. The cars of Groups 1 and 3 are relatively close to the series models, while in Groups 2 and 4 the number of permitted modifications to all components related to power and driving dynamics is considerable, enabling what is in many cases a dramatic transformation of a once-tame, everyday set of wheels into a fiery racing machine. More exciting yet, and not just for racing aficionados, are the brawny specimens of group 5, which are undeniably race cars tethered to their series namesakes by the slenderest of threads – cars whose genetic ancestry can be traced back to either touring cars or GTs (Gran Turismo). For the other groups, by contrast, distinguishing between the two is their raison d'être – Groups 1 and 2 are for touring cars, and Groups 3 and 4 are for GTs. To be more precise, Group 1 is reserved for four-door series touring cars. The homologation is fulfilled if the manufacturer can demonstrate that it has produced 5,000 units of the model within one year. There is an exception to the space requirements for vehicles with a displacement under 1,000 cc; it would scarcely make much sense, after all, to throw these generally comparatively modestly motorized cars in with the muscular GT sports cars. For tuners and dedicated racing teams, or even manufacturers' works teams, this Group, with its vanishingly small scope of permitted modifications and high homologation numbers, is relatively

unappealing. For amateurs, by contrast, it offers a manageable and relatively inexpensive means of scratching the racing itch. Prime examples of this include the Ford Escort and the Opel Kadett coupés, which are entered in countless circuit races, rallies and slalom competitions.

Group 2 is a more spectacular affair. This is where one finds the "enhanced touring cars" whose homologation in the 1970s requires proof of having built a mere 1,000 vehicles in the twelve-month period. Indeed, in the early 1960s the homologation requirement is only half that number. Yet in every era, some manufacturers accept the homologation challenge with special model variants and thereby create optimal base vehicles for their racing ambitions. One such car is the legendary GTA, of which only just enough are built to satisfy the homologation rules.

Driving pleasure and competitiveness are guaranteed by the numerous – legal – technical optimization efforts. The measures touch practically all component assemblies: engines, cylinder heads, camshafts, pistons,

Some manufacturers clear homologation hurdles with great creativity

valves, oil pressure systems, exhaust systems, clutches, transmissions, differentials, suspensions, brakes, electrical equipment, springs, etc. This free-spiritedness applies to Group 4 as well. Although even before the war complications increasingly arise in the approval processes for racing events on public roadways – the development of circuit races such as the Targa Florio and track races such as Brooklands and the Nurburgring bear witness to that – racing events in a public space ever more cramped with traffic and a growing, albeit often misguided, sense of environmental awareness gradually become an almost unthinkable indulgence. To this day, rallies remain an exception, though they too are much curtailed in terms of time and space compared to the days of yore. Even before the energy crisis in the early 1970s, the comparatively pure racing machines are far from universally appreciated thanks to their boisterous noise levels. Based upon a ruling by the former International Sporting Committee, or CSI, homologated cars in Groups 1 through 4 remain legal through the beginning of the 1980s. The only exception: all-wheel drive vehicles

➤ "Papa" Hähn, the Alfa Romeo dealer from Mannheim, is also a successful team owner and manager. His GTA cars always bear distinguishing marks. In this photo, "HE" stands for Harald Ertl, one of his drivers for whom he opens the door to Formula 1. Jochen Mass also begins his racing career with successful outings in Helmut Hähn's squad.

The BMW 635 CSi with its 3.5-liter, straight-six power plant from the mid-engine M1 sports car is one of the top dogs in the early days of the Group A, launched in 1982. In 1984, Volker Strycek is the first champion of the young DTM driving a 635 CSi.

are not permitted. But back to the Group designations ... Like Group 1, the cars homologated in Group 3 are still relatively series-like vehicles. However, this group does include GT cars, the so-called series Grand Turismo cars, of which 1,000 units per model have to be manufactured within the year. The Group 4 regulations call for sports and Gran Turismo cars with a significantly lower homologation threshold. Moreover, the scope of permitted modifications – as in Group 2 – is considerably more expansive. Until the mid-1960s, a scant 100 units of the respective GT is enough to clear the homologation hurdle. But even the later threshold of 400 units of the base version within two years was not too high a barrier for small-series manufacturers such as Ferrari, Maserati and the like to join the ranks of the homologated racers.

lfa Romeo, or more precisely the works sport department Autodelta, takes this hurdle with the Giulia TZ. The dozen of the subsequently manufactured – and even more uncompromising – TZ2s are regarded by the functionaries there as a permitted enhancement of the previously homologated base model. It's a loophole that will be stretched to its limits with some regularity as time goes on: The Ferrari 250 GTO (Gran Turismo Omologato), for example, is classified as a mere model variant of the homologated 250 GT. Otherwise, the Squadra Rossa from Maranello would scarcely have been given the green light for the hot-blooded GTO, with a mere 38 units produced.

For Group 5, which caused a massive stir towards the end of the 1970s in the endurance racing world and the Deutsche Rennsport-Meisterschaft (DRM), the conditions are different. This group is reserved for the "special production cars" for which no minimum unit numbers are prescribed. Nevertheless, the models transformed into Group 5 racing machines must originate with cars homologated in Groups 1 through 4. The most spectacular manifestations in this Group emerge in the late 1970s. They include the Porsche 935, the BMW 2002 Turbo and 320 Turbo, the Ford Capri and the Lancia Beta Montecarlo. Technically and aerodynamically, the permitted changes appear all but unlimited. Only the exterior body shape must be retained. Hence the moniker "silhouette race cars" in the motorsport jargon of the day. In addition to the production cars classified in category A, the purebred race cars of category B are also included.

This, in turn, is subdivided into Groups 6, 7 and 8. Group 6 is designated for two-seater race cars. In layman's terms: sports cars or sports car prototypes. Group 7 governs the technical regulations of monoposto race cars such as those of Formula 1, Formula 2 and Formula 3. And Group 8 encompasses non-formula race cars (including monoposti).

At the beginning of the 1982 racing season, an entirely new classification goes into effect with which the FIA attempts to circumvent the existing abuses in Groups 1 through 5. Spelling is the name of the game from now on ...

Group A is for touring cars. It is roughly comparable to the previous Group 3 and therefore allows relatively substantial modifications. For homologation, manufacturers need to prove production of 5,000 cars within 12 months. The homologation rules also specify a required weight. The cars can be slimmed down somewhat, but only down to the displacement-based minimum thresholds. The vehicle components can be reworked, balanced, scaled down or modified in their shape. In the process, however, their derivation from the original part must remain identified. Of course, the engine could be modified and the brakes adjusted. When it comes to aerodynamics, the authorities stay firm: subsequently added spoilers and flares remain forbidden. After all, the cars are homologated with their precise appearance – notwithstanding the rearview mirrors. As the representatives of the individual manufacturers come to find that the sales prospects of 5,000 decidedly race-worthy base cars are too low to merit the expense, loopholes soon begin to appear in Group A as well. Meanwhile, so-called evolution models have been approved that – if just 500 of them are produced in a series – are permitted for racing use as well. For the Mercedes Benz 190E 2.5-16, for instance – a car used primarily in the DTM – the carmaker introduces two evolution models with the "Evo 1" and "Evo 2," bringing an influx of race-ready aerodynamics to the otherwise rather dull appearance and aerodynamic standards prevalent in staid Group A. The Group A touring cars such as the Alfa 75, BMW M3, Ford Sierra Cosworth, etc., race predominantly in the different national championships as well as the World and European Touring Car Championships.

The near-series contingent of production vehicles, meanwhile, find themselves covered by the regulations of Group N. Their playground is the

series and races reserved for semi-professionals and amateurs, such as the 24 Hours Nürburgring. The conditions are the same as for Group A. Here, too, the rules call for 5,000 units to be produced within twelve months. Yet the racing machines prepared according to the rules of Group N remain – notwithstanding the safety-related components such as roll cages, fire extinguishers, harness belt, and racing bucket seats – quite close to the series models. Here the boundaries of what is possible are even more tightly circumscribed than in Group 1.

For Group N, the classifications are made by the respective national sport authorities and precisely described in the homologation specifications in the respective countries. In Germany, the governing body is initially the ONS (Oberste Nationale Sportbehörde), and later, from the 1990s onwards, the Deutsche Motor-Sport-Bund (DMSB). This precise homologation prevents the use of vehicles with elements such as extravagantly dimensioned wheel wells, for example, which are declared a "rough driving package," or cars ostensibly designed for release on the African market, which can confer a competitive advantage as such body modifications can enable the use of larger wheels and brakes. For the four-seater Group N cars, engine modifications are limited to changes in the accelerator cable, spark plugs, thermostat, speed limiters and cables. The suspensions are practically identical to those of the series vehicles, though the dampers are exempted, provided that the shell of the series standard McPherson spring strut is retained.

◄ In the mid-1990s, the two-liter Class 2 touring cars are the popular choice in many national touring car series, with the European Touring Car Championship and the FIA World Touring Car Championship (from 2005) representing the international stage. Between 2000 and 2003, the Alfa 156 proves unbeatable.

G roup B ranges somewhere between the previous Groups 4 and 5. It encompasses Gran Turismo sports cars and brings its march of triumph to the rally world as well, where the homologation rules are comparatively easy to fulfill, with just 200 cars to be manufactured within the twelve-month period. Not least in the mid-1980s, when the racing crowd is joined by a sizable group of collectors who are prepared to pay heretofore inconceivable sums for these irresistibly alluring, yet also technologically sophisticated gems of automotive engineering. Many manufacturers are drawn to the notion of designing and producing these usually all-wheel-drive turbo speedsters – a combination of qualities all but predestined for the traction-challenging arena of rally racing. Rally-shy, by contrast, are such sports car manufacturers as Porsche and Ferrari, for which the street-legal, high-tech Group B hot-rods prove to provide a well-paid, image-burnishing campaign for their impressive wares. Outstanding examples of this stratagem include the Porsche 959 and the Ferrari 288 GTO, paired against the likes of the Peugeot 205 turbo 16 and Audi quattro Sport S1.

The Group B racing machines are as unbridled as they are captivating to watch in action: Restricted to 20 units, these evolution models enable the implementation of thoroughbred racers of sometimes precariously fragile constructions. After some severe accidents with the highly-charged Group B cars, their use is prohibited in rallying from 1987 onwards. The Rally World Championship is subsequently opened to cars under the regulations of Group A. And since the Group B cars are almost exclusively used in the rally ranks, the car category practically goes extinct on the spot. B must be followed by C, of course – so, in keeping with this compelling maxim, the rule-makers declare the creation of a Group C, in which sports car prototypes receive their rules of the game. Here, there are no specifications in terms of the unit numbers, but there is no shortage of framework conditions, such as minimum dimensions of 4.80 x 2.00 x 1.10 meters (length x width x height) and a minimum weight of 800 kilograms. To offer space for two passengers – for the sake of appearances, at any rate, though in reality the passenger's side accommodates the emerging control units of the electronic age –, a windshield size of 80 centimeters is prescribed. On the engine side, there are no restrictions whatsoever for these aerodynamically sophis-

Group B sets off a fascinating, yet dangerous fireworks display

ticated sports car-flounders with ground-effect underbodies. Amazingly, in spite of their higher weight and narrower tire widths, the driving performance of these spectacular racing machines actually surpasses that of Formula 1 cars for a time. However, the sports car prototypes assigned to the Group C classes C1 and C2 are ultimately slowed by strict consumption regulations. With a maximum of 60 liters per 100 kilometers allowed for the long-distance pursuit, power is effectively limited in spite of the absence of restrictions on turbochargers and compressors. At the same time, the development of economical engines and engine control units is accelerated. The now ubiquitous series-production Motronic technology is just one example of many.

It is the GT1 and GT2 race cars that emerge as the successors to Group C. The GT regulations reach the pinnacle of their run in the late 1990s, following the demise of the high-tech International Touring Car Championship that had emerged from the flagging DTM (Deutsche Tourenwagen-Meisterschaft). The classifications for the international FIA GT series extended to the relatively series-like GT3 classes. These classifications also apply at Le Mans, of course, where the GT sports cars also pick up where Group C left off. The endurance classic on the Sarthe also includes the Le Mans prototypes – divided into LMP1 and LMP2 depending on their displacement and output. In the United States, the race cars already go by the designations GTP (for Grand Tourisme prototypes) and GTN for the series-like sports cars even during Group C era. Following the end of the IMSA (International Motor-Sport Association), the sports car and prototype racing milieu begins its successful comeback, initially with the American Le Mans Series (ALMS) initiated by Don Panoz. Unlike in the FIA Group C regulations, the consumption formula is not accepted by the IMSA. Instead there is a handicap regulation which – albeit in a somewhat different form – also ushers in a renaissance for touring car racing in the Group A era. First the French, and then the German "Deutsche Produktionswagen-Meisterschaft" (after 1986, the DTM), become a "classless society" in which, thanks to differently dimensions air restrictors and handicap weights, all starters are placed in a single classification. At long last, every race spectator can immediately identify the overall winner …

In spite of the continuation of the Group A rules, the elite echelon of touring car racing splits into two classes in 1993. Here we find C1 and C2 – not to be mistaken for the sports car designations– standing for Class 1 and Class 2 touring race cars.

etween 1993 and 1996, Class 1 develops into the undisputed heavyweight class of touring car racing. The homologation requirements call for proof of production of 25,000 units of a base model within 12 months. In order to offer drivers and spectators authentic, fascinating race cars in spite of the considerable unit requirements, there is a rule that allows for substantial modifications compared to the sometimes less-than-scintillating base models. Though the drive concept was not prescribed, the cars were limited to a six-cylinder, 2.5-liter engine with engine speeds of no greater than 12,000 rpm. Maximum fuel consumption for the just under 100-kilometer race circuits is limited to 55 liters. The restrictions on the size and position of the rear wing forestall the development of elaborate aerodynamic concoctions and obviate the need for costly testing and development in the wind tunnels of the automotive and aviation industries. Aerodynamics engineers and developers are permitted, however, to work their magic with practically no restrictions below the wheel centerline. And fender flares are – to a certain extent, anyway – also permitted. The base weight is limited to 1,040 kilograms. To that is added the obligatory twelve kilos for the TV equipment, including a camera and transponder, or compensatory weights, for all starters. The underlying idea is clear: an even playing field with the fewest possible number of restrictions – a precept that applies equally to suspensions and leads to a sophisticated monocoque design and numerous, highly complex electronic developments. Yet ultimately these fascinating race cars go the way of the dodo: When Opel announces its exit from this exclusive racing club – a racing fraternity in which the cars could be crafted with the aid of just a handful of technicians, engineers and mechanics – late in the summer of 1996, the series' days are numbered. The young drivers like Alexander Wurz and Giancarlo Fisichella, who have gained profound knowledge of electronic differentials and telemetry recordings in the series, are later welcomed to the Formula 1 circus with open arms.

Stuffed with high technology, the Class 1 machines are used in the increasingly international DTM, which in 1995 becomes the European and 1996 the global ITC (International Touring Car Cup). No less global in its outlook is Class 2, which establishes itself as the benchmark for touring car racing and continues until the European Super Touring Championship is established for Class 2-like Superturismo cars in 2001.

To prevent cost explosions of the sort that had dogged the DTM/ITC, the engine speed level (maximum 8,500 rpm) of the two-liter, four-cylinder race cars and the aerodynamics (initially completely series standard, including exterior mirrors, later exactly defined) are set at relatively low levels. Elaborate detail solutions such as ABS and telemetry recordings are prohibited. Even the tire warmers that are mandatory in Formula 1 and the DTM are out of bounds in the STW league.

In Germany, after their premier year in the DTM field, starting in 1994 the two-liter cars find their home in the ADAC STW Cup, which becomes a bona fide super touring car championship. Not to be outdone, the Class 2 sedans do indeed become bona fide super touring cars as well: On the one hand they, too, reveal themselves – typically for works team racing – to be technologically sophisticated and anything but cheap race cars, while on the other hand offering exhilarating, top-flight racing, notwithstanding mixed reviews for the touring cars among the driving professionals. Many manufacturers join the fray in this Class, which enjoys worldwide popularity in a variety of national championship series, which in turn culminate each year in something of a touring car Olympics, with a Touring Car World Final contested by Class 2 cars. A point of contention – a perpetually recurring theme in motor racing – emerges concerning the classification of the different drive variants. For vehicles with rear-wheel drive, for example, there is initially a weight handicap of 100 kilograms, later reduced to 50 in 1995. In numerical terms, the largest contingent of the roughly 300-hp machines is comprised of front-wheel drive cars, which have to weigh at least 975 kilograms. This amounts to a base weight of 1,025 kilograms for the rear-wheel drive faction, hailing primarily from Munich, and 1,040 kilograms for the all-wheel drive cars developed in Ingolstadt. Yet in spite of, or perhaps because of, the different base weights, the super touring field turns out to be fascinatingly balanced.

After a few manufacturers circumvent the aerodynamics restrictions through the series bodies with evolution models, spoilers are subjected

to precise dimension limits. This puts paid to the Alfa 155 1.8 Silverstone, or Formula, presented by Alfa Romeo. Yet before this happens, this evolution model, with its expansive front spoiler and rather crass-looking rear wing mounted on adapter pieces, does its part in securing the title victory in what is, at the time, the most competitive Class 2 championship going, the British Touring Car Championship (BTCC).

fter the demise of the Class 1 dinosaurs, the Class 2 racers rise to become the top league of touring car racing worldwide. With their precarious differentials and complicated, lightweight mechanical solutions, these speedsters are by now anything but inexpensive. Thus emerges a new class above Group N, which proves rather less than fascinating for spectators. The DTC (Deutsches Tourenwagen Championat) serves as the forerunner for the FIA-governed Group N plus, which is soon replicated around the world. The homologation rules call for a mere 2,500 units produced within a year. Here, too, a maximum of 2,000 cc of displacement is allowed. Compression is limited to a maximum ratio of 11:1 and turbochargers are – as was the case in Classes 1 and 2 – not permitted. The tires for the either front-wheel (1,100-kilogram minimum weight) or rear-wheel (1,130 kilograms) powered touring cars are restricted to a maximum of 7 x 15 inches and countless of the – for outsiders imperceptible – detail solutions from the STW era are taboo.

This series quickly becomes the preferred racing class worldwide – including for the FIA. After the Euro-SPC Cup (Europa-Superproduzione-Cup) in 2000, this FIA Group N plus becomes an FIA-operated series featuring Superproduzione cars as part of the officially revived European Touring Car Championship. Above that there is still the Superturismo, the super touring cars, with which a European Super Touring Championship is first carried out again in 2001 after the Euro STC 2000 (European Super Touring

Evolution models come to the Class 2 super touring car scene as well

Cup) in 2000. After 2002, the the title is no longer contested in two classes but with enhanced Superproduzione or slimmed-down Superturismo race cars, depending on one's point of view. The so-called Super 2000 cars are two-liter vehicles for which the aerodynamic modification options are once again loosened considerably. In keeping with the legal modifications to the engine and suspension, as well as the large-format, wheel well-filling wheels, they give these speedsters from the likes of Alfa, BMW, Nissan, Honda and Volvo some genuine race car characteristics. With some exciting racing in the field, the series actually becomes a world championship event as of 2005.

One constant on the racing scene is the Formula 1 World Championship, held since 1950. The series emerges from the Grand Prix format begun in 1906. Over the decades, even the Grand Prix racing machines have faced ever-changing conditions through the regulations. The regulations are primarily in place to restrict the immense speeds to manageable dimensions. To exclude over-heavy, powerful designs, in 1906 the cars can weigh no more than a metric ton. The following year, a maximum consumption of 30 liters per 100 kilometers is defined. By 1908, the cars are permitted a minimum weight of 1,100 kilograms and a piston surface of no more than 155 mm. Following the formula-less period from 1909 to 1911, vehicle width is restricted to 1.75 meters. The vehicle weight must fall between 800 and 1,100 kilograms and consumption may not exceed 20 liters per 100 kilometers. Furthermore, streamlined tails are prohibited. In 1914, compressors are banned and displacement is limited to 4,500 cc. The rules continually adapt to the state of the technology and become increasingly complex and extensive as the years go by. A printout of the current FIA Formula 1 regulations would burst the seams of this tome ...

Among royalty

___ Formula 1 is the heavyweight class of motorsport and has developed into a globe-spanning sporting stage of the first order. Under the firm guiding hand of the FIA and Bernie Ecclestone, this circus of speed is flourishing and expanding into new countries every year. For decades, the automobile producing nations of Europe are the focus, though as time goes by the emphasis increasingly shifts toward new markets with obvious appeal for the sponsors and Formula 1 itself. Countries such as Turkey, Bahrain and China have long since joined the establishment. States like India and Russia already have a foot firmly in the door.

The roughly dozen-and-a-half races each year captivate over a billion TV viewers around the world. This wasn't always the case. It is only with the rise of the former Brabham team owner (1971–1987) Bernie Ecclestone, who unifies the teams' interests, represents them as a negotiating partner vis-a-vis organizers and charts a course toward offering a unified "Formula 1 product" package, that the success of Formula 1 as we know it today takes shape. An unforgettable test of wills ensues between the Ecclestone-led grouping of mainly British teams in Formula One Constructors' Association (FOCA) and the automobile association FISA (forerunner of the FIA), under whose auspices the manufacturers' teams are organized. At the European kick-off in 1982, the San Marino Grand Prix, the FOCA teams boycott the event and the Tifosi in Imola experience a race in which only the works team cars from Alfa Romeo, Ferrari and Renault and a handful of strike-breakers vie for the win.

Formula 1 is a global show and sporting spectacle of the first order

Formula 1 owes its very inception to a convergence of interests. With the introduction of the World Championship title starting in the 1950 season, a compelling merger of a series of international events is created that has operated under the Grand Prix designation ever since. Until well into the 1970s, there are other races staged for Formula 1 cars in addition to the Grand Prix races included in the Formula 1 World Championship. With attractive prize winnings for drivers and teams, these events are a lucrative affair. This changes with Ecclestone's initiative, for now the teams are in a considerably more favorable position thanks to their participation in the entire World Championship series. The participation and prize money is now augmented by a share of the revenues from the sale of the television rights.

Technologically, Formula 1 has shown itself through the decades to be wholly amenable to adaptation. The 4.5-liter naturally aspirated engines and the 1.5-liter supercharged racers of the first two years are followed, in economically turbulent times, by two years in which Formula 1 contents itself with two liters of displacement and cars whose technology draws heavily on Formula 2 cars. In 1954, a displacement boost to two-and-a-half liters is introduced. The race distance of at least 300 kilometers or three hours of racing in the early days is shortened to 200–300 kilometers or at least two hours in 1958. In 1961, Formula 1 and Formula 2 go their separate ways again: The combustion chamber volume is set at 1.5 liters of displacement until 1965. This scarcely affects the speed of the cars, at any rate; with a race duration of two hours, the Grand Prix distances now range between 300 and 500 kilometers. From 1966, three-liter engines are introduced, all of which are mounted behind the driver. The rules also allow for supercharged 1.5-liter engines, but this chapter will only begin with the introduction of the Renault Turbo in 1977. The race distance is shortened to a maximum of 325 kilometers in 1971. In the early 1980s, almost all teams deploy turbo engines, leading to an effort to limit power by restricting the tank volume.

Starting in 1986, only turbos are allowed. Yet the power escalation (in spite of the charge pressure restriction) leads to a ban on turbocharged engines for the 1989 season. Since 1987, naturally aspirated engines with a maximum of 12 cylinders and 3,500 cc are allowed. From 1990, the race distance is limited to 305 kilometers and cannot exceed two hours in duration. In the FIA's endless struggle to ensure that speeds and lap times for the monoposti stay within reasonable bounds from a safety perspective, displacement is restricted to three liters in 1995, and 2.5 liters in 2006. While designers deploy ten-cylinder engines in the new three-liter era, they opt for eight-cylinder engines in 2006. In order to keep financial outlays and engine power from rising ever further (roughly 900 hp at 19,000 rpm), the rules prescribe driving times and penalties – for instance the loss of places on the grid – for unscheduled changes of components from the drivetrain. Since 2009, the heavyweight class is contested with hybrid vehicles in which a KERS system (Kinetic Energy Recovery System) recuperates braking energy and stores it in a battery, which in turn supplies an electric motor with additional energy.

From 2010, the race winner pockets 25 points and even the tenth-place finisher comes away with a point. 2011 sees the advent of a Drag Reduction System (DRS), an adjustable rear wing that eases overtaking maneuvers. The 2014 introduction of a new 1.6-liter, V6 turbo engine caused quite a commotion on the scene – albeit only among fans and within the Formula 1 family; otherwise the modern and highly efficient turbos are exceptionally quiet compared to previous Formula 1 engine generations. The aim of efficiency and environmental friendliness is also supported by the restriction of the fuel quantity to 100 kilograms. In addition to the brake energy recuperation (KERS), the thermal energy of the turbocharger (ERS-H) is also recuperated. ___

In 1975, Niki Lauda is crowned world champion with the Ferrari 312T. As was customary at this time, he and his teammate Clay Regazzoni sit virtually on top of the gas tank in a monocoque made of riveted aluminum sheets. At his tragic fire accident on the Nürburgring in 1976, Lauda experiences firsthand just how dangerous these race car constructions are.

► Michael Schumacher dominates Formula 1 and gains fame with seven world championship titles. The supreme discipline of his era enjoys record numbers of spectators – both live at the racetracks and on television.

Year	Drivers' champion	Car	Constructors' champion
2017	Lewis Hamilton (GB)	Mercedes F1 W08 Hybrid	Mercedes AMG Petronas F1 Team
2016	Niko Rosberg (D)	Mercedes F1 W07 Hybrid	Mercedes AMG Petronas F1 Team
2015	Lewis Hamilton (GB)	Mercedes F1 W06 Hybrid	Mercedes AMG Petronas F1 Team
2014	Lewis Hamilton (GB)	Mercedes F1 W05 Hybrid	Mercedes AMG Petronas F1 Team
2013	Sebastian Vettel (D)	Red Bull Renault RB9	Red Bull Racing
2012	Sebastian Vettel (D)	Red Bull Renault RB8	Red Bull Racing
2011	Sebastian Vettel (D)	Red Bull Renault RB7	Red Bull Racing
2010	Sebastian Vettel (D)	Red Bull Renault RB6	Red Bull
2009	Jenson Button (GB)	Brawn-Mercedes BGP001	Brawn
2008	Lewis Hamilton (GB)	McLaren-Mercedes MP4-23	Ferrari
2007	Kimi Räikkönen (FIN)	Ferrari F2007	Ferrari
2006	Fernando Alonso (E)	Renault R26	Renault
2005	Fernando Alonso (E)	Renault R25	Renault
2004	Michael Schumacher (D)	Ferrari F2004	Ferrari
2003	Michael Schumacher (D)	Ferrari F2002 & F2003-GA	Ferrari
2002	Michael Schumacher (D)	Ferrari F2002	Ferrari
2001	Michael Schumacher (D)	Ferrari F1-2001	Ferrari
2000	Michael Schumacher (D)	Ferrari F1-2000	Ferrari
1999	Mika Häkkinen (FIN)	McLaren-Mercedes MP4/14	Ferrari
1998	Mika Häkkinen (FIN)	McLaren-Mercedes MP4/13	McLaren
1997	Jacques Villeneuve (CDN)	Williams-Renault FW19	Williams
1996	Damon Hill (GB)	Williams-Renault FW18	Williams
1995	Michael Schumacher (D)	Benetton B195-Renault	Benetton
1994	Michael Schumacher (D)	Benetton B194-Ford	Williams
1993	Alain Prost (F)	Williams-Renault FW15C	Williams
1992	Nigel Mansell (GB)	Williams-Renault FW14B	Williams
1991	Ayrton Senna (BR)	McLaren-Honda MP4/6	McLaren
1990	Ayrton Senna (BR)	McLaren-Honda MP4/5B	McLaren
1989	Alain Prost (F)	McLaren-Honda MP4/5	McLaren
1988	Ayrton Senna (BR)	McLaren-Honda MP4/4	McLaren
1987	Nelson Piquet (BR)	Williams-Honda FW11B	Williams
1986	Alain Prost (F)	McLaren-TAG-Porsche MP4/2C	Williams
1985	Alain Prost (F)	McLaren-TAG-Porsche MP4/2B	McLaren
1984	Niki Lauda (A)	McLaren-TAG-Porsche MP4/2	McLaren
1983	Nelson Piquet (BR)	Brabham BMW BT52	Ferrari
1982	Keke Rosberg (FIN)	Williams-Cosworth FW07C & FW08	Ferrari
1981	Nelson Piquet (BR)	Brabham-Cosworth BT49C	Williams
1980	Alan Jones (AUS)	Williams-Cosworth FW07 & FW07B	Williams
1979	Jody Scheckter (ZA)	Ferrari 312T3	Ferrari
1978	Mario Andretti (USA)	Lotus-Cosworth 78 & 79	Lotus
1977	Niki Lauda (A)	Ferrari 312T2	Ferrari
1976	James Hunt (GB)	McLaren-Cosworth M23	Ferrari
1975	Niki Lauda (A)	Ferrari 312B3 & 312T	Ferrari
1974	Emerson Fittipaldi (BR)	McLaren-Cosworth M23	McLaren
1973	Jackie Stewart (GB)	Tyrrell-Cosworth 005 & 006	Lotus
1972	Emerson Fittipaldi (BR)	Lotus-Cosworth 72D	Lotus
1971	Jackie Stewart (GB)	Tyrrell-Cosworth 001 & 003	Tyrrell
1970	Jochen Rindt (A)	Lotus-Cosworth 49C & 72C	Lotus
1969	Jackie Stewart (GB)	Matra-Cosworth MS10 & MS80	Matra
1968	Graham Hill (GB)	Lotus-Cosworth 49 & 49B	Lotus
1967	Denis Hulme (NZ)	Brabham-Repco BT20 & BT24	Brabham
1966	Jack Brabham (AUS)	Brabham-Repco BT19 & BT20	Brabham
1965	Jim Clark (GB)	Lotus-Climax 33	Lotus
1964	John Surtees (GB)	Ferrari 158	Ferrari
1963	Jim Clark (GB)	Lotus-Climax 25	Lotus
1962	Graham Hill (GB)	BRM P57	BRM
1961	Phil Hill (USA)	Ferrari 156	Ferrari
1960	Jack Brabham (AUS)	Cooper-Climax T53	Cooper
1959	Jack Brabham (AUS)	Cooper-Climax T51	Cooper
1958	Mike Hawthorn (GB)	Ferrari Dino 246	Vanwall
1957	Juan-Manuel Fangio (RA)	Maserati 250F	(Constructors' title since 1958)
1956	Juan-Manuel Fangio (RA)	Lancia Ferrari D50	
1955	Juan-Manuel Fangio (RA)	Mercedes-Benz W196	
1954	Juan-Manuel Fangio (RA)	Maserati 250F/Mercedes-Benz W196	
1953	Alberto Ascari (I)	Ferrari 500	
1952	Alberto Ascari (I)	Ferrari 500	
1951	Juan-Manuel Fangio (RA)	Alfa Romeo Tipo 159 "Alfetta"	
1950	Dr. Giuseppe "Nino" Farina (I)	Alfa Romeo Tipo 158 "Alfetta"	

➤ In motorsport, the triple crown of F1, Le Mans and Indy 500 victories has a very special ring. Graham Hill is the only racing driver by now to manage all three. In 2017, Fernando Alonso attempted to follow in his footsteps with his Indianapolis outing – without success.

What goes around comes around

____ In the Indianapolis 500 – that is, 500 miles of racing –, cars do 200 laps around the oval. With average speeds of 350 km/h, the 804.5-kilometer distance takes roughly three hours – assuming a reasonably small number of yellow flags, at any rate. The only thing capable of shortening the distance is the vicissitudes of the weather; formerly staged on a slick brick surface, the race is only run on a dry track. If no restart of the race is possible, the standings at the time of the postponement are declared the official result. Precisely this occurs in 2007, when strong rainfall after 113 laps brings the race to a halt and doesn't allow for a resumption. With over 300,000 spectators, the race is the largest one-day sporting event worldwide.

When the race first starts on May 30, 1911, the Indianapolis Motor Speedway is already two years old. Completely new, however, is the track constructed of bricks, replacing the unreliable gravel and tar surface and giving the world's first car race track its nickname, the "Brickyard." Since 1935, the oval and its four 10.75° banked corners have been topped with a tarmac surface. Only a short section of bricks at the start/finish line still bears witness to the original surface.

For ten years, the Indy 500 was part of the Formula 1 World Championship

From 1950 to 1960, the race is part of the Formula 1 World Championship. But since the cars differ from each other quite substantially, the degree of exchange between the heavily European-tilted Formula 1 scene and the American racers remains minimal. Jim Clark and Graham Hill do manage to win the race, but by the mid-1960s there are no longer any Formula 1 points awarded for the feat. The list of successful Formula 1 drivers to win at Indy as well include Emerson Fittipaldi, Mario Andretti, Jacques Villeneuve and Juan Pablo Montoya.

For many years, a series of wins in Indy and Le Mans, capped by the F1 title, is regarded as the greatest hat-trick in the motorsport world. But Graham Hill remains the only driver to pull it off. Mario Andretti tries to follow in his footsteps, but can't conquer Le Mans. As a Peugeot works driver, Jacques Villeneuve currently has the best prospects of achieving the hat-trick.

Montoya, Villeneuve, Andretti, and Fittipaldi are some of the Indy 500 winners who also manage to take top honors in the monoposti Champ Car series, the North American counterpart to Formula 1. The cars themselves are referred to as IndyCars. Yet the issue is the reason behind a falling out that leads the Champ Car series and the Indy 500 to part ways in 1996. As the name rights for Indy reside with the operators of the Indianapolis Motor Speedway, but disagreements emerge between the track operators and the Champ Car organizers, the Indy Racing League (IRL) is formed and is held in parallel with the still operating Champ Car series. As for the legendary 500-mile race at the Brickyard, from now on only IRL cars are allowed to take part.

The cars are bought by teams with the established chassis manufacturers, such as Dallara. Also uniform are the tires, the sequential six-speed gearbox, the engines and the prescribed wing configurations. Until 2006, the permitted displacement for the V8 engines is 3.0 liters. Since 2007, 3.5-liter engines are used. The cars of the Indy Racing League are operated with ethanol.

The Champ Car series goes by several different names. IndyCar and CART series are also common names for the most prestigious formula

racing series in America. The CART name stands for "Championship Auto Racing Teams" and marks the beginning of a reorientation in 1979 of the top racing class staged by the USAC (United States Auto Club) since 1956. Due to the severe accident at Le Mans in 1955, the American Automobile Association (AAA) relinquishes control of the organization it formed in 1909. The IndyCars name becomes established in the 1960s, and it's no great surprise considering that the series is driven with the cars used at the legendary race. Staged between 1909 and 1955, the AAA National Championship becomes the USAC National Championship. In 1979, America's top-tier racing series goes by the name SCCA/CART Indy Series and from 1980 (through 1996) becomes the PPG IndyCar World Series, with races in the USA, Canada, Japan, Australia and the United Kingdom. Later, a stop is added in Germany as well. In 1997, the series is called the PPG CART World Series. PPG stands for the title sponsor, an automotive supplier that makes windshields. In 1998, the FedEx delivery service steps in as the sponsor of the FedEx Championship Series, which in turn operates as the Champ Car World Series starting in 2003.

Compared to Formula 1, the technical regulations remain remarkably stable over time. Since 1969, turbocharged 2.65-liter engines are used.

As a rule, the methanol used as fuel is injected into eight combustion chambers. In the 1980s, four- and six-cylinder models are also used. The use of uniform parts keeps costs low, while the conservativeness of the regulations is the foundation for outstanding reliability.

Recently the series has used a uniform series car with a 750-hp V8 whose power can be boosted by 20 hp for 60 seconds using a "turbo-boost" button. This eases passing maneuvers on the mainly oval tracks, but also for monoposti used on city circuits. The chassis comes from Panoz (DP01). The top speeds are around 380 km/h, and the cars can sprint from a standstill to 100 km/h in just 2.4 seconds. ___

Indianapolis 500

Year	Driver	Car
2017	Takuma Sato (JPN)	Dallara-Honda
2016	Alexander Rossi (USA)	Dallara-Honda
2015	Juan Pablo Montoya (CO)	Dallara-Chevrolet
2014	Ryan Hunter-Reay (USA)	Dallara-Honda
2013	Tony Kanaan (BR)	Dallara-Chevrolet
2012	Dario Franchitti (GB)	Dallara-Honda
2011	Dan Wheldon (GB)	Dallara-Honda
2010	Dario Franchitti (GB)	Dallara-Honda
2009	Hélio Castroneves (BR)	Penske-Honda
2008	Scott Dixon (USA)	Ganassi-Honda
2007	Dario Franchitti (GB)	Dallara-Honda
2006	Sam Hornish jr. (USA)	Dallara-Honda
2005	Dan Wheldon (GB)	Dallara-Honda
2004	Buddy Rice (USA)	Panoz G-Force-Honda
2003	Gil de Ferrarn (BR)	Panoz G-Force-Toyota
2002	Hélio Castroneves (BR)	Dallara-Chevrolet
2001	Hélio Castroneves (BR)	Dallara-Aurora
2000	Juan Pablo Montoya (CO)	G-Force-Aurora
1999	Kenny Bräck (S)	Dallara-Aurora
1998	Eddie Cheever (USA)	Rachel`s Dallara-Aurora
1997	Arie Luyendyk (NL)	G-Force-Aurora
1996	Buddy Lazier (USA)	Hemelgarn-Reynard-Cosworth
1995	Jacques Villeneuve (CDN)	Reynard-Cosworth
1994	Al Unser jr. (USA)	Penske PC23 Mercedes-Benz
1993	Emerson Fittipaldi (BR)	Penske PC22 Chevrolet
1992	Al Unser jr. (USA)	Galmer G92 Chevrolet
1991	Rick Mears (USA)	Penske PC20 Chevrolet
1990	Arie Luyendyk (NL)	Lola T90/00 Chevrolet
1989	Emerson Fittipaldi (BR)	Penske PC18 Chevrolet
1988	Rick Mears (USA)	Penske PC17 Chevrolet
1987	Al Unser (USA)	March 86C-Cosworth
1986	Bobby Rahal (USA)	March 86C-Cosworth
1985	Danny Sullivan (USA)	March 85C-Cosworth
1984	Rick Mears (USA)	March 84C-Cosworth
1983	Tom Sneva (USA)	March 83C-Cosworth
1982	Gordon Johncock (USA)	Wildcat Mk88-Cosworth
1981	Bobby Unser (USA)	Penske PC9B-Cosworth
1980	Johnny Rutherford (USA)	Chaparral 2K-Cosworth
1979	Rick Mears (USA)	Penske PC6-Cosworth
1978	Al Unser (USA)	Lola T500-Cosworth
1977	A.J. Foyt (USA)	Coyote-Foyt Fore
1976	Johnny Rutherford (USA)	McLaren M16E-Offenhauser
1975	Bobby Unser (USA)	Eagle 75 Offenhauser
1974	Johnny Rutherford (USA)	McLaren M16C-D-Offenhauser
1973	Gordon Johncock (USA)	Eagle 73 Offenhauser
1972	Mark Donohue (USA)	McLaren M16B-Offenhauser
1971	Al Unser (USA)	Colt 71 Ford
1970	Al Unser (USA)	Colt 70 Ford
1969	Mario Andretti (USA)	Brawner-Hawk III Offenhauser
1968	Bobby Unser (USA)	Eagle 68 Drake-Offenhauser
1967	A.J. Foyt (USA)	Coyote/Lotus 34 Ford
1966	Graham Hill (GB)	Lola T90-Ford

Indianapolis 500

Year	Driver	Car
1965	Jim Clark (GB)	Lotus 38 Ford
1964	A.J. Foyt (USA)	Watson-Offenhauser
1963	Parnelli Jones (USA)	Watson-Offenhauser
1962	Rodger Ward (USA)	Watson-Offenhauser
1961	A.J. Foyt (USA)	Watson-Trevis Offenhauser
1960	Jim Rathmann (USA)	Watson-Offenhauser
1959	Rodger Ward (USA)	Watson-Offenhauser
1958	Jimmy Bryan (USA)	Kuzma-Offenhauser
1957	Sam Hanks (USA)	Epperly-Offenhauser
1956	Pat Flaherty (USA)	Watson-Offenhauser
1955	Bob Sweikert (USA)	Kurtis Kraft 500D-Offenhauser
1954	Bill Vukovich (USA)	Kurtis Kraft 500A-Offenhauser
1953	Bill Vukovich (USA)	Kurtis Kraft 500A-Offenhauser
1952	Troy Ruttman (USA)	Kuzma-Offenhauser
1951	Lee Wallard (USA)	Kurtis Kraft-Offenhauser
1950	Johnnie Parsons (USA)	Kurtis Kraft-Offenhauser
1949	Bill Holland (USA)	Deidt-Offenhauser
1948	Mauri Rose (USA)	Deidt-Offenhauser
1947	Mauri Rose (USA)	Deidt-Offenhauser
1946	George Robson (USA)	Adams-Sparks
1941	Floyd Davis & Mauri Rose (USA)	Wetteroth-Offenhauser
1940	Wilbur Shaw (USA)	Maserati SC
1939	Wilbur Shaw (USA)	Maserati SC
1938	Floyd Roberts (USA)	Wetteroth-Miller
1937	Wilbur Shaw (USA)	Shaw-Stevens Offenhauser
1936	Louis Meyer (USA)	Stevens-Miller
1935	Kelly Petillo (USA)	Wetteroth-Offenhauser
1934	Bill Cummings (USA)	Miller
1933	Louis Meyer (USA)	Miller
1932	Fred Frame (USA)	Wetteroth FD-Miller
1931	Louis Schnieder (USA)	Stevens-Miller
1930	Billy Arnold (USA)	Summers-Miller
1929	Ray Keech (USA)	Miller
1928	Louis Meyer (USA)	Miller
1927	George Souders (USA)	Duesenberg
1926	Frank Lockhart (USA)	Miller
1925	Peter DePaolo & Neil Batten (USA)	Duesenberg
1924	Lora L- Corum & Joe Boyer (USA)	Duesenberg
1923	Tommy Milton (USA)	Miller
1922	Jimmy Murphy (USA)	Duesenberg-Miller
1921	Tommy Milton (USA)	Frontenac
1920	Gaston Chevrolet (USA)	Frontenac
1919	Howdy Wilcox (USA)	Peugeot
1916	Dario Resta (GB)	Peugeot EX5
1915	Ralph DePalma (USA)	Mercedes
1914	René Thomas (F)	Dealge
1913	Jules Goux (F)	Peugeot L76
1912	Joe Dawson (USA)	National
1911	Ray Harroun (USA)	Marmon Wasp

Indy Racing League (IRL), since 2003 IndyCar Series

Year	Champion	Team
2017	Josef Newgarden (USA)	Team Penske
2016	Simon Pagenaud (F)	Team Penske
2015	Scott Dixon (AUS)	Chip Ganassi Racing
2014	Will Power (AUS)	Team Penske
2013	Scott Dixon (AUS)	Chip Ganassi Racing
2012	Ryan Hunter-Reay (USA)	Andretti Autosport
2011	Dario Franchitti (GB)	Chip Ganassi Racing
2010	Dario Franchitti (GB)	Andretti Green Racing
2009	Dario Franchitti (GB)	Andretti Green Racing
2008	Scott Dixon (AUS)	Chip Ganassi
2006	Sam Hornish jr. (USA)	Marlboro Team Penske
2005	Dan Wheldon (GB)	Andretti Green Racing
2004	Tony Kanaan (BR)	Andretti Green Racing
2003	Scott Dixon (AUS)	Target Chip Ganassi Racing
2002	Sam Hornish jr. (USA)	Panther Racing
2001	Sam Hornish jr. (USA)	Panther Racing
2000	Buddy Lazier (USA)	Hemelgarn Racing
1999	Greg Ray (ISA)	Team Menard
1998	Kenny Bräck (S)	A.J. Foyt Enterprises
1997	Tony Stewart (USA)	Team Menard
1996	Buzz Calkins & Scott Sharp (USA)	Bradley Motorsports & A.J. Foyt Enterprises

ChampCar

Year	Champion	Rookie of the year
2007	Sébastien Bourdais (F)	Robert Doornbos (NL)
2006	Sébastien Bourdais (F)	Will Power (AUS)
2005	Sébastien Bourdais (F)	Timo Glock (D)
2004	Sébastien Bourdais (F)	A.J. Allmendinger (USA)
2003	Paul Tracy (CDN)	Sébastien Bourdais (F)
2002	Christiano da Matta (BR)	Mario Dominguez (MEX)
2001	Gil de Ferran (BR)	Scott Dixon (AUS)
2000	Gil de Ferran (BR)	Kenny Bräck (S)
1999	Juan Pablo Montoya (CO)	Juan Pablo Montoya (CO)
1998	Alex Zanardi (I)	Tony Kanaan (BR)
1997	Alex Zanardi (I)	Patrick Carpentier (CDN)
1996	Jimmy Vasser (USA)	Alex Zanardi (I)
1995	Jacques Villeneuve (CDN)	Gil de Ferran (BR)
1994	Al Unser jr. (USA)	Jacques Villeneuve (CDN)
1993	Nigel Mansell (GB)	Nigel Mansell (GB)
1992	Bobby Rahal (USA)	Stefan Johansson (S)
1991	Michael Andretti (USA)	Jeff Andretti (USA)
1990	Al Unser jr. (USA)	Eddie Cheever (USA)
1989	Emerson Fittipaldi (BR)	Bernard Jourdain (MEX)
1988	Danny Sullivan (USA)	John Jones (CDN)
1987	Bobby Rahal (USA)	Fabrizio Barbazza (I)
1986	Bobby Rahal (USA)	Chip Robinson (USA)
1985	Al Unser (USA)	Arie Luyendyk (NL)
1984	Mario Andretti (USA)	Roberto Guerrero (CO)
1983	Al Unser (USA)	Teo Fabi (I)
1982	Rick Mears (USA)	Bobby Rahal (USA)
1981	Rick Mears (USA)	Tony Bettenhausen jr. (USA)
1980	Johnny Rutherford (USA)	Dennis Firestone (USA)
1979	Rick Mears (USA)	

USAC National Championship

Year	Champion
1979	A.J. Foyt
1978	Tom Sneva
1977	Tom Sneva
1976	Gordon Johncock
1975	A.J. Foyt
1974	Bobby Unser
1973	Roger McCluskey
1972	Joe Leonard
1971	Joe Leonard
1970	Al Unser
1969	Mario Andretti
1968	Bobby Unser

USAC National Championship

Year	Champion
1967	A.J. Foyt
1966	Mario Andretti
1965	Mario Andretti
1964	A.J. Foyt
1963	A.J. Foyt
1962	Rodger Ward
1961	A.J. Foyt
1960	A.J. Foyt
1959	Rodger Ward
1958	Tony Bettenhausen
1957	Jimmy Bryan
1956	Jimmy Bryan

AAA National Championship

Year	Champion
1955	Bob Sweikert
1954	Jimmy Bryan
1953	Sam Hanks
1952	Chuck Stevenson
1951	Tony Bettenhausen
1950	Henry Banks
1949	Johnnie Parsons
1948	Ted Horn
1947	Ted Horn
1946	Ted Horn
1941	Rex Mays
1940	Rex Mays
1939	Wilbur Shaw
1938	Floyd Roberts
1937	Wilbur Shaw
1936	Mauri Rose
1935	Kelly Petillo
1934	Bill Cummings
1933	Louis Meyer
1932	Bob Carey
1931	Louis Schneider
1930	Billy Arnold
1929	Louis Meyer
1928	Louis Meyer
1927	Pete DePaolo
1926	Harry Hartz
1925	Pete DePaolo
1924	Jimmy Murphy
1923	Eddie Hearne
1922	Jimmy Murphy
1921	Tommy Milton
1920	Gaston Chevrolet (changed to Tommy Milton in 1951)
1916	Dario Resta (subsequently awarded)
1919	Howard Wilcox
1918	Ralph Mulford
1917	Earl Cooper
1915	Earl Cooper
1914	Ralph DePalma
1913	Earl Cooper
1912	Ralph DePalma
1911	Ralph Mulford
1910	Ray Harroun
1909	Bert Dingley (changed to George Robertson in 1951)
1908	Louis Strang
1907	Eddie Bald
1906	Joe Tracy
1905	Victor Hemery
1904	George Heath
1903	Barney Oldfield
1902	Harry Harkness

Electrifying racing action

___ On September 13, 2014, the world's first electric racing series celebrated its premiere. The site of the spectacle: the Olympic grounds in Beijing. And the names of the protagonists are promising indeed: Virgin Racing, e.dams Renault, Andretti, and ABT Schaeffler are just a few of the teams. Piquet, Prost, Senna, Heidfeld, Trulli, Sato, Buemi and di Grassi are just a few of the 36 drivers who will test their mettle in the new electric monoposti over the 2014/2015 season. Altogether the field has room for ten teams of two drivers each and – because drivers bring in a second car halfway through the race – a total of 40 cars. The logistics are handled by DHL, who guarantee environmentally friendly transport, storage between the races in a nearby logistics center as well as punctual delivery on the short racing weekend. Alejandro Agag, a charismatic businessman with a political background, an unmistakable affinity for motor racing and a nose for good opportunities, stories and communication, is the mastermind behind the world's first fully electric racing series. In FIA president Jean Todt, he finds an influential supporter in the early going.

It soon becomes clear that Formula E is extremely demanding from a driving perspective. Not so much in terms of the lateral-acceleration forces, however; the races, after all, are staged on tight urban circuits in which top speeds and cornering speeds are less prominent factors due to the course layout alone. And the identical aerodynamics for all cars, as well as the use of uniform, non-slick tires, on the "green," – that is, covered with ordinary road dust – circuits also counteract the effect. But the format calls for a good deal of brainpower, for energy management, measured panache when overtaking, and exceptional vehicle control with the vital recuperation function working only on the rear axle. The latter works like a brake and also recuperates kinetic energy. It's made possible by the electric drive unit mounted on the real axle.

In the first season, the electric drive unit – which is identical for all teams – is provided by McLaren and is identical to the one in the McLaren P1 super sports car. McLaren is also responsible for providing the power electronics. The 28 kWh-capacity batteries, by contrast, come

Formula E is drawing completely new fans to motor racing

from Williams Engineering – yet another illustrious partner in on the ground floor. The series standard chassis is manufactured by Dallara and goes by the designation Spark SRT_01E. Starting in season two, the teams have a free hand in the development of the drivetrain – electric motor and transmission – as well as the rear suspension. The new racing series is extremely popular with the carmakers and suppliers from the outset, and almost all teams field custom solutions. The most efficient drivetrains turn out to be the systems from Renault and ABT, which are built with the substantial support of Continental subsidiary Zytek (Renault) and Schaeffler, and Schaeffler subsidiary Compact Dynamics (ABT Schaeffler Audi Sport). Beyond the restrictively regulated logistics and relatively small team sizes on site, the step-by-step opening of the technological development fields practically guarantees the notably modest budgets in this global series – at least compared to Formula 1 and the LMP1 category in the WEC.

What this gradual opening means in concrete terms, for example, is that the available engine power is raised from 170 and 150 kW (in training and races) to 200 and 170, and then 200 and 180 kW (season four). In season five, the previous 28-kWh batteries are replaced by a 54-kWh unit. This obviates the need for a mid-race car-switch. And the recuperable energy also rises from 100 to 150 (season three), then 200 (season four) and finally 250 kW (season five).

Not only the proximity to the spectators in the urban centers around the world draws new fans, but also the wide-ranging communications via various social media channels and the FanBoost. This novel idea gives fans the chance to provide their favorite driver with additional engine power through an online voting process. The three most popular drivers in the vote get an extra boost of 100 kJ. It's often enough for an additional passing maneuver.

Season	Meister	Team	Car
2016/2017	Lucas di Grassi	ABT Schaeffler Audi Sport	ABT Schaeffler FE02
2015/2016	Sébastien Buemi	e.dams Renault	Renault Z.E. 15
2014/2015	Nelson Piquet jr	NEXTEV ETCR	Spark SRT_01E

➤ At the third attempt, the ABT-Schaeffler pilot Lucas di Grassi is crowned the Formula E champion of the 2016/2017 season. The ongoing duel between Sébastien Buemi and the Schaeffler contender makes its mark on Formula E right from the outset. In season four (upper left photo), Audi takes the lead. The racer's drivetrain still comes from Schaeffler.

The shine of silver

___ Curiosity to ascertain which nation builds the best automobile inspires James Gordon Bennett to organize a race the likes of which no one has ever seen before.

James Gordon Bennett grows up in France and lives in Paris. Beginning in the year 1866, he stands at the helm of the "New York Herald," a paper founded by his father and one of the large New York papers. Furthermore, he also founds another major media corporation from his base in Europe, the "International Herald Tribune." His life partner is Baroness von Reuter, daughter of the news agency founder Paul Reuter.

The media manager has a prescient sense of the appeal emanating from the recent invention, the automobile. Yet it is less a passion for the new form of mobility than a businessman's calculated venture that leads to the establishment of the Gordon Bennett Cup. The competition he initiates is the perfect way to draw spectators, gain readers and keep them on the line as the exclusive source of information about the contest. It is with the same idea in mind that Gordon Bennett has Henry Morton Stanley search for the marooned missionary and Africa explorer David Livingstone in 1869. Then there are the polo tournaments and aviation contests.

James Gordon Bennett is 59 years old when the first of six races ultimately staged in his name is held. The rules for the once-annual race state that the vehicle, vehicle parts and driver must hail from the same nation that enters the vehicle. For the Gordon Bennett Cup, the cars must also bear the colors designated for the various nations. This leads to the designation that persists in Grand Prix racing as well, until advertising sponsors join the fray. The dark green color known as British Racing Green is actually thanks to the Irish, however, notwithstanding the name. Because, with the victory of British driver Selwyn Francis Edge

in 1902, the right to host the next year's race goes to the United Kingdom. The British view of cars at the time, however, is decidedly skeptical, and hosting a race on public roads is out of the question. The organizing automobile club therefore shifts the event to Ireland, and as a sign of gratitude – so goes the legend, in any case – all British race cars thereafter are painted in the dark color.

One typical nuisance at the time is the dust kicked up on unpaved roads. Organizers attempt to get the situation under control by a variety of means. For a race held in the Taunus range in Germany, the dust binding agent invented by the German Westrum von Schade is used. It goes by the name Westrumit and consists of a 5% admixture of petroleum and ammonia in water. The idea is to spread the agent evenly across the gravel of the 140-kilometer circuit. The coachmen hired to do the job are enticed to carry out the night work with whiskey. However, a series of barrels dumped in ditches bear testament to the short-lived motivational properties of the tipple.

Incomparably shinier than the dusty track is the prize for the winner of the race for the Gordon Bennett Cup: The winner's trophy weighs 17 kilograms, consists of pure silver and has a value of 20,000 francs. It is, however, a challenge cup.

In 1906, the Grand Prix, organized by the automobile club of France and originally staged once annually as well, follows in the footsteps of the Gordon Bennett Cup. As a member of the ACF, James Gordon Bennett is one of the co-founders of the races which would be carried on in the tradition of his cup. ___

Year	Winner	Car	Route, distance
1905	Léon Théry (F)	Richard-Brasier 96 HP	Circuit d'Auvergne, 548 km
1904	Léon Théry (F)	Richard-Brasier 80 HP	Taunus-Ring, 512 km
1903	Camille Jenatzy (B)	Mercedes 60 HP	Circuit near Athy (Northern Ireland), 527 km
1902	Selwyn Francis Edge (GB)	Napier 40 HP	Paris–Innsbruck, 565 km
1901	Leonce Girardot (F)	Panhard et Levassor 40 HP	Paris–Bordeaux, 527 km
1900	Fernand Charron (F)	Panhard et Levassor 24 HP	Paris–Lyon, 562 km

Leading the pack in America

___ Like James Gordon Bennett Jr., the initiator of the Gordon Bennett Cup, William Kassam Vanderbilt II enjoys a degree of financial comfort that enables him to while away the days indulging his interests in automobiles and yachts. The young Vanderbilt owes his independence to his grandfather Cornelius, the "Railroad King" who embodies an era of burgeoning prosperity and goes down in American history.

"Willie K." Vanderbilt tries his hand as a racing and record-setting driver. He wins a few races and in January 1904 wrests the land speed record from Henry Ford behind the wheel of a Mercedes 90 HP. He reaches the speed of 147.5 km/h. The year before he takes part in the road race from Paris to Madrid and recognizes the advertising impact of these events, which he then aims to establish in America as well.

The Vanderbilt family hails from New York. Long Island, to be precise. This is also the location at which a number of race car drivers from the old and new worlds gather in October 1904. William Vanderbilt is offering a silver cup fashioned by the New Yorker jeweler Tiffany and a stately prize sum. This coup enables Vanderbilt to bring the motor racing passion so present in Europe across the Atlantic to the New World. He thereby unleashes a passion that spreads rapidly stateside as well.

Organizationally, the American Automobile Association (AAA), later the Automobile Club of America (ACA), is on hand to assist and will later pro-

Motorsport in this era is mainly a pastime of the rich

mote open-wheel racing, which in turn will receive a vigorous counterpart from the country's south, with the stock car-focused NASCAR organization. With regard to regulations, the Vanderbilt Cup (from 1909) diverges from the Grand Prix rules and develops toward the technical specs that will come to apply for Indy cars. Starting in 1911, the race for the Vanderbilt Cup is held in conjunction with the American Grand Prix. After the outbreak of the First World War in Europe, the Vanderbilt Cup race is held a further two times. While at home motor racing is an unthinkable frivolity, Peugeot is victorious far from France on the American west coast. Only with the entry of the Americans into WWI in 1917, the history of this race goes into hiatus.

Twenty long years will pass before the race – now organized by nephew George Washington Vanderbilt III – is revived and held once again at Roosevelt Field on Long Island. But there are only two more stagings of the race, which are won by Nuvolari in an Alfa Romeo and Rosemeyer in an Auto Union. At this point, the Americans don't quite manage to demonstrate their competitiveness versus the cars from the Old World. Rather, the Europeans make good use of the event to advertise the merits of their products. The upshot is that American develops its own identity, which after the war leads to the incompatibility between the European Grand Prix cars and American Indy cars. ___

Year	Drivers' champion	Car	Event (place)
1937	Bernd Rosemeyer (D)	Auto Union Porsche Typ C	Vanderbilt Cup (Long Island)
1936	Tazio Nuvolari (I)	Alfa Romeo 12C	Vanderbilt Cup (Long Island)
1916	Dario Resta (I)	Peugeot EX5	Vanderbilt Cup (Santa Monica)
1915	Dario Resta (I)	Peugeot	Vanderbilt Cup (San Francisco)
1914	Ralph de Palma (USA)	Mercedes	Vanderbilt Cup (Santa Monica)
1912	Ralph de Palma (USA)	Mercedes	Vanderbilt Cup (Milwaukee)
1911	Ralph Mulford (USA)	Lozier	Vanderbilt Cup (Savannah)
1910	Harry Grant (USA)	Alco	Vanderbilt Cup (Long Island)
1909	Harry Grant (USA)	Alco	Vanderbilt Cup (Long Island)
1908	George Robertson (USA)	Locomobile 90HP "Old 16"	Vanderbilt Cup (Long island
1906	Louis Wagner (F)	Darracq 120HP	Vanderbilt Cup (Long Island)
1905	Victor Héméry (F)	Darracq 80HP	Vanderbilt Cup (Long Island)
1904	George Heath (USA)	Panhard 70HP	Vanderbilt Cup (Long Island)
1916	Howdy Wilcox (USA)	Peugeot EX5	American Grand Prix (Santa Monica)
1915	Dario Resta (I)	Peugeot EX3	American Grand Prix (Santa Monica)
1914	Eddie Pullen (USA)	Mercer	American Grand Prix (Santa Monica)
1912	Celeb Bragg (USA)	Fiat S.61 Corsa	American Grand Prix (Milwaukee)
1911	David Bruce-Brown (USA)	Fiat S.74 Corsa	American Grand Prix (Savannah)
1910	David Bruce-Brown (USA)	Benz	American Grand Prix (Savannah)
1908	Louis Wagner (F)	Fiat 100HP Corsa	American Grand Prix (Savannah)

Formulas for success

___ The first Grand Prix in the history of motorsports is staged at Le Mans in 1906. Held annually thereafter, the over 500-kilometer races follow in the footsteps of the competitions around the Gordon Bennett Cup. The race takes a hiatus for economic reasons between 1909 and 1911 before the First World War puts an end to the race staged by the French automobile club ACF. After the war, there is a series of events held under the banner of the Grand Prix designation, but none of them can match the exclusivity and class of the annual test of prowess among the best representatives from many nations that is held at Le Mans. In terms of technology, every edition of the GP has a new set of regulations. The rules start with a maximum weight formula (1,000 kilograms plus seven kilos for ignition magnetos). It is replaced in 1907 by a consumption formula (a maximum of 30 liters per 100 kilometers) and in 1908 makes way for the Ostende formula (1,100 kg minimum weight without operating materials, tools and tires; the bore for four-cylinders cannot exceed 155 mm; for vehicles with more cylinders, the same overall piston surface is prescribed). In 1912, only the vehicle width of no more than 1.75 meters is prescribed. For the following year, the weight window is between 800 and 1,100 kilograms, fuel consumption is limited to a maximum of 20 liters per 100 km and streamlined tails are prohibited. For 1914, the use of compressors is prohibited for the engines, which are themselves limited to 4.5 liters. The cars can weigh no more than 1.1 metric tons.

With the formation of a series of various GP races, which between 1925 and 1927 carries the World Championship title to boot, the Grand Prix designation regains its original luster. The regulations for the 1925 season are taken from the year 1922. Two seats, two liters of displacement and at least 650 kilograms are the salient figures. The minimum width of the body is set at 80 centimeters. To limit the inexorable advance

Ever-changing rules attempt to tame the top tier

of engine power, the displacement is restricted to 1.5 liters for the following two years, the weight initially lowered to 600 kg, but raised again to 700 kilograms for the 1927 campaign.

With the end of the World Championship, weight prescriptions (between 550 and 750 kg, and at least 900 kg from 1929) once again replace the displacement rules. The short-lived era of the Formula Libre or free formula begins in 1931. In 1934, the 750-kilogram formula ushers in a new and attractive chapter in the history of motor racing. From now on, it is primarily the Silver Arrows from Mercedes Benz and the Auto Unions that vie for victory with the red racers of Alfa Romeo. For four years the rules specify the minimum dry weight (without operating materials and tires), minimum body width (85 cm) and race length (at least 500 km). Starting in 1935, selected Grand Prix are combined to create a European Championship.

For the 1938 and 1939 campaigns a new formula comes into effect: Now the rules allow for three liters of displacement with a compressor, or 4.5 liters without a supercharger. The minimum weight in this era of lightweight construction lies – depending on the combustion chamber volume – between 400 and 850 kilograms. Alongside the silver speedsters from southern and eastern Germany, supercharged 1.5-liter race cars emerge under the Voiturette regulations. A non-factor on the Grand Prix scene before the war, once hostilities cease and racing operations resume, these 1.5-liter supercharged race cars form the technological backbone of Formula 1 as introduced in 1947 and the history of the Formula 1 World Championship that begins in 1950. ___

Year	Drivers' champion	Car	Championship
1939	Hermann Lang (D)	Mercedes-Benz W163	Grand Prix, European Championship
1938	Rudolf Caracciola (D)	Mercedes-Benz W154	Grand Prix, European Championship
1937	Rudolf Caracciola (D)	Mercedes-Benz W125	Grand Prix, European Championship
1936	Bernd Rosemeyer (D)	Auto Union Porsche Typ C	Grand Prix, European Championship
1935	Rudolf Caracciola (D)	Mercedes-Benz W25B	Grand Prix, European Championship
1927	(Robert Benoist (F))	Delage* (15-S-8)	Grand Prix, World Championship
1926	(Jules Goux (F))	Bugatti* (T35 & T39A)	Grand Prix, World Championship
1925	(Gastone Brilli-Peri (I))	Alfa Romeo* (P2)	Grand Prix, World Championship
	* The World Championship title is awarded exclusively to the manufacturer		
1914	Christian Lautenschlager	Mercedes Grand-Prix	GP ACF Lyon
1913	Georges Boillot	Peugeot EX5	GP ACF Amiens
1912	Georges Boillot	Peugeot S76	GP ACF Dieppe
1908	Christian Lautenschlager	Mercedes	GP ACF Dieppe
1907	Felice Nazzaro	Fiat 130 HP	GP ACF Dieppe
1906	François Szisz	Renault AK 90 CV	GP ACF Le Mans

The legendary thousand miles

___ The Mille Miglia is the dinosaur among the open-road races. While the race from Brescia to Rome and back cannot boast of quite so long a tradition as the Targa Florio, the Mille Miglia remains a brand name to this day, and its popularity unbroken.

The race is held 24 times between 1927 and 1957 before Alfonso de Portago suffers a fatal crash after a tire blowout on a straight section of country road between Mantova and the finish line in Brescia in 1957 – also killing his co-driver Edmund Nelson and ten spectators. From the very beginning, the Po Valley is regarded as a merciless stretch; its long, flat straightaways allow the muscular race cars to attain exceptionally high speeds. After the mountainous passages in the Apennines, the roads of the Po Valley are taken at top speeds around the 300 km/h barrier. It would otherwise scarcely be possible to achieve the average speeds of well over 150 km/h – on public roads of varying quality, no less.

The tragic accident marks the end of the legendary road race. As early as 1938, the future of the event is already up in the air. Bologna is the site of an accident in which a Lancia Aprilia careers out of control at a multi-track railway crossing and runs into the surrounding spectators. Here, too, there are ten fatalities and 23 injured all told. In response, the government bans all race events held on public roads – a move that also affects the Targa Florio, which this year is staged solely as a regularity rally for series production compact cars. In 1940, the "Mille" makes its way back into the racing calendar by way of a detour as the "Gran Premio

di Brescia." The last staging before the war is held on a nine-lap circuit from Brescia via Cremona and Castellucchio back to Brescia.

From 1927 to 1947, the history of this Italian festival for motorsport Tifosi – and who isn't one in Italy – is written by Alfa Romeo. The Milan-based brand dominates the race 11 times. The victors included Carlo Pintacuda, Achille Varzi, Mario Umberto Borzacchini, Giuseppe Campari and Tazio Nuvolari – the last of which, by the way, is the first to post an average speed of over 100 km/h, on unpaved roads, in his Alfa Romeo 6C 1750 in 1930. When Alfa Romeo race director Enzo Ferrari founds his own brand in the late 1940s, the man from Modena dedicates the lion's share of his attention to the "Mille" in addition to Formula 1. Ferrari now takes overall victory eight times, followed by the series-like Alfa Romeos that are still dominating various displacement classes.

Since 1977, the Mille Miglia is staged as a historical motorsport event and regularity rally. Its one-of-a-kind mix of sports cars from four decades of motor racing history make it now the largest rolling museum worldwide. Theoretically, participation is limited to the models that once took place in the 1,000-mile chase. So it's a pity, really, when PR strategists from other automobile brands attempt to finagle misplaced brands and cars into the field in exchange for lucre with a sort of nouveau-riche and historically oblivious air. ___

Year	Winner	Car	Race duration, distance
1957	Pierro Taruffi (I)	Ferrari 315 S	10.27'47/998 mls
1956	Eugenio Castelotti (I)	Ferrari 290 MM	11.37'10/998 mls
1955	Stirling Moss (GB)/Denis Jenkinson (GB)	Mercedes-Benz 300 SLR	10.07'48/998 mls
1954	Alberto Ascari (I)	Lancia D24	11.26'10/998 mls
1953	Giannino Marzotto (I)/Marco Crosara (I)	Ferrari 340 MM	10.37'19/945 mls
1952	Giovanni Bracco (I)/Alfonso Rolfo (I)	Ferrari 250 S	12.09'45/978 mls
1951	Luigi Villoresi (I)/Piero Cassani (I)	Ferrari 340 America	12.50'18/978 mls
1950	Giannino Marzotto (I)/Marco Crosara (I)	Ferrari 195 S	13.39'20/1.022 mls
1949	Clemente Biondetti (I)/Ettore Salani (I)	Ferrari 166 MM	12.07'05/996 mls
1948	Clemente Biondetti (I)/Giuseppe Navone (I)	Ferrari 166 S	15.05'44/1.137 mls
1947	Clemente Biondetti (I)/Emilio Romano (I)	Alfa Romeo 8C 2900 B	16.16'39/1.137 mls
1940	Fritz Huschke von Hanstein (D)/Walter Bäumer (D)	BMW 328	8.54'54/9x103 mls
1938	Clemente Biondetti (I)/Aldo Stefani (I)	Alfa Romeo 8C 2900 B	11.58'29/1.013 mls
1937	Carlo Pintacuda (I)/Paride Mambelli (I)	Alfa Romeo 8C 2900 A	14.17'32/1.009 mls
1936	Antonio Brivio (I)/Carlo Ongaro (I)	Alfa Romeo 8C 2900 A	13.07'51/998 mls
1935	Carlo Pintacuda (I)/Alessandro della Stufa (I)	Alfa Romeo 8C 2900 B	14.04'47/1.009 mls
1934	Achille Varzi (I)/Antonio Bignami (I)	Alfa Romeo 8C 2600	14.08'05/1.009 mls
1933	Tazio Nuvolari (I)/Decimo Compagnoni (I)	Alfa Romeo 8C 2300	15.11'50/1.022 mls
1932	Mario Umberto Borzacchini (I)/Antonio Bignami (I)	Alfa Romeo 8C 2300	14.55'19/1.022 mls
1931	Rudolf Caracciola (D)/Wilhelm Sebastian (D)	Mercedes-Benz SSKL	16.10'10/1.022 mls
1930	Tazio Nuvolari (I)/Giovanni Battista Guidotti (I)	Alfa Romeo 6C 1750	16.18'59/1.018 mls
1929	Giuseppe Campari (I)/Giulio Ramponi (I)	Alfa Romeo 6C 1750	18.04'25/1.018 mls
1928	Giuseppe Campari (I)/Giulio Ramponi (I)	Alfa Romeo 6C 1500	19.14'05/1.018 mls
1927	Ferdinando Minoia (I)/Giuseppe Morandi (I)	OM 665	21.04'48/1.018 mls

An island with a roller-coaster

___ "Children and dogs," announce large signs, "must be kept away from the road." From 1906 to 1973, or ultimately 1977, the Sicilians along the Madonie circuit live especially dangerously. For seven decades the Sicilians have the chance to experience international racing stars and their racing machines up close.

The idea for the race can be traced back to Vincenzo Florio at the beginning of the twentieth century. The automobile enthusiast and son of a Sicilian shipowner, merchant and major land holder wants to enhance the profile of the southern Italian island, stimulate tourism and increase the traffic on the family shipping line.

Florio creates the world's first circuit race. The circuit is situated in the thinly populated region to the east of Palermo. After initial circuit variants of 148 and 108 kilometers, from 1951 onwards the circuit stretches for 72 kilometers and includes over 800 corners between Cerda near the coastline and up to Caltavuturo in the mountains, before heading back down to the Tyrrhenian Sea. The former "Grande Madonie" becomes the "Piccola Madonie," though it, too, is driven in a counterclockwise direction. The circuit is still characterized by the driving challenges posed by the demanding switches between high-speed sections, tight switchbacks and difficult-to-read corner passages. The Buonfornello straightaway that runs parallel to the coast, incidentally, is over six kilometers in length and thus even longer than the Mulsanne Straight, which at the time is uninterrupted by chicanes. Overtaking maneuvers on the narrow course are difficult; a mass start on the winding circuit is unthinkable. So, the cars start staggered at 20-second intervals. The prize awaiting the victor is a challenge cup that – as at Le Mans –

The Targa Florio becomes one of the biggest race events worldwide

is permanently awarded in the event of a third consecutive win, a feat accomplished at the "Targa" by Bugatti, Alfa Romeo, Maserati, and Porsche.

The first contests take place on unpaved trails. This gives rise to races like the one in 1911, which sees the cars sink into the mud following rainy weather, and no small number of the participants throw in the towel long before they've spotted the finish line after nearly 450 kilometers. It is a typical race distance for the time. In the early days, the Targa Florio runs to some 500 kilometers, and in the late 1940s and early 1950s it extends to a stately 1,080 kilometers. With the final course layout, the races cover five, ten or eleven laps at 72 kilometers a pop. After the 1973 running, the living legend of the "Targa" loses its World Championship status, though the race itself does not lose its attractiveness for participants, who populate a field of up to 80 cars in the race's golden age.

While the cities are soon too tight to warrant further inclusion in racing scenarios, and the Mille Miglia meets its demise due to accidents in the mid-1950s, the "Targa" survives thanks to its geographic, and demographic, characteristics. In the Madonie, the circuit passes through only a few sections of village roads, which are heavily signposted with warnings well before the race arrives. By the late 1970s, however, the days of open-road racing are numbered – even in Sicily. The sleek Group 6 race cars are far from suitable for the uneven, narrow trails in the Madonie. The number of victims lost due to the lack of run-off areas is, thankfully, substantially lower than in the Mille Miglia. But the development of modern race cars and circuits cannot be halted. ___

Year	Winner	Car	Average speed
1977*	Alfonso Merendino (I)/Franco Restivo (I)	Chevron B 36-BMW	107,14 km/h
1976*	Eugenio Renna (I)/Armando Floridia (I)	Osella PA 4-BMW	99,09 km/h
1975*	Arturo Merzario (I)/Nino Vaccarella (I)	Alfa Romeo 33TT12	115,46 km/h
1974*	Amilcare Ballestrieri (I)/Gérard Larrousse (F)	Lancia Stratos	109,95 km/h
1973	Hermann Müller (CH)/Gijs van Lennep (NL)	Porsche 911 Carrera RSR	114,69 km/h
1972	Arturo Merzario (I)/Sandro Munari (I)	Ferrari 312 P	122,54 km/h
1971	Nino Vaccarella (I)/Toine Hezemans (NL)	Alfa Romeo 33/3	120,07 km/h
1970	Jo Siffert (CH)/Brian Redman (GB)	Porsche 908/3	120.15 km/h
1969	Gerhard Mitter (D)/Udo Schütz (D)	Porsche 908/2	117,44 km/h
1968	Vic Elford (GB)/Ugo Maglioli (I)	Porsche 907/8	111,09 km/h
1967	Paul Hawkins (AUS)/Rolf Stommelen (D)	Porsche 910/8	108,78 km/h
1966	Willy Mairesse (B)/Hermann Müller (CH)	Porsche 906 (Carrera 6)	98,96 km/h
1965	Nino Vaccarella (I)/Lorenzo Bandini (I)	Ferrari 275 P2	102,56 km/h
1964	Colin Davis (GB)/Antonio Pucci (I)	Porsche 904 GTS	100,26 km/h
1963	Joakim Bonnier (S)/Carlo Mario Abate (I)	Porsche 718 RS61	103,89 km/h
1962	Willy Mairesse (B)/Pedro Rodríguez (MEX)/Olivier Gendebien (F)	Ferrari Dino 246 SP	102,14 km/h
1961	Wolfgang von Trips (D)/Olivier Gendebien (F)	Ferrari Dino 246 SP	103,43 km/h
1960	Joakim Bonnier (S)/Hans Herrmann (D)	Porsche 718 RS60	95,32 km/h
1959	Edgar Barth (D)/Wolfgang Seidel (D)	Porsche 718 RSK	91,29 km/h
1958	Luigi Musso (I)/Olivier Gendebien (F)	Ferrari 250 TR	94,79 km/h
1956	Ugo Maglioli (I)/Fritz Huschke von Hanstein (D)	Porsche 550 A	90,97 km/h
1955	Stirling Moss (GB)/Peter Collins (GB)	Mercedes-Benz 300 SLR	96,29 km/h
1954	Piero Taruffi (I)	Lancia D24	89,96 km/h
1953	Ugo Maglioli (I)	Lancia D20	80,64 km/h
1952	Felice Bonetto (I)	Lancia Aurelia B20 Competizione	80,02 km/h
1951	Franco Cortese (I)	Frazer-Nash Le Mans-BMW	76,62 km/h
1950	Franco Bornigia (I)/Mario Bornigia (I)	Alfa Romeo 6C 2500 Competizione	86,80 km/h
1949	Clemente Biondetti (I)/Aldo Benedetti (I)	Ferrari 166 MM	81,49 km/h
1948	Clemente Biondetti (I)/Igor Troubetskoy (I)	Ferrari 166 S	88,76 km/h
1940	Luigi Villoresi (I)	Maserati 4CL	142,29 km/h
1939	Luigi Villoresi (I)	Maserati 6CM	136,45 km/h
1938	Giovanni Rocco (I)	Maserati 6CM	114,30 km/h
1937	Francesco Severi (I)	Maserati 6CM	107,70 km/h
1936	Costantino Magistri (I)	Lancia Augusta	67,08 km/h
1935	Antonio Brivio (I)	Alfa Romeo Tipo B (P3)	79,15 km/h
1934	Achille Varzi (I)	Alfa Romeo Tipo B (P3)	69,22 km/h
1933	Antonio Brivio (I)	Alfa Romeo 8C 2300 Monza	76,52 km/h
1932	Tazio Nuvolari (I)	Alfa Romeo 8C 2300 Monza	79,28 km/h
1931	Tazio Nuvolari (I)	Alfa Romeo 8C 2300	64,83 km/h
1930	Achille Varzi (I)	Alfa Romeo P2-1930	78,00 km/h
1929	Albert Divo (F)	Bugatti T35	74,35 km/h
1928	Albert Divo (F)	Bugatti T35	73,45 km/h
1927	Emilio Materassi (I)	Bugatti T35	71,06 km/h
1926	Meo Constantini (I)	Bugatti T35	73,51 km/h
1925	Meo Constantini (I)	Bugatti T35	71,61 km/h
1924	Christian Werner (D)	Mercedes Indy	66,00 km/h
1923	Ugo Sivocci (I)	Alfa Romeo RL	59,17 km/h
1922	Giulio Masetti (I)	Mercedes Grand Prix 1914	63,09 km/h
1921	Giulio Masetti (I)	Fiat S.57/14 B	58,23 km/h
1920	Guido Meregalli (I)	Nazarro Grand Prix	51,08 km/h
1919	André Boilliot (F)	Peugeot L25	55,03 km/h
1914	Ernesto Ceirano (I)	Scat 22/32 HP/4,4	58,07 km/h
1913	Felice Nazzaro (I)	Nazzaro 4,4	50,69 km/h
1912	Cyril Snipe (I)/Pedrini (I)	Scat 25/35 HP/4,7	41,44 km/h
1911	Ernesto Ceirano (I)	Scat 22/32 HP/4,4	46,80 km/h
1910	Franco Tullio Cariolato (I)	Franco 35/50 HP/4,9	47,27 km/h
1909	Francesco Ciuppa (I)	SPA 28/40 HP/7,8	54,37 km/h
1908	Vincenzo Trucco (I)	Isotta-Fraschini50 HP/8,0	57,06 km/h
1907	Felice Nazzaro (I)	Fiat 28/40 HP/7,4	53,83 km/h
1906	Alessandro Cagno (I)	Itala 35/40 HP/8,0	46,80 km/h

*Without World Championship status from 1974

➤ View of the cockpit of the Le Mans-winning car of 1971, the Porsche 917 of Marko/ van Lennep.

Twice around the clock

___ The Circuit de la Sarthe first gains world fame in 1906. It becomes the site of the first Grand Prix and thus the cradle of a Grand Prix tradition that, thanks to Formula 1, is still popular around the world today. The race run back then, staged outside the gates of Le Mans, covers 1,238 kilometers. The winner needs just over 12 hours for the feat. Today home to some 140,000 inhabitants, the name of the small city becomes legendary in 1923 with the holding of the 24-hour race, which from then on is staged (with a few exceptions) every year, providing the classic backdrop for demonstrations of automotive reliability and power.

The length of circuit, which even today includes some stretches of public rural roads, changes from over 103 kilometers (1906) to 17.25 (1923–1928) and 16.3 (1929–1931) kilometers. Starting in 1932, the course shifts to the outskirts of Le Mans and shortens to the length it still has today, at just over 13 kilometers. The old sand walls, which in the 1960s slow cars careering off the course (leading to a good deal of time-wasting shoveling thereafter), and the chicane-less Mulsanne Straight, on which the World Champ Peugeot reaches a top speed of 405 km/h in 1988, are history. Since 1990, two chicanes cap the top speeds on the famous straightaway that formerly stretched for almost six kilometers. The traditional pit lane, formerly located directly at the road's edge, is replaced in time for the 1991 race with a more modern configuration that combines the pits, the race directors, press center, VIP lounges, and grandstand, and serves as the center of what is still the greatest of all 24-hour races.

The race experiences ups and downs, but always remains a legend

While the race is initially reserved for four-seater touring cars, by the late 1930s Gran Turismo, sports cars and prototypes are all vying for overall victory and class wins. Le Mans thus becomes a Mecca for the sports car scene and the products from the likes of Jaguar, Ferrari and Porsche and Le Mans make and burnish their sports car reputations right here. Bentley and Alfa Romeo, too, lay the foundation for their status as sports car makers with success at Le Mans. With a recent win in the modern age, Bentley even manages to pick up where the "Bentley Boys" of old left off, and Audi demonstrates that brand images can be built in the here and now, and not just in the distant past: With 13 victories, the Ingolstadt-based company has already bested the number of triumphs posted by Alfa Romeo, Ford and Bentley and has even knocked Ferrari off the second step of the podium. Only the 19 overall victories by Porsche seem certain to go unchallenged for the immediate future.

Technically interesting events include the first win by a diesel by the Audi R10 TDI with Biela, Pirro, and Werner behind the wheel in 2006 and a win by a car with a rotary engine, whilst, in 1991, Gachot, Herbert, and Weidler win in their Wankel-powered Mazda. Le Mans experiences further innovations with gas turbines and hybrid drives. The gas turbine-outfitted BRM Rovers fielded by the carmaker in the 1960s (1963 and 1965) actually reach the finish line and garner the accolades accorded to such a feat – not least after Graham Hill and Richie Ginther take the prize in the consumption category. The car is, however, from the outset by no means a contender for overall victory. In 1965, Graham Hill and Jackie Stewart start in the two-liter class and finish in tenth place. In 1998, a hybrid Panoz Esperante GTR-1 going by the designation Q9 and equipped with a hybrid drive fails to qualify by a mere ten seconds. With the LMP1 hybrid sports cars from Audi, Porsche and Toyota, motor racing experiences its moment of greatest technological sophistication. The sleek, 1,000-hp all-wheel-drive rockets show how a sporting contest and rivalry between engineers can yield significant developments in terms of efficiency. In 2015, the average speed in qualifying, on a course comprised primarily of sections of public roads, tops 250 km/h. And the competitiveness at the top of the field means that an average speed just minimally below that figure is achieved for the whole 24-hour race. One dispiriting incident occurs in 2016, when Toyota relinquishes its all-but-certain victory to Porsche not five minutes before the finish line.

Year	Winner 24 hours of Le Mans	Car	Distance
2017	Timo Bernhard/Nick Tandy/Brendon Hartley	Porsche 919 hybrid	5.001,990 km
2016	Neel Jani/Romain Dumas/Marc Lieb	Porsche 919 hybrid	5.233,536 km
2015	Nico Hülkenberg/Nick Tandy/Earl Bamber	Porsche 919 hybrid	5.382,820 km
2014	André Lotterer/Benoit Tréluyer/Marcel Fässler	Audi R18 e-tron quattro	5.165,391 km
2013	Tom Kristensen/Allan McNish/Loic Duval	Audi R18 e-tron quattro	4.742,892 km
2012	André Lotterer/Benoit Tréluyer/Marcel Fässler	Audi R18 e-tron quattro	5.151,800 km
2011	André Lotterer/Benoit Tréluyer/Marcel Fässler	Audi R18	4.838,295 km
2010	Timo Bernhard/Romain Dumas/Mike Rockenfeller	Audi R15 TDI Plus	5.410,73 km
2009	David Brabham/Marc Gené/Alexander Wurz	Peugeot 908 HDI FAP	5.206,27 km
2008	Rinaldo Capello/Allan McNish/Tom Kristensen	Audi R10 TDI	5.192,65 km
2007	Frank Biela/Emanuele Pirro/Marco Werner	Audi R10 TDI	5.029,10 km
2006	Frank Biela/Emanuele Pirro/Marco Werner	Audi R10 TDI	5.179,02 km
2005	Tom Kristensen/Marco Werner/JJ Lehto	Audi R8	5.050,50 km
2004	Seiji Ara/Rinaldo Capello/Tom Kristensen	Audi R8	5.169,97 km
2003	Rinaldo Capello/Tom Kristensen/Guy Smith	Bentley EXP Speed 8 GT	5.145,40 km
2002	Emanuele Pierro/Frank Biela/Tom Kristensen	Audi R8	5.118,75 km
2001	Emanuele Pierro/Frank Biela/Tom Kristensen	Audi R8	4.367,20 km
2000	Emanuele Pierro/Frank Biela/Tom Kristensen	Audi R8	5.007,99 km
1999	Pierluigi Martini/Yannick Dalmas/Joachim Winkelhock	BMW V12 LMR	4.967,99 km
1998	Alan McNish/Stéphane Ortelli/Laurence Aiello	Porsche 911 GT1 98	4.775,33 km
1997	Michele Alboreto/Stefan Johansson/Tom Kristensen	TWR-Joest Porsche WSC	4.909,60 km
1996	Manuel Reuter/Davy Jones/Alexander Wurz	TWR-Joest Porsche WSC	4.814,40 km
1995	Yannick Dalmas/JJ Lehto/Masanori Sekiya	McLaren-BMW F1 GTR	4.055,80 km
1994	Yannick Dalmas/Hurley Haywood/Mauro Baldi	Dauer 962 LM Porsche	4.685,70 km
1993	Geoff Brabham/Christoph Bouchut/Eric Hélary	Peugeot 905 Evo 1C	5.100,00 km
1992	Derek Warwick/Yannick Dalmas/Marc Blundell	Peugeot 905 Evo 1 LM	4.787,20 km
1991	Bertrand Gachot/Johnny Herbert/Volker Weidler	Mazda 787 B	4.922,81 km
1990	Martin Brundle/John Nielsen/Price Cobb	Jaguar XJR 12	4.882,40 km
1989	Jochen Mass/Stanley Dickens/Manuel Reuter	Sauber C9/88-Mercedes	5.265,11 km
1988	Jan Lammers/Johnnie Dumfries/Andy Wallace	Jaguar XJR 9 LM	5.319,96 km
1987	Derek Bell/Hans-Joachim Stuck/Al Holbert	Porsche 962C	4.791,77 km
1986	Derek Bell/Hans-Joachim Stuck/Al Holbert	Porsche 962C	4.972,73 km
1985	Klaus Ludwig/Paolo Barilla/John Winter	Porsche 956	5.088,50 km
1984	Henri Pescarolo/Klaus Ludwig	Porsche 956	4.900,27 km
1983	Al Holbert/Hurley Haywood/Vern Schuppan	Porsche 956	5.047,93 km
1982	Jacky Ickx/Derek Bell	Porsche 956	4.899,08 km
1981	Jacky Ickx/Derek Bell	Porsche 936/81	4.825,34 km
1980	Jean Rondeau/Jean-Pierre Jaussaud	Rondeau-Cosworth M 379B	4.608,02 km
1979	Klaus Ludwig/Don Whittington/Bill Whittington	Porsche 935 K3	4.173,93 km
1978	Didier Pironi/Jean-Piere Jaussaud	Renault 369-Alpine A 442B	5.044,53 km
1977	Jürgen Barth/Hurley Haywood/Jacky Ickx	Porsche 936	4.671,63 km
1976	Jacky Ickx/Gijs van Lennep	Porsche 936	4.769,92 km
1975	Jacky Ickx/Derek Bell	Gulf-Mirage-Ford GR8	4.595,57 km

Year	Winner 24 hours of Le Mans	Car	Distance
1974	Henri Pescarolo/Gérard Larrousse	Matra-Simca MS 670B	4.606,57 km
1973	Henri Pescarolo/Gérard Larrousse	Matra-Simca MS 670B	4.853,94 km
1972	Henri Pescarolo/Graham Hill	Matra-Simca MS 670	4.691,34 km
1971	Helmut Marko/Gijs van Lennep	Porsche 917 K	5.335,31 km
1970	Richard Attwood/Hans Herrmann	Porsche 917 K	4.607,81 km
1969	Jacky Ickx/Jackie Oliver	Ford GT40	4.998,00 km
1968	Pedro Rodriguez/Lucien Bianchi	Ford GT40	4.452,88 km
1967	Dan Gurney/Antony Joseph Foyt	Ford GT40 Mk IV	5.232,90 km
1966	Chris Amon/Bruce McLaren	Ford GT40 Mk II	4.843,09 km
1965	Masten Gregory/Jochen Rindt	Ferrari 275 LM	4.677,11 km
1964	Nino Vaccarella/Jean Guichet	Ferrari 275 P	4.695,31 km
1963	Ludovico Scarfiotti/Lorenzo Bandini	Ferrari 250 P	4.561,71 km
1962	Olivier Gendebien/Phil Hill	Ferrari 330 LM TRI	4.451,25 km
1961	Olivier Gendebien/Phil Hill	Ferrari 250 TR 61	4.476,58 km
1960	Olivier Gendebien/Paul Frére	Ferrari 250 TR 59/60	4.217,52 km
1959	Roy Salvadori/Carroll Shelby	Aston Martin DBR1	4.347,90 km
1958	Olivier Gendebien/Phil Hill	Ferrari 250 TR	4.101,92 km
1957	Ivor Bueb/Ron Flockhart	Jaguar D-Type	4.397,10 km
1956	Ninian Sanderson/Ron Flockhart	Jaguar D-Type	4.034,92 km
1955	Mike Hawthorn/Ivor Bueb	Jaguar D-Type	4.135,38 km
1954	Maurice Trintignant/José Froilan Gonzales	Ferrari 375 Plus	4.061,15 km
1953	Tony Rolt/Duncan Hamilton	Jaguar XK 120 C-Type	4.088,06 km
1952	Hermann Lang/Fritz Riess	Mercedes-Benz 300 SI	3.733,80 km
1951	Peter Walker/Peter Whitehead	Jaguar XK 120 C-Type	3.611,19 km
1950	Louis Rosier/Jean-Louis Rosier	Talbot Lago T266-GS	3.465,12 km
1949	Luigi Chinetti/Lord Selsdon (Peter Mitchell-Thompson)	Ferrari 166 MM	3.178,27 km
1939	Jean-Pierre Wimille/Pierre Veyron	Bugatti T57C	3.354,76 km
1938	Eugène Chaboud/Jean Tremoulet	Delahaye 135S	3.180,94 km
1937	Jean-Pierre Wimille/Robert Benoist	Bugatti T57G	3.287,93 km
1935	John Hindmarsh/Louis Fontes	Lagonda Rapide	3.006,79 km
1934	Philippe Etancelin/Luigi Chinetti	Alfa Romeo 8C 2300	2.886,93 km
1933	Raymond Sommer/Tazio Nuvolari	Alfa Romeo 8C 2300	3.144,03 km
1932	Raymond Sommer/Luigi Chinetti	Alfa Romeo 8C 2300	2.954,03 km
1931	Lord Howe/Henry Birkin	Alfa Romeo 8C 2300	3.017,65 km
1930	Woolf Barnato/Glen Kidston	Bentley Speed Six	2.930,66 km
1929	Woolf Barnato/Henry Birkin	Bentley Speed Six	2.834,83 km
1928	Woolf Barnato/Bernard Rubin	Bentley4.4	2.669,27 km
1927	"Sammy" Davis/Dr. John Benjafield	Bentley 3.0 "Sport"	2.369,80 km
1926	Robert Bloch/André Rossignol	Lorraine-Dietrich B3-6	2.552,41 km
1925	Gérard de Courcelles/André Rossignol	Lorraine-Dietrich B3-6	2.233,98 km
1924	John Duff/Frank Clement	Bentley 3.0 "Sport"	2.077,34 km
1923	André Lagache/René Leonhard	Chenard & Walcker "Sport"	2.209,53 km

Two seats and for a good long time

___ The sports car racing scene cannot, of course, look back on a history of comparable constancy to that of Formula 1. Yet these generally long-distance contests with their open and closed two-seaters remain amongst the most fascinating of all competitions in the field of motorsport. Races like the Targa Florio, the Mille Miglia, the 1,000-kilometer race on the Nürburgring, the 24 Hours of Le Mans, the Tourist Trophy and battles of endurance in Sebring and Daytona very quickly become stalwart elements in the repertoire of that august theater whose actors sit in cars from the manufacturers Alfa Romeo, Cobra, Ford, Ferrari, Jaguar, Porsche and the like.

Starting in 1953, the results of selected races such as the "Mille," the "Targa" and the "TT" are added to a title competition. In addition to the great track events and tradition-rich open-road races, hill climb races soon prove both attractive and lucrative for sports car drivers. Until 1968, the title is divided into multiple classes (above and below two liters, both for sports cars and GT cars). Combined with a concentration a manufacturer's title, the sports car milieu becomes a major spectacle. A golden era, if you will. Ford, Ferrari and Porsche engage in a staggering technological arms race that culminates in the emergence of bulging muscle-cars like the almost five-liter Porsche 917 or the Ferrari 512. Manufacturers that just opt for a displacement boost from two to three liters simply cannot keep up. One such car is the Alfa Romeo Tipo 33/3.

The elegant sports cars are amongst the most attractive race cars

In the World Sportscar Championship, a displacement restriction puts a damper on the power explosion – the arms race only continues in the North American CanAm series and leads to over 1,100 hp in the bi-turbocharged Porsche 917 Spyder. With three liters of displacement and engines identical to those in Formula 1, the sports car prototypes experience a golden age in the 1970s, before a split into Groups 5 and 6 takes place in 1976. While the World Championship title is still awarded for sports cars, the manufacturer's title is decided in Group 5. These silhouette sports cars are also used as the racing machines in the then-popular Deutsche Rennsport-Meisterschaft (DRM).

In 1982, the Group C era begins. A stage for the sleek sports cars from Lancia, Porsche and others is provided by the World Endurance Championship. But the impressive turbo speedsters, which actually outmatch the power of Formula 1 cars for a time, also thrill spectators in the recently internationalized IRDM and invitation races such as those on the Norisring in Nuremberg, the "Supercup" races staged between 1986 and 1989 and, of course, at Le Mans. To keep a handle on the power and speed, the Group C sports cars are subjected to a consumption rule. At Le Mans, the kilometers-long Mulsanne Straight is de-fanged through the placement of two chicanes.

Nevertheless, the route leads inexorably toward a realignment. From 1994, the BPR series established by Jürgen Barth, Patrick Peter and Stéphane Ratel offers a new home for GT sports cars. This series enjoys growing popularity, with a fascinating McLaren F1 inspiring Porsche, Mercedes-Benz, Nissan and Toyota to create GT1 sports cars homologated for street use. In reality, it is a choice selection of purebred racing machines that face off against each other from 1997 in the FIA-accredited, World Championship-awarding GT series. Subdivided into different GT categories, the GT scene enjoys rude health to this day. At the 24 Hours of Le Mans, the GTs (LM GT1 and near-series LM GT2) race in harmony with the Le Mans prototypes preferred by the organizer ACO, which – also subdivided into LMP1 and LMP2 – are also raced in the American (ALMS) and European Le Mans Series (ELMS). While the Audi R10 TD1 is amongst the representatives of LMP1, Porsche joins the fray in the smaller-displacement and lighter-weight LMP2 class with the Spyder.

Starting in 2014, Porsche returns to the top tier and joins the FIA-sanctioned World Endurance Championship (WEC) established in 2012 with an LMP1 car. In the LMP1 category, exceptionally technologically advanced hybrid race cars from the brands Audi (until 2015), Toyota and Porsche contest the title. A highly complex rule-book illustrates how very distinct technological approaches can lead to very comparable solutions.

The field of competitors in the WEC (World Endurance Championship) races is provided by a bevy of different prototypes (LMP1 Hybrid, LMP1 and LMP2) as well as GT cars (LMGTE Pro and LMGTE Am). One season encompasses seven six-hour championship rounds as well as the 24 Hours of Le Mans, which counts double. Still occupied only by Porsche and Toyota in 2016, the thin field in the LMP1 category will – once again – confront the top category in the sports car field with a difficult challenge. ___

Year	World Sportscar Champion	Car	Manufacturer's World Champion
2017	Earl Bamber (NZ)/Timo Bernhard (D)/Brendon Hartley (NZ)	Porsche 919 hybrid (WEC)	
2016	Neel Jani (CH)/Romain Dumas (F)/Marc Lieb (D)	Porsche 919 hybrid (WEC)	
2015	Timo Bernhard (D)/Brendon Hartley (AUS)/Mark Webber (AUS)	Porsche 919 hybrid (WEC)	
2014	Sébastien Buemi (CH)/Anthony Davidson (GB)	Toyota TS040 Hybrid (WEC)	
2013	Loic Duval (F)/Tom Kristensen (DK)/Allan McNish (GB)	Audi R18 e-tron quattro (WEC)	
2012	Marcel Fässler (CH)/André Lotterer (D)/Benoit Tréluyer (F)	Audi R18 e-tron Quattro (WEC)	
2010	Michael Bartels (D)/Andrea Bertolini (I)	Maserati MC12	Maserati (FIA-GT)
2009	Michael Bartels (D)/Andrea Bertolini (I)	Maserati MC12	Ferrari (FIA-GT)
2008	Michael Bartels (D)/Andrea Bertolini (I)	Maserati MC12	Maserati (FIA-GT)
2007	Michael Bartels (D)/Andrea Bertolini (I)	Maserati MC12	Maserati (FIA-GT)
2006	Michael Bartels (D)/Andrea Bertolini (I)	Maserati MC12	Maserati (FIA-GT)
2005	Gabriele Gardel (CH)	Ferrari F550 Maranello	Larbre Ferrari (FIA-GT)
2004	Luca Cappellari (I)/Fabrizio Gollin (I)	Ferrari F550 Maranello	Ferrari (FIA-GT)
2003	Thomas Biagi (I)/Matteo Bobbi (I)	Ferrari F550 Maranello	BMS Scuderia Italia Ferrari (FIA-GT)
2002	Christophe Bouchut (F)	Chrysler Viper GTS-R	Larbre Chrysler (FIA-GT)
2001	Christophe Bouchut (F)/Jean Philippe Belloc (F)	Chrysler Viper GTS-R	Larbre Chrysler (FIA-GT)
2000	Julian Bailey (GB)/Jamie Campbell-Walter (GB)	Lister Storm	Lister (FIA-GT)
1999	Olivier Beretta (I)/Karl Wendlinger (A)	Chrysler Viper GTS-R	Chrysler Team Oreca (FIA-GT)
1998	Klaus Ludwig (D)/Riccardo Zonta (BR)	Mercedes CLK GTR	AMG-Mercedes (FIA-GT)
1997	Bernd Schneider (D)	Mercedes CLK GTR	AMG-Mercedes (FIA-GT)
1996	Ray Bellm (GB)/James Weaver (GB)	McLaren F1 GTR-BMW	Gulf McLaren-BMW (BPR)
1995	Thomas Bscher (D)/John Nielsen (DK)	McLaren F1 GTR-BMW	West McLaren-BMW (BPR)
1992	Derek Warwick (GB)/Yannick Dalmas (F)	Peugeot 905 Evo 1	Bis Peugeot Talbot Sport
1991	Teo Fabi (I)	Jaguar XJR-14	Silk Cut Jaguar
1990	Jean-Louis Schlesser (F)/Mauro Baldi (I)	Sauber C9 & C11-Mercedes	Sauber-Mercedes
1989	Jean-Louis Schlesser (F)	Sauber C9-Mercedes	Sauber-Mercedes
1988	Martin Brundle (GB)	Jaguar XJR-9	Silk Cut Jaguar
1987	Raul Boesel (BR)	Jaguar XJR-8	Silk Cut Jaguar
1986	Derek Bell (GB)	Porsche 962C	Brun-Porsche
1985	Derek Bell (GB)	Porsche 962C	Rothmans-Porsche
1984	Stefan Bellof (D)	Porsche 956	Porsche
1983	Jacky Ickx (B)	Porsche 956	Porsche
1982	Jacky Ickx (B)	Porsche 956	Porsche
1981	Bob Garretson (USA)*	Porsche 935	Porsche
1980	John Fitzpatrick (GB)	Porsche 935 K3	Lancia
1979	Don Whittington (USA)	Porsche 935 K3 & AMC Spirit	Porsche
1978	John Paul sr. (USA)	Porsche 911 RSR & 935 & Mazda RX2	Porsche
1977		Porsche 935	Porsche (Manufacturer)
1977	Arturo Merzario (I)	Alfa Romeo 33SC12	Alfa Romeo (Sportscar)
1976		Porsche 935	Porsche (Manufacturer)
1976	Jochen Mass (D)	Porsche 936	Porsche (Sportscar)
1975	Arturo Merzario (I)	Alfa Romeo 33TT12	Alfa Romeo
1974	Gérard Larrousse (F)	Matra-Simca MS 670C	Matra
1973	Gérard Larrousse (F)/Henri Pescarolo (F)	Matra-Simca MS 670B	Matra
1972	Jacky Ickx (B)	Ferrari 312 PB	Ferrari
1971	Pedro Rodríguez (MEX)	Porsche 917	Porsche
1970	Pedro Rodríguez (MEX)/Leo Kinnunen (SF)	Porsche 917 & 908/3	Porsche
1969	Jo Siffert (CH)	Porsche 908 & 917	Porsche
1968	Hans Herrmann (D)	Porsche 907 & 908	Ford
1967	Gerhard Mitter (D)/Jo Siffert (CH)/Paul Hawkins (AUS)	Porsche 910 & Lola-Chevrolet Ferrari (Class over 2,0l) & Porsche	T70 & Ford GT40
1966	Gerhard Mitter (D)	Porsche 906	Ford (over 2.0l) & Porsche (under 2,0l)
1965	Gerhard Mitter (D)	Porsche 904/8 & 904 GTS	Shelby Cobra Ford & Porsche
1964	Ludovico Scarfiotti (I)	Ferrari 250 GTO & 330 P	Ferrari & Porsche
1963	Hans Herrmann (D)	Abarth-Simca 1300 Bialbero & Abarth 2000	Ferrari
1962	Olivier Gendebien (F)	Ferrari 250 GTO & 330 TRI LM & Dino 246 SP	Ferrari
1961	Olivier Gendebien (F)	Ferrari Dino 246 SP	Ferrari
1960	Olivier Gendebien (F)	Ferrari 250 TR & Porsche 718 RS60	Ferrari
1959	Olivier Gendebien (F)	Ferrari 250 TR	Aston Martin
1958	Olivier Gendebien (F)	Ferrari 250 TR	Ferrari
1957	Peter Collins (GB)	Ferrari 335S	Ferrari
1956	Eugenio Castelotti (I)/Stirling Moss (GB)	Ferrari 860 Monza & 290 MM/Maserati 300S	Ferrari
1955	Stirling Moss (GB)	Mercedes-Benz 300 SLR	Mercedes-Benz
1954	Maurice Trintignant (F)	Ferrari 375 Plus	Ferrari
1953	Giuseppe Farina (I)	Ferrari 375 MM	Ferrari

*No official title awarded through 1981

A grand tour

___ Exciting duels in which the cars zip down the track with their door handles practically touching, and starting grids bursting at the seams: Such are the charms of touring car racing. International race tracks, home to the European Touring Car Championship for two decades from 1963, as well as the World Touring Car Championship held in 1987 and since 2005, have also served as the stage for the ace touring car drivers to test their mettle all around the world.

The European Touring Car Championship is first staged in 1963. In view of the great demand and rather unbalanced field, the European title is divided into three divisions between 1965 and 1969. In the small Division 1, the field consists primarily of Mini Coopers and the Fiat 600-based Abarth 1000 TC. Division 2 represents the hotly contest mid-range contenders. This group is led by the Lotus Ford Cortina, Alfa Romeo Giulia Sprint GTA and Lancia Flavia Sport Zagato. And in the big-engine Division 3, proceedings are initially dominated by the likes of the Ford Mustang, and later the two-liter BMW 2000 TI and 2002.

Touring car racing under the aegis of the FIA has a rich and varied history

The top of the international touring car scene is reserved for the involved teams and works squads. Alfa Romeo, BMW and Ford bedeck themselves in laurels in the 1970s, and their sporting reputations still rest to some extent on them to this day. The Ford Capri and Escort, and above all the big BMW Coupés (3.0 and 3.5 CSL), are the outstanding cars of these years.

In 1982, touring car racing enters the Group A era. The period lasts until 1988 and reaches its high-water mark in 1987 with a parallel staging of the European and World Championships. Due to squabbling on the functionary level, the World Championship for Group A touring cars remains a one-off event, with the BMW-M3 driver Ravaglia taking the title by a one-point margin over the Ford Sierra Cosworth RS 500, which, however, takes the manufacturer's title. The entry fee for the European Championship is US$ 6,000, though ten times that much is required to collect points in the title race. In the 1980s, too, the three touring car divisions are retained, and points are assigned by groups. However, the title still goes to one driver and one manufacturer, as has been the custom since 1970. Consistently racking up wins in Division 2, the Alfa Romeo Alfetta GTV6

wins the title on the trot between 1982 and 1985. The overall victories, meanwhile, are contested in these years between the representatives of the big division, the BMW 635 CSi, Jaguar XJ-S, Volvo 240 and Rover Vitesse.

As for the touring car racing scene itself, the end of the 1980s sees a shift toward the DTM. A European Championship is not held again until the year 2000. However, the two-liter touring cars built under the Class 2 rules racing in several different national championships do also compete against each other in the FIA-initiated Touring Car World Cup in 1994 and 1995. The Class 1 cars used in the DTM also aspire to race abroad. So, in 1995, an international championship is held alongside the DTM, and in 1996 actually replaces it. Unfortunately, this technologically advanced championship turns out to be a dead end due to the vertiginously spiraling costs in a period of economic turmoil for carmakers.

But the internationally popular Class 2 touring cars pass through several stages of development, from super touring cars to Super 2000 touring cars, and ultimately the perfect machines for the European Touring Car Championship revived in the 2000 season and the World Touring Car Championship brought back in 2005 as the pinnacle of the international touring car racing series. After the era of the Super Touring Car regulations, the WTCC adopts the FIA Super 2000 rules. What that means is that beyond the 2,500 series units required for homologation, the Group A base cars based on them are equipped with the supplementary Super 2000 kit. The weight for front-wheel drive cars is set at 1,140 kilograms. Rear-wheel drive models have to weigh an additional 30 kilos. The same applies to vehicles with sequential transmissions. All-wheel drive, ABS and ESP are strictly forbidden. The two-liter and just under 300-hp engines can rev to between 8,500 (four-cylinders) and 9,000 rpm (six-cylinders).

With brands such as Lada, Chevrolet and Citroen, however, the globally staged sprint series ranks somewhat below the manufacturer-controlled "DTM" marketing platform, in which premium brand manufacturers such as Audi, BMW and Mercedes-Benz compete against each other. ___

Year	Drivers' champion	Car	Championship	Manufacturers' champion (car)
2016	José Maria López (ARG)	Citroen C-Elysée WTCC	WTCC	Citroen (C-Elysée WTCC)
2015	José Maria López (ARG)	Citroen C-Elysée WTCC	WTCC	Citroen (C-Elysée WTCC)
2014	José Maria López (ARG)	Citroen C-Elysée WTCC	WTCC	Citroen (C-Elysée WTCC)
2013	Yvan Muller (F)	Chevrolet Cruze	WTCC	Honda (Civic)
2012	Robert Huff (GB)	Chevrolet Cruze	WTCC	Chevrolet (Cruze)
2011	Yvan Muller (F)	Chevrolet Cruze	WTCC	Chevrolet (Cruze)
2010	Yvan Muller (F)	Chevrolet Cruze	WTCC	Chevrolet (Cruze)
2009	Gabriele Tarquini (I)	Seat Léon TDI	WTCC	Seat (Léon TDI)
2008	Yvan Muller (F)	Seat Léon TDI	WTCC	Seat (Léon TDI)
2007	Andy Priaulx (GB)	BMW 320si	WTCC	BMW (320si)
2006	Andy Priaulx (GB)	BMW 320si	WTCC	BMW (320si)
2005	Andy Priaulx (GB)	BMW 320i	WTCC	BMW (320i)
2004	Andy Priaulx (GB)	BMW 320i	ETCC	BMW (320I)
2003	Gabriele Tarquini (I)	Alfa Romeo 156 GTA	ETCC	
2002	Fabrizio Giovanardi (I)	Alfa Romeo 156 GTA	ETCC (Super 2000 regulations)	
2001	Fabrizio Giovanardi (I)	Alfa Romeo 156	STC (Europe)	
2000	Fabrizio Giovanardi (I)	Alfa Romeo 156	Euro-STW-Cup (ultimate Classe 2)	
1996	Manuel Reuter (D)	Opel Calibra V6	ITC	
1995	Bernd Schneider (D)	Mercedes-Benz C-Class	ITC	
1995	Frank Biela (D)	Audi A4 STW	FIA Touring Car World Cup	
1994	Paul Radisich (NZ)	Ford Mondeo STW	FIA Touring Car World Cup	
1988	Roberto Ravaglia (I)	BMW M3	TW-EM	Ford (Sierra Cosworth RS 500)
1987	Roberto Ravaglia (I)	BMW M3	TW-WM	Ford (Sierra Cosworth RS 500)
1987	Winni Vogt (D)	BMW M3	TW-EM	BMW (M3)
1986	Roberto Ravaglia (I)	BMW 635 CSi	TW-EM	Toyota (Corolla GT)
1985	Gianfranco Brancatelli (I)	Volvo 240 Turbo	TW-EM	Alfa Romeo (Alfetta GTV6)
1984	Tom Walkinshaw (GB)	Jaguar XJ-S	TW-EM	Alfa Romeo (Alfetta GTV6)
1983	Dieter Quester (A)	BMW 635 CSi	TW-EM	Alfa Romeo (Alfetta GTV6)
1982	Umberto Grano (I)/Helmut Kelleners (D)	BMW 528i	TW-EM	Alfa Romeo (Alfetta GTV6)
1981	Umberto Grano (I)/Helmut Kelleners (D)	BMW 635CSi	TW-EM	Škoda (130 RS)
1980	Helmut Kelleners (D)/Sigfried Müller jr. (D)	BMW 320	TW-EM	Audi (80 GTE)
1979	Martino Finotto (I)/Carlo Facetti (I)	BMW 3.5 CSL	TW-EM	BMW (3.5 CSL)
1978	Umberto Grano (I)	BMW 3.5 CSL	TW-EM	BMW (3.5 CSL)
1977	Dieter Quester (A)	BMW 3.5 CSL	TW-EM	Alfa Romeo (Alfetta GTV & Alfasud & Alfasud Sprint)
1976	Jean Xhenceval (B)/Pierre Dieudonné (B)	BMW 3.5 CSL	TW-EM	Alfa Romeo (GTA & Giulia GTV & Alfetta GTV)
1975	Alain Peltier (F)/Siegfried Müller sen. (D)	BMW 3.5 CSL	TW-EM	BMW (3.5 CSL)
1974	Hans Heyer (D)	Ford Capri & Escort RS	TW-EM	Ford (Escort RS)
1973	Toine Hezemans (NL)	BMW 3.0 CSL	TW-EM	BMW (3.0 CSL)
1972	Jochen Mass (D)	Ford Capri RS	TW-EM	Alfa Romeo (GTA)
1971	Dieter Glemser (D)	Ford Capri RS	TW-EM	Alfa Romeo (GTA)
1970	Toine Hezemans (NL)	Alfa Romeo Giulia Sprint GTA	TW-EM	BMW (2002 & 2800 CS)
1969	Dieter Quester (A)	BMW 2002 ti	(EM-Division3)	
	Spartaco Dini (I)	Alfa Romeo Giulia Sprint GTA	(EM-Div.2)	
	"PAM" (I)	Fiat Abarth	(EM-Div.1)	
1968	Dieter Quester (A)	BMW 2002	(EM-Div.3)	
	John Rhodes (GB)	BMC Cooper Mini	(EM-Div.2)	
	John Handley (GB)	BMC Cooper	(EM-Div.1)	
1967	Karl Freiherr von Wendt (D)	Porsche 911	(EM-Div.3)	
	Andrea de Adamich (I)	Alfa Romeo Giulia Sprint GTA	(EM-Div.2)	
	Willibert Kauhsen (D)	Abarth 1000 TC Corsa	(EM-Div.1)	
1966	Hubert Hahne (D)	BMW 2000 TI	(EM-Div.3)	
	Andrea de Adamich (I)	Alfa Romeo Giulia Sprint GTA	(EM-Div.2)	
	Gian Carlo Baghetti (I)	Fiat Abarth 1000	(EM-Div.1)	
1965	Jacky Ickx (B)	Ford Mustang	(EM-Div.3)	
	Sir John Whitmore (GB)	Ford Lotus Cortina	(EM-Div.2)	
	Ed Swart (NL)	Fiat Abarth 1000	(EM-Div.1)	
1964	Warwick Banks (GB)	Austin Mini Cooper S		
1963	Peter Nöcker (D)	Jaguar Mk II 3,8 Litre S		

Full house and puffy cheeks

___ Riveting duels and fascinating race cars whose fundamental characteristics derive from series cars prove irresistible for the viewing public. Not to mention the stately prize money sums such as the over 100,000 German marks offered by the organizers of Nuremberg's Norisring race to draw teams and drivers.

The history of the Deutsche Rennsport-Meisterschaft, translated in English as the German Racing Championship, begins in 1972, and it is shaped by Hans-Joachim Stuck, the driver who, in addition to starting in Formula 2 at the same time, takes nine of 12 races, and thus the championship title, in his Ford Capri RS. Stuck's Capri is one of the cars in the big division, while later titles go to drivers of cars in the small division. In most cases, both fields are sent off onto the roughly 100–150 kilometer journeys together. And so it is that the two Ford Escort drivers Dieter Glemser and Hans Heyer frequently fail to take overall victory, yet take home the titles all the same. The Escort is one of the cars assigned to the small division, which is subject to a two-liter displacement limit. The big division, by contrast, has a more capacious four liters to work with.

The technical data for the Escort with which Heyer takes top honors six times in 1975 and thus paves his way to the title are 275 hp, 1,974 cc of displacement and 880 kilograms. Teams like Zakspeed take the lightweight construction maxim to such extremes that they use razor-thin telephone wires for the wiring harness. All told, the team sinks 70,000 marks into the Class 2 car. The members of the big division, the muscular Porsche 911 Carrera RSR and BMW 3.5 CSL, by contrast, boast sale prices of between 100,000 and 150,000 marks. In 1976, the output of the Zakspeed Escort gets a five-horsepower boost to 280 hp from now 1,965 cc of displacement. Though it also boosts the price by 10,000 marks.

The puffy-cheeked turbo monsters put on a great show

1977 goes into the history books as the year of the juniors. The BMW Junior Team provokes both admiration and animosity with its fiery race performances. But this early example of junior talent promotion by a manufacturer bears fruit. Manfred Winkelhock, Marc Surer and Eddie Cheever later all make the jump to Formula 1. The DRM racing machines are now built according to Group 5 regulations. That translates into retaining the series production silhouette while outfitting the cars with spoilers and extremely prominent fender flares. In the big division, the turbocharged Porsche 935s come to rule the roost. The displacement of the then three-liter Porsche 911 Carrera RSR shrinks to 2,587 cc, which with a turbo factor of 1.4 amounts to 3,999.8 cc, just a hair's breadth below the four-liter limit. The output of the "flat nose" car is listed at roughly 640 hp. Depending on the position of the charge pressure-regulating "boost controller," additional horses can be rustled up. With the juniors and their team colleagues stealing points from each other, Porsche driver Stommelen emerges the laughing victor: He takes the title.

After the 1978 title goes again to the ranks of the small division and BMW 320 Turbo driver Ertl, in 1979 Klaus Ludwig takes ten of eleven races in his Kremer-built Porsche 953 K3, with a second-place finish in the eleventh for good measure. His manufacturer colleagues Bob Wollek, "John Winter", Rolf Stommelen and Manfred Schurti, as well as the drivers of the Ford Capri Turbo (Hans Heyer, Harald Ertl, Klaus Niedzwiedz) and BMW 320 Turbo (Manfred Winkelhock, Markus Höttinger, Harald Grohs) battling it out in the small division are left in the dust. Also, naturally, in the title race.

Before sell-out crowds at the Norisring, Mainz-Finthen, Diepholz, Hockenheim or the Nürburgring and the Avus, the 1980 GS team races

the Beta Montecarlo Turbo, which Lancia is also racing in the Manufacturer's World Championship and World Endurance Championship. The small division gains yet another model. The 1,425 cc four-cylinder puts an outstanding 430 hp on the tarmac while tipping the scales at just 780 kilograms. But there is growth in the big division as well. The BMW M1 used the year before in the Formula 1-associated Procar series joins the field. Manfred Winkelhock, Hans-Georg Bürger and Helmut Kelleners are among the speedier M1 drivers. The distribution of the field remains as it was: While a good dozen of the big-engined cars vie for overall victory, in the small division some two dozen participants regularly battle it out for the class win and points. After Klaus Ludwig has to concede victory in a Turbo Capri built for the big division in 1980, in 1981 he tries his luck in a smaller Ford Capri Turbo and promptly takes the title. The season marks the end of the "grand days of the DRM."

In 1982, Group C sports cars follow the footsteps of the massive Group 5 turbos. The DRM is recast as a sports car championship under the name IDRM – I as in international. In a transitional phase for the first year, Group 6 prototypes are also allowed. Bob Wollek cruises to victory in the mature and Le Mans-tested 936. Teammate Volkert Merl drives a closed Joest Porsche 936C built under Group C regulations for a spell, and Kremer fields a closed flat-six-powered car as well. The car is known as the Kremer-Porsche CK5. Its traditional venue, however, is in the classic sports car races.

Before the IDRM is subsumed into the "Supercup" (1986–1989), Bob Wollek, Stefan Bellof and Jochen Mass take home the series titles – drivers who are equally adept at piloting the Group C speedsters to victory in World Championship races. —

Year	Champion	Car	Team
1985	Jochen Mass (D)	Porsche 956 (Gr.C)	Joest
1984	Stefan Bellof (D)	Porsche 956 (Gr.C)	Brun
1983	Bob Wollek (F)	Porsche 956 (Gr.C)	Joest
1982	Bob Wollek (F)	Porsche 936 (Gr.6)	Joest
1981	Klaus Ludwig (D)	Ford Capri Turbo (Gr.6)	Zakspeed
1980	Hans Heyer (D)	Lancia Beta Montecarlo Turbo (Gr.5)	GS/Lancia Corse
1979	Klaus Ludwig (D)	Porsche 935 K3 (Gr.5)	Kremer
1978	Harald Ertl (D)	BMW 320 Turbo (Gr.5)	Schnitzer
1977	Rolf Stommelen (D)	Porsche 935 (Gr.5)	Georg Loos
1976	Hans Heyer (D)	Ford Escort (Gr.2)	Zakspeed
1975	Hans Heyer (D)	Ford Escort (Gr.2)	Zakspeed
1974	Dieter Glemser (D)	Ford Escort (Gr.2)	Zakspeed
1973	Dieter Glemser (D)	Ford Esort (Gr.2)	Zakspeed
1972	Hans-Joachim Stuck (D)	Ford Capri RS (Gr.2)	Zakspeed

Door to door

___The DTM goes back to the year 1984, initially going by the name Deutsche-Produktionswagen-Meisterschaft – the German production car championship. With a handicap weight and intake air restrictors ensuring a level playing field, the regulations do away with the multi-class setups employed by previous touring car races. Like the French production car championship on which it is modeled, the DTM is a classless society. And a highly successful one. The ever-rising number of spectators and the regular, and popular, televised broadcasts of the races lead to growing engagement on the part of the manufacturers. The annual season highlight in the late 1980s is the event held on the North Loop of the Nürburgring, the infamous Nordschleife. The DTM is a regular presence here, taking part in the 24-hour race, until 1993. And healthy numbers of the teams enter their Ford Sierra Cosworths and BMW M3s in this unique endurance race, this "festival of motorsport," as well.

> ## The late 1980s to the mid-1990s are the wildest years

The appearance and the dominance of the powerful all-wheel drive sedans from Ingolstadt, the Audi A8, unsettles the competition, which has already been severely rattled by the "contest of equals" pitting of the turbocharged Ford Cosworths against the high-revving four-valve faction from Stuttgart and Munich, the Mercedes 190E 2.5-16 and BMW M3, as well as lightweight front-wheel drive cars like the Opel Kadett GSI. Today, we know for certain what could only be assumed back then: The "Cossies" muster up to 500-plus hp in spite of the air restrictors ...

The approval of evolution models gives the carmakers the opportunity to react to the sporting requirements. The works in Stuttgart, Munich, Rüsselsheim and Cologne soon retort with elaborately modified model versions in 500-unit runs of the original 5,000 produced units of the racing sedans homologated in Group A.

For the 1993 season, a new set of Class 1 rules replace the Group A regulations of 1982. These race-built touring cars are all equipped with a 2.5-liter six-cylinder engine whose crankshaft is restricted to a maximum of 12,000 revolutions per minute. Engineers have a variety of technical possibilities at their disposal. All-wheel drive is allowed. With the Class 1 speedsters, the racing series experiences a boom that gains it a wide following abroad as well. The fascinating high-tech touring cars are associated with accelerating expenditures, of course. Ample reason for the manufacturers to strive for an internationalization of the series. With the blessing of the FIA, the DTM morphs into the ITC (International

Touringcar Championship), before the departures of Opel and Alfa Romeo at the end of 1996 stop the series in its tracks at the pinnacle of its technological prowess.

For the 2000 season, the DTM has a renaissance as the Deutsche Tourenwagen Masters – the German Touring Car Masters. Mercedes-Benz, Opel and Audi bring powerful eight-cylinder prototypes to the series, cars that embody a combination of cost-saving uniform parts and fascinating high-tech creations. Though they optically resemble series vehicles, beneath their carbon bodies these racing machines conceal carbon-fiber monocoques with steel roll cages. The rear-wheel drive powered DTM speedsters are propelled by four-liter V8 engines boasting up to 480 hp. The rear wings, transmissions, suspension components, and brakes are uniform.

Mercedes-Benz, for decades the stalwart player and driving force behind the DTM – not least thanks to the substantial efforts of Mercedes motorsport boss Norbert Haug – delivers a new landmark moment for the series with its announcement in summer 2017 that it will withdraw from the DTM. At a time when electric and hybrid vehicles are becoming increasingly important, the FIA Formula E is admittedly a more fitting prospect than a racing series based on an increasingly archaic-sounding contest between four-liter V8s. The most serious weakness of the series, however, turns out to be the lacking championship status and the steering hand of a governing body. Instead, the dedicated manufacturers take matters into their own hands. And as such, they are duty-bound to represent the interests of their respective employers. It's no way to reach agreement. Instead, the result is regulations with penalty weights that are utterly inscrutable to spectators, and ultimately even the mechanics of the teams. At times, the DTM makes more headlines with its internal squabbling than its racing events, which is all the more a pity when the 2016 season – discussions about handicap weights notwithstanding – again offers up a series of extremely exciting races. Here, the diligent work of the new DTM boss, former Formula 1 driver and BMW Motorsport manager Gerhard Berger pays dividends.

Through the end of 2018, the DTM retains the technical regulations it introduced for the 2000 season. For the 2012 season, the involved manufacturers and their teams receive a new DTM standard monocoque resembling that of Formula 1. The car is essentially built around a cage. The technology modules for the drive and suspension are added in the

front and rear, with the manufacturer-specific bodyshell topping things off. In each case the car recalls the appearance of series models, but in terms of frontal area they are tuned for maximum equality.

In the mid-1990s, in addition to the powerful and technologically sophisticated DTM Class 1 touring cars, numerous championships emerge around the world featuring touring cars operating under Class 2 rules. In Germany, the Class 2 cars still compete with the stronger Class 1 cars in the 1993 season of the DTM; starting in 1994, they start in the Tourenwagen or Super Tourenwagen Cup (German Touring Car or German Super Touring Car Cup). This series, in turn, becomes an STW Championship in 1998. The advantage of this super touring car with two-liter displacement is its ability to be used in different regions. The number of involved manufacturers is accordingly large.

Initially conceived as a series-based super touring car series with 18-, and later 19-inch wheels, practically every sport-oriented manufacturer in the industry took the chance to field a car in the series. While the Class 1 speedsters are most comparable with silhouette prototypes, Class 2 takes its lead more from the former Group A. Among race car drivers, however, the 300-hp front-wheel drive machines are far from universally beloved. As the number of participants grows, so too the level of competition and pressure to innovate. Unsurprisingly, elaborate differential solutions, high-volume evolution models and labor-intensive aerodynamics solutions also lead to rising costs, which ultimately put paid to Class 2 and the super touring cars to which it gave rise.

In the pantheon of championships held in Germany, Italy (CIVT), France and many other countries, the British Touring Car Championship (BTCC) ranks as the most hotly contested title. The number of involved manufacturers and the quality of the field lends the BTCC title a gravitas that cannot be matched by the FIA STW World Cup title, which is decided in just a few final races.

That changes with the granting of European and World Championship status. In the context of this highest-ranking racing series in the world, touring cars built under the super touring regulations are used until 2002, when they are displaced by more technologically austere two-liter racing touring cars. These Super 2000 cars – so named for the regulations on which they are based – feature 17-inch wheels, while the more near-series Group N-based cars under the Super Production rules grip the track with 15-inch tires. The engine speed restriction for the "STW light"-dubbed Super 2000 cars is pegged, as for Class 2 touring

cars, at 8,500 rpm. The transmission is limited to five speeds and the weight for front-wheel drive models is initially set at 1,140 kilograms, while rear-wheel drive models can tip the scales with an additional 30 kilos.

Revived in 2005, the field in the WTCC is long populated by the likes of sporty mid-level sedans along the lines of the BMW 3-series or the Alfa 156. Seat launches the successful León into the fray, a compact compact-class model, leading the way, in turn, for further compact models from Lada (Granta), Volvo (S60), Honda (Civic), Chevrolet (first Lacetti, then Cruze) or Citroën (C-Elysée). And successfully so, it must be said, for the victories and titles henceforth go exclusively to the compact speedsters. From 2011, only turbocharged 1.6-liter engines are used. Initially the manufacturers choose them voluntarily, as the series models are also all sold with the smaller engines. The rule-makers react and, starting in 2012, make the 1.6-liter displacement limit mandatory.

The rules of the WTCC are widely adopted by national racing series as well, including the BTCC. In 2015 a further touring car category emerges with the TCR and quickly spreads both domestically and internationally. The idea behind the classification is once again the objective of creating competitive touring race cars at a reasonable cost. The entry price for a race-ready car comes in at less than 100,000 euros. The initiator is the longtime head of the WTCC Marcello Lotti. The cars, based on series-production bodyshells outfitted with all the requisite racing components and powered by near-series two-liter turbo engines with about 330 hp under the hood come from numerous venerable names in the automotive industry, including Alfa Romeo, Audi, Ford, Honda, Hyundai, Kia, Opel, Peugeot, Seat, Subaru and Volkswagen. Flamboyant fenders and substantially dimensioned spoilers lend the cars a striking appearance as their drivers battle for motor racing supremacy on the many tracks that stage the races.

In view of the DTM withdrawal of Mercedes at the end of the 2018 DTM season that was announced in mid-2017, the arguably most prestigious touring car racing series in the world is facing a test of its own. The FIA is also working feverishly to restore the WTCC to former glory. Ongoing deliberations focus on the inevitability of including hybrid vehicles, which are powered both by combustion engines and electric energy. The subject of autonomous driving will also most likely play a role, albeit only for demonstration purposes, for instance having the cars drive themselves into their start positions on the grid. ⎯⎯

Year	DTM-Champion	Car
2017	René Rast (D)	Audi RS5 DTM
2016	Marko Wittmann (D)	BMW M4 DTM
2015	Pascal Wehrlein (D)	Mercedes-AMG C 63 DTM
2014	Marko Wittmann (D)	BMW M3 DTM
2013	Mike Rockenfeller (D)	SCHAEFFLER-Audi RS5 DTM
2012	Bruno Spengler (CD)	BMW M3 DTM
2011	Martin Tomczyk (D)	SCHAEFFLER-Audi A4 DTM
2010	Paul di Resta (GB)	Mercedes-Benz C-Class
2009	Timo Scheider (D)	Audi A4 DTM
2008	Timo Scheider (D)	Audi A4 DTM
2007	Matthias Ekström (S)	Audi A4 DTM
2006	Bernd Schneider (D)	Mercedes-Benz C-Class
2005	Gary Paffett (GB)	Mercedes-Benz C-Class
2004	Mattias Ekström (S)	Audi A4 DTM
2003	Bernd Schneider (D)	Mercedes-Benz CLK-DTM
2002	Laurent Aiello (F)	ABT-Audi TT-R
2001	Bernd Schneider (D)	Mercedes-Benz CLK-DTM
2000	Bernd Schneider (D)	Mercedes-Benz CLK-DTM
1996	Manuel Reuter (D)	Opel Calibra V6 (ITC)
1995	Bernd Schneider (D)	Mercedes C-Class
1994	Klaus Ludwig (D)	Mercedes C-Class
1993	Nicola Larini (I)	Alfa Romeo 155 V6 TI
1992	Klaus Ludwig (D)	Mercedes 190E 2.5-16 Evo 2
1991	Frank Biela (D)	Audi V8 quattro Evolution
1990	Hans-Joachim Stuck (D)	Audi V8 quattro
1989	Roberto Ravaglia (I)	BMW M3 Evolution
1988	Klaus Ludwig (D)	Ford Sierra Cosworth RS500
1987	Eric van de Poele (B)	BMW M3
1986	Kurt Thiim (DK)	Rover Vitesse
1985	Per Stureson (S)	Volvo 240 Turbo
1984	Volker Strycek (D)	BMW 635 CSi

Year	STW-Champion	Car	
1999	Uwe Alzen/Christian Abt*	Opel Vectra/Audi A4*	(German STW Championship) (*title decided at the green table)
1998	Johnny Cecotto (YV)	BMW 320i	(German STW Championship)
1997	Laurent Aiello (F)	Peugeot 406	(German STW Cup)
1996	Emanuele Pirro (I)	Audi A4	(German STW Cup)
1995	Joachim Winkelhock (I)	BMW 318i	(German STW Cup)
1994	Johnny Cecotto (YV)	BMW 318i	(German Touring Car Cup)

Year	BTCC-Champion	Car
2017	Ashley Sutton (GB)	Subaru Levorg GT
2016	Gordon Shedden (GB)	Honda Civic Type R
2015	Gordon Shedden (GB)	Honda Civic Type R
2014	Colin Turkington (GB)	BMW 125 M Sport
2013	Andrew Jordan (GB)	Honda Civic
2012	Gordon Shedden (GB)	Honda Civic
2011	Matt Neal (GB)	Honda Civic
2010	Jason Plato (GB)	Chevrolet Cruze
2009	Colin Turkington (GB)	BMW 320si
2008	Fabrizio Giovanardi (I)	Vauxhall Vectra
2007	Fabrizio Giovanardi (I)	Vauxhall Vectra
2006	Matt Neal (GB)	Honda Integra-R
2005	Matt Neal (GB)	Honda Integra-R
2004	James Thompson (GB)	Vauxhall/Opel Astra Coupé
2003	Yvan Muller (F)	Vauxhall/Opel Astra Coupé
2002	James Thompson (GB)	Vauxhall/Opel Astra Coupé
2001	Jason Plato (GB)	Vauxhall/Opel Astra Coupé (Super 2000 regulations)
2000	Alain Menu (CH)	Ford Mondeo
1999	Laurent Aiello (F)	Nissan Primera
1998	Rickard Rydell (S)	Volvo S40
1997	Alain Menu (CH)	Renault Laguna
1996	Frank Biela (D)	Audi A4
1995	John Cleland (GB)	Opel/Vauxhall Vectra
1994	Gabriele Tarquini (I)	Alfa Romeo 155 TwinSpark
1993	Joachim Winkelhock (D)	BMW 318i

Holding the line

___ A movement is born in the American south. Racing with series production cars, or stock cars, as they're also known, emerges from the then illegal milieu of moonshiners and bootleggers, late-night whiskey distilleries, and smuggling runs to the buyers of the contraband. Popular speedsters come from the carmakers Chevrolet and – above all – Ford.

The first races take place before the 1930s are out, and in 1949 the inaugural season of the NASCAR (National Association for Stock Car Auto Racing) series is held. The founding fathers include the likes of Bill France, who in 1936 drove home a 300-dollar prize for a fifth-place finish in Daytona – a month's rent for a house in those days is 15 dollars.

The first races are held on the beach in Daytona or on the red clay of Atlanta. The course layout is an oval from the outset. And that remains the same long after tarmac has replaced sand and clay as the driving surface. What remains is the immense public interest in the sport, which today is organized in a sophisticated league system and whose top-flight performers face off against each other 40 times a year. In the States, NASCAR is regarded as a "200-mph billboard," a 320 km/h advertising surface that provides rich rewards for both the teams and drivers.

From 1950 to 1971, the top league goes by the name Grand National. Since 1972 it has adopted the name of the title sponsor: the Winston Cup until 2003, and the Nextel Cup ever since. The races are contested in cars with a near-series silhouette slipped over the tubular frame.

No national racing series draws more fans than NASCAR

Under the lightweight chassis lies a heart of American V8 technology. It is inexpensive and illustrates the down-to-earth character of NASCAR, which has always maintained a more approachable air than the northern-based AAA and its open-wheel racing series. Today the league system also includes NASCAR Busch Series for touring cars and (since 1995) the NASCAR Craftsman Truck Series for pick-up trucks.

As early as the 1950s, NASCAR looks to expand into new types of cars. But the convertible class launched in the second half of the decade proves a flop.

In the early 1980s, the world's most popular touring car series makes the leap from stick cars in the original sense to NASCAR speedsters with near-series silhouettes. What that means is that the cars are built around a tube frame clad in an aluminum or plastic bodyshell. This proves both a safer and cheaper option than the cars like the Dodge Charger Daytona and the Plymouth Road Runner Superbird, elaborately and therefore expensively developed homologation cars that also found their way into the "noodle pots," as oval tracks are evocatively called in German, of the wild southwest.

With 200 wins, 126 pole positions and seven titles (like Dale Earnhardt), Richard Petty remains the most successful NASCAR driver of all time. Of course, he did enter no fewer than 1,177 races in a career that spanned from 1958 to 1992. ___

Year	Champion	Car	Team	Rookie of the year
2016	Jimmie Johnson	Chevrolet	Rick Hendrick	Chase Elliott
2015	Kyle Bush	Toyota	Joe Gibbs	Brett Moffitt
2014	Kevin Harvick	Chevrolet	Stewart-Haas-Racing	Kyle Larson
2013	Jimmie Johnson	Chevrolet	Rick Hendrick	Ricky Stenhouse Jr.
2012	Brad Keselowski	Dodge	Roger Penske	Stephen Leicht
2011	Tony Stewart	Chevrolet	Stewart-Haas-Racing	Andy Lally
2010	Jimmie Johnson	Chevrolet	Rick Hendrick	Kevin Convey
2009	Jimmie Johnson	Chevrolet	Rick Hendrick	Joey Logano
2008	Jimmie Johnson	Chevrolet	Rick Hendrick	Regan Smith
2007	Jimmie Johnson	Chevrolet	Hendrick Motorsports	Juan Pablo Montoya
2006	Jimmie Johnson	Chevrolet Monte Carlo SS	Rick Hendrick	Danny Hamlin
2005	Tony Stewart	Chevrolet Monte Carlo	Joe Gibbs	Kyle Bush
2004	Kurt Busch	Ford Taurus	Georgetta Roush	Kasey Kahne
2003	Matt Kenseth	Ford Taurus	Jack Roush	Jamie McMurray
2002	Tony Stewart	Pontiac Grand Prix	Joe Gibbs	Ryan Newman
2001	Jeff Gordon	Chevrolet Monte Carlo	Rick Hendrick	Kevin Harvick
2000	Bobby Labonte	Pontiac Grand Prix	Joe Gibbs	Matt Kenseth
1999	Dale Jarrett	Ford Taurus	Robert Yates	Tony Stewart
1998	Jeff Gordon	Chevrolet Monte Carlo	Rick Hendrick	Kenny Irwin
1997	Jeff Gordon	Chevrolet Monte Carlo	Rick Hendrick	Mike Skinner
1996	Terry Labonte	Chevrolet Monte Carlo	Rick Hendrick	Johnny Benson
1995	Jeff Gordon	Chevrolet Monte Carlo	Rick Hendrick	Ricky Craven
1994	Dale Earnhardt	Chevrolet Lumina	Richard Childress	Jeff Burton
1993	Dale Earnhardt	Chevrolet Lumina	Richard Childress	Jeff Gordon
1992	Alan Kulwicki	Ford Thunderbird	Alan Kulwicki	Jimmy Hensley
1991	Dale Earnhardt	Chevrolet Lumina	Richard Childress	Bobby Hemilton
1990	Dale Earnhardt	Chevrolet Lumina	Richard Childress	Bob Moroso
1989	Rusty Wallace	Pontiac Grand Prix	Raymond Beadle	Dick Trickle
1988	Bill Elliott	Ford Thunderbird	Harry Melling	Ken Bouchard
1987	Dale Earnhardt	Chevrolet Monte Carlo	Richard Childress	Davey Allison
1986	Dale Earnhardt	Chevrolet Monte Carlo	Richard Childress	Alan Kulwicki
1985	Darrell Waltrip	Chevrolet Monte Carlo	Junior Johnson	Ken Schrader
1984	Terry Labonte	Chevrolet Monte Carlo	Billy Hagan	Rusty Wallace
1983	Bobby Allison	Buick Regal	Bill Gardner	Sterling Marlin
1982	Darrell Waltrip	Buick Regal	Junior Johnson	Geoffrey Bodine
1981	Darrell Waltrip	Buick Regal	Junior Johnson	Ron Bouchard
1980	Dale Earnhardt	Chevrolet Monte Carlo	Rod Osterlund	Jody Ridley
1979	Richard Petty	Chevrolet Monte Carlo	Petty Enterprises	Dale Earnhardt
1978	Cale Yarborough	Oldmobile	Junior Johnson	Ronnie Thomas
1977	Cale Yarborough	Chevrolet Malibu	Junior Johnson	Ricky Rudd
1976	Cale Yarborough	Chevrolet Chevelle	Junior Johnson	Skip Manning
1975	Richard Petty	Dodge Charger	Petty Enterprises	Bruce Hill
1974	Richard Petty	Dodge Charger	Petty Enterprises	Earl Ross
1973	Benny Parsons	Chevrolet Chevelle	L.G. DeWitt	Lennie Pond
1972	Richard Petty	Plymouth Road Runner Superbird	Petty Enterprises	Larry Smith
1971	Richard Petty	Plymouth Road Runner Superbird	Petty Enterprises	Walter Ballard
1970	Bobby Isaac	Dodge Charger Daytona	Nord Krauskopf	Bill Dennis
1969	David Pearson	Ford Torino Talladega	Holman-Moody	Dick Brooks
1968	David Pearson	Ford Torino	Holman-Moody	Pete Hamilton
1967	Richard Petty	Plymouth Satellite GTX	Petty Enterprises	Donnie Allison
1966	David Pearson	Dodge Charger	Cotton Owens	James Hylton
1965	Ned Jarrett	Ford Galaxie	Bondy Long	Sam McQuagg
1964	Richard Petty	Plymouth Belvedere	Petty Enterprises	Doug Cooper
1963	Joe Weatherly	Pontiac Catalina	Bud Moore	Billy Wade
1962	Joe Weatherly	Pontiac Catalina	Bud Moore	Tom Cox
1961	Ned Jarrett	Chevrolet Impala	W.G. Holloway Jr.	Woodie Wilson
1960	Rex White	Chevrolet Impala	White-Clements	David Pearson
1959	Lee Petty	Plymouth Hardtop	Petty Enterprises	Richard Petty
1958	Lee Petty	Oldmobile 88 Hardtop	Petty Enterprises	Shorty Rollins*
1957	Buck Baker	Chevrolet Bel Air	Buck Baker	
1956	Buck Baker	Chrysler 300-B	Carl Kiekhaefer	
1955	Tim Flock	Chrysler 300	Carl Kiekhaefer	
1954	Lee Petty	Chrysler New Yorker	Petty Enterprises	
1953	Herb Thomas	Hudson Hornet	Herb Thomas	
1952	Tim Flock	Hudson Hornet	Ted Chester	
1951	Herb Thomas	Hudson Hornet	Herb Thomas	
1950	Bill Rexford	Oldsmobile Futuramic 88	Julian Buesink	
1949	Red Byron	Oldsmobile Futuramic 88	Raymond Parks	
1949	Red Byron	Oldsmobile Futuramic 88	Raymond Parks	

*Rookie of the year is officially awarded by NASCAR since 1958.

Rallying the troops

___ Though the differences are legion, there are a few notable similarities between the military and rally racing milieus: Chief among them is the need to traverse nearly any type of terrain as quickly as possible. Gravel, snow and ice, mud and scree, and sometimes asphalt, provide the driving surface for these globally-staged competitions. It all begins with the Rallye Monte Carlo, the "mother of rally racing." The ideal 'midwife' for this winter drive is represented by the rallies held Italy in those days, initially reserved for the bicycle-bound. Beyond speed, reliability is the watchword in this discipline. First staged in 1911, for the tiny principality the rally is a welcome opportunity to draw guests to the Côte d'Azur in the bleak midwinter as well. For the participants starting in Berlin, Boulogne-sur-Mer, Brussels, Geneva, Paris and Vienna, the prize money of 10,000 francs is more than inviting. The entry fee, by contrast, is a measly 50 francs.

There quickly emerges a bevy of competitions that bring together competitors from different cities and countries at a single location and finish with a raft of identical trials for all participants. Then there are events, such as the Acropolis and RAC rallies, whose character, with an identical course for all participants, resembles that of the "Monte" finale and thus the format that is still practiced today.

There are also rallies in the road race format such as Spa-Sofia-Liège, or the Carrera Pan-americana. Ultimately, the long-distance races no longer find the space they require amid the ever-denser traffic and are discontinued for safety reasons or moved to race tracks. The venerable Liège-Sofia-Liège race, for example, becomes the up-to-96-hour trial known as the "Marathon de la Route." The race is held on the Nürburgring. In 1970, the once four-day, then three-and-a-half day, then three-day "Marathon de la Route" becomes the 24-hour race on the Nürburgring's Nordschleife that today is known as the "festival of motorsport."

Until the era of the muscular "monsters" of Group B, the "Monte" is still organized in the old style, with participants "rallying" to meet at the site, although the conceit is more of a publicity exercise by now. The actual racing competition takes place above the Riviera in the Maritime Alps, and indeed well into the French hinterland.

The rally scene has long since developed into a series of challenging racing competitions. The competitors face off in special stages, dueling for supremacy against both the circuit and the clock. And in most cases, the races are decided by fractions of a second.

Since 1979 – like the Formula 1 World Championship – the most successful driver in the events that make up the championship series is awarded the title. In earlier times there is the champion's laurel wreath – a novelty in 1973 – for the most successful manufacturer. Continual changes to the formerly different formats of rallies worldwide have deprived the Rallye Monte Carlo of former highlights such as the "Night of the Long Knives" and the stages in the Ardèche. Today it is – like the other World Championship races held between Finland and New Zealand, Japan and Argentina, Germany and Cyprus – a compact three-day event with a central rally center and short service distances. Now, the "Monte" is comparable to other events in the calendar, and a highly telegenic one at that.

The attractiveness for television and its viewers is an important key to the success of rally racing, which has long since become a grueling, stage-based sprint competition. Impressive technological advancements include the now commonplace computer graphics that make it possible to superimpose the data from different vehicles on top of one another. This, in turn, enables fascinating comparisons of the races of competitors starting at different times. Modern communication technology and GPS make it all possible, whether the competitors are at the "Monte," the "Acropolis," in Australia or Sweden, on gravel, snow, mud, scree or asphalt. ___

Rallying is regarded as one of the original forms of automotive competition

Year	Rally champion	Car	Manufacturers' champion (model)
2017	Sébastien Ogier (F)	Ford Fiesta WRC	M-Sport World Rallye Team (Ford Fiesta)
2016	Sébastien Ogier (F)	Volkswagen Polo WRC	Volkswagen (Polo WRC)
2015	Sébastien Ogier (F)	Volkswagen Polo WRC	Volkswagen (Polo WRC)
2014	Sébastien Ogier (F)	Volkswagen Polo WRC	Volkswagen (Polo WRC)
2013	Sébastien Ogier (F)	Volkswagen Polo WRC	Volkswagen (Polo WRC)
2012	Sébastien Loeb (F)	Citroën DS3 WRC	Citroën (DS3 WRC)
2011	Sébastien Loeb (F)	Citroën DS3 WRC	Citroën (DS3 WRC)
2010	Sébastien Loeb (F)	Citroën C4 WRC	Citroën (C4 WRC)
2009	Sébastien Loeb (F)	Citroën C4 WRC	Citroën (C4 WRC)
2008	Sébastien Loeb (F)	Citroën C4 WRC	Citroën (C4 WRC)
2007	Sébastien Loeb (F)	Citroën C4 WRC	Ford (Focus WRC)
2006	Sébastien Loeb (F)	Citroën Xsara WRC	Ford (Focus WRC)
2005	Sébastien Loeb (F)	Citroën Xsara WRC	Citroën (Xsara WRC)
2004	Sébastien Loeb (F)	Citroën Xsara WRC	Citroën (Xsara WRC)
2003	Petter Solberg (N)	Subaru Impreza WRC	Citroën (Xsara WRC)
2002	Marcus Grönholm (FIN)	Peugeot 206 WRC	Peugeot (206 WRC)
2001	Richard Burns (GB)	Subaru Impreza WRC	Peugeot (206 WRC)
2000	Marcus Grönholm (FIN)	Peugeot 206 WRC	Peugeot (206 WRC)
1999	Tommi Mäkinen (FIN)	Mitsubishi Lancer Evo VI	Toyota (Corolla WRC)
1998	Tommi Mäkinen (FIN)	Mitsubishi Lancer Evo IV/Evo V	Mitsubishi (Lancer Evo IV & V Gr.A)
1997	Tommi Mäkinen (FIN)	Mitsubishi Lancer Evo IV	Subaru (Impreza WRC)
1996	Tommi Mäkinen (FIN)	Mitsubishi Lancer Evo III	Subaru (Impreza WRX Gr.A)
1995	Colin McRae (GB)	Subaru Impreza 555 WRX	Impreza 555 WRX/Subaru (Impreza WRX Gr.A)
1994	Didier Auriol (F)	Toyota Celica Turbo 4WD	Toyota (Celica Turbo 4WD Gr.A)
1993	Juha Kankkunen (FIN)	Toyota Celica Turbo 4WD	Toyota (Celica Turbo 4WD Gr.A)
1992	Carlos Sainz (E)	Toyota Celica Turbo 4WD	Lancia (Delta HF Integrale Gr.A)
1991	Juha Kankkunen (FIN)	Lancia Delta Integrale 16V	Lancia (Delta Integrale 16V Gr.A)
1990	Carlos Sainz (E)	Toyota Celica Turbo 4WD	Lancia (Delta Integrale 16V Gr.A)
1989	Miki Biasion (I)	Lancia Delta Integrale 16V	Lancia (Delta Integrale 16V Gr.A)
1988	Miki Biasion (I)	Lancia Delta Integrale	Lancia (Delta Integrale Gr.A)
1987	Juha Kankkunen (FIN)	Lancia Delta HF 4WD	Lancia (Delta HF 4WD Gr.A)
1986	Juha Kankkunen (FIN)	Peugeot 205 turbo 16	Peugeot (205 turbo 16 Gr.B)
1985	Timo Salonen (FIN)	Peugeot 205 turbo 16	Peugeot (205 turbo 16 Gr.B)
1984	Stig Blomqvist (S)	Audi quattro	Audi (quattro Gr.B)
1983	Hannu Mikkola (S)	Audi quattro	Lancia 037 (Rally Gr.B)
1982	Walter Röhrl (D)	Opel Ascona 400	Audi (quattro Gr.4)
1981	Ari Vatanen (FIN)	Ford Escort	Talbot (Lotus 2.2 Gr.2)
1980	Walter Röhrl (D)	Fiat 131 Abarth	Fiat (131 Abarth)
1979	Björn Waldegaard (S)	Ford Escort RS	Ford (Escort RS)

Until 1978, only a manufacturer's world championship or international manufacturer's championship is staged

1978	(Markku Alen)	Fiat (131 Abarth)
1977	(Björn Waldegaard)	Fiat (131 Abarth)
1976	(Sandro Munari)	Lancia (Stratos)
1975	(Hannu Mikkola)	Lancia (Stratos)
1974	(Sandro Munari)	Lancia (Stratos)
1973	(Jean-Luc Therier)	Alpine-Renault (A110)

In 1973, the previous European Rally Championship becomes the International Championship for Manufacturers

1972 (European Rally Championship)	Lancia (Fulvia HF)
1971 (International Manufacturer's Championship)	Alpine-Renault (A110)
1970 (International Manufacturer's Championship)	Porsche (911, 911S)
1969 (European Rally Championship)	Ford (20M, Escort TC)
1968 (European Rally Championship)	Ford (Escort TC)

Adventures in the desert

___ "Today I'll make men of you!" It is with such words that Dakar Rally organizer Thierry Sabine breathes life into the Dakar legend and becomes immortal – though he met his death at the 1986 Dakar, the victim of a helicopter crash. The rally lives on. And is still considered the hardest rally in the world. "The Dakar is comparable with a Formula 1 World Championship," says Volkswagen Motorsport Director Kris Nissen, "except that after crossing the finish line of a race, a daily stage, in the Dakar the cars have to be ready to go again the very next day. And they do that until they cross the finish line, that is, for the entire duration of the race, they can't allow themselves the slightest weakness."

Sahara expeditions with automobiles have been on the books since 1901. A pair of aristocratic brothers set off with accompaniment and two Panhard et Levassor 12 HPs. In 1922/23 the Sahara is crossed for the first time by the Citroën expedition (with 20-hp half-track models based on the B2 compact car). Time and again the desert draws adventurers and holds them in thrall. The Sahara is principally a destination for intrepid French explorers; small wonder in view of their colonialist incursions there and another legacy, that of their language, which that period leaves in its wake. The drives of the "friends of the Sahara" (les amies d'Sahara) are followed from December 26, 1978 to January 14, 1979, by the first rally from Paris to Dakar. 182 cars take part in the first rally, which brings motor racing to the Sahara for the first time.

The rally was originally the idea of adventurous desert wanderers

The rally skitters from stage finish to stage finish, year by year. The route is first sketched out in late autumn and announced each evening before the next day's stage in the form of road books. Although today's GPS technology would simplify navigation, the participants are provided only the information in GPS system provided by the organizer. Only when one waypoint is reached does the next waypoint become visible. This keeps the route challenging and the corridor specified by the organizers narrow. In spite of different vehicle concepts – for instance, all-wheel drive prototypes custom-built for the race such as the Volkswagen Race Touareg or the Mitsubishi Pajero Evolution, as well as two-wheel drive buggies and so-called ProTrucks, such as those used in the Baja races in Mexico – the "Dakar" offers competition of the highest level. Even after several hundred kilometers and hours of relentless pursuit, the frontrunners are often separated by mere seconds.

The long special stages stretch nearly from stage finish to stage finish. Thus the Dakar Rally resembles rally and long-distance racing as it is practiced in Europe into the 1960s , with events like the original "Monte" and competitive races like the Liège–Sofia–Liège.

In the beginning, there is only one classification. The winner is whoever reaches the finish at Lac Rose before the gates of Dakar in the shortest time, be it by car, motorcycle or truck. By now, however, the organizers have long since taken to minimizing the risk for the respective groups through technical specifications and there is a separate classification for each vehicle type. The cars garner the most attention. After the 2008 Dakar had to be cancelled due to security concerns, all races beginning with 2009 were held in South America. This doesn't deter the die-hard fans: a large number of the field is typically made up of amateurs. ___

Year	Winner	Car	Route
2017	Stéphane Peterhansel (F)/Jean-Paul Cottret (F)	Peugeot Buggy	Asuncion-La Paz-Buenos Aires
2016	Stéphane Peterhansel (F)/Jean-Paul Cottret (F)	Peugeot Buggy	Buenos Aires-Rosario
2015	Nasser Al Attiyah (KAT)/ Matthieu Baumel (F)	Mini	Buenos Aires-Iquique-Buenos Aires
2014	Nani Roma (SP)/Michel Périn (F)	Mini	Rosario-Valparaiso
2013	Stéphane Peterhansel (F)/Jean-Paul Cottret (F)	Mini	Lima-Santiago de Chile
2012	Stéphane Peterhansel (F)/Jean-Paul Cottret (F)	Mini	Mar del Plata-Lima
2011	Nasser Al-Attiyah (KAT)/Timo Gottschalk (D)	Volkswagen Race Touareg 3	Argentinien Chile
2010	Carlos Sainz (E)/ Lucas Cruz (E)	Volkswagen Race Touareg 2	Argentinien-Chile
2009	Gimiel de Villiers (SA)/Dirk von Zitzewitz (D)	Volkswagen Race Touareg 2	Argentinien-Chile
2008	(cancelled due to security concerns in Northern Africa)		
2007	Stéphane Peterhansel (F)/Jean-Paul Cottret (F)	Mitsubishi Pajero	Lisboa-Dakar
2006	Luc Alphand (F)/Gilles Picard (F)	Mitsubishi Pajero	Lisboa-Dakar
2005	Stéphane Peterhansel (F)/Jean-Paul Cottret (F)	Mitsubishi Pajero	Barcelona-Dakar
2004	Stéphane Peterhansel (F)/Jean-Paul Cottret (F)	Mitsubishi Pajero	Clermont-Ferrand-Dakar
2003	Hiroshi Masuoka (J)/Andreas Schulz (D)	Mitsubishi Pajero	Marsaille-Sharm El Sheikh
2002	Hiroshi Masuoka (J)/Pascal Maimon (F)	Mitsubishi Pajero	Arras-Dakar
2001	Jutta Kleinschmitt (D)/Andreas Schulz (D)	Mitsubishi Pajero	Paris-Dakar
2000	Jean-Louis Schlesser (F)/Henri Magne (F)	Schlesser-Renault	Granada-Dakar
1999	Jean-Louis Schlesser (F)/Philippe Monnet (F)	Schlesser-Renault	Dakar-Kairo
1998	Jean-Pierre Fonenay (F)/Gilles Picard (F)	Mitsubishi Pajero	Paris-Dakar
1997	Kenjiro Shinozuka (J)/Henri Magne (F)	Mitsubishi Pajero	Dakar-Dakar
1996	Pierre Lartigue (F)/Michel Périn (F)	Citroën ZX	Paris-Dakar
1995	Pierre Lartigue (F)/Michel Périn (F)	Citroën ZX	Paris-Dakar
1994	Pierre Lartigue (F)/Michel Périn (F)	Citroën ZX	Paris-Dakar-Eurodisney
1993	Bruno Saby (F)/Dominique Series (F)	Mitsubishi Pajero	Paris-Dakar
1992	Hubert Auriol (F)/Philippe Monnet (F)	Mitsubishi Pajero	Paris-Kapstadt
1991	Ari Vatanen (FIN)/Bruno Berglund (S)	Citroën ZX	Paris-Dakar
1990	Ari Vatanen (FIN)/Bruno Berglund (S)	Peugeot 405 turbo 16	Paris-Dakar
1989	Ari Vatanen (FIN)/Bruno Berglund (S)	Peugeot 405 turbo 16	Paris-Dakar
1988	Juha Kankkunen (FIN)/ Juha Piironen (FIN)	Peugeot 205 turbo 16	Paris-Dakar
1987	Ari Vatanen (FIN)/Bernard Giroux (F)	Peugeot 205 turbo 16	Paris-Dakar
1986	René Metge (F)/Dominique Lemyne (F)	Porsche 959	Paris-Dakar
1985	Patrick Zaniroli (F)/Jean da Silva (F)	Mitsubishi Pajero	Paris-Dakar
1984	René Metge (F)/Dominique Lemoyne (F)	Porsche 911 4x4	Paris-Dakar
1983	Jacky Ickx (B)/Claude Brasseur (F)	Mercedes-Benz 280 GE	Paris-Dakar
1982	Claude Marreau (F)/Bernard Marreau (F)	Renault 20	Paris-Dakar
1981	René Metge (F)/Bernard Giroux (F)	Range Rover	Paris-Dakar
1980	Freddy Kottulinski (S)/Gerd Löffelmann (D)	Volkswagen Iltis	Paris-Dakar
1979	Joseph Terbiaut (F)/Jean Lemordant (F)/Genestier (F)	Range Rover	Paris-Dakar

Special thanks goes out to the people close to me for their infinite patience, and to many obliging people for their support, especially: Peter Gutzmer, Lucas di Grassi and Edwin Baaske, Uwe Baldes, Claudia Berger, Hans-Gerd Bode, Alan Bodfish, Marco Brinkmann, Walter Demel, Dieter Dressel, Malte Dringenberg, Thomas May-Englert, Paul Entwhistle, Lutz Gernert, Nina Göllner, Manfred Grunert, Jan de Haas, Jake Harris, Jörn Heese, Dr. Arno Homburg, Alexandra Hoppe, Christoph Horn, Dirk Johae, Sabine Kehm, Thomas Kern, Davide Kluzer, Julius Kruta, Bettina Lüttgen, Andreas Männer, Lesley Ann Miller, Stefan Müller, Kris Nissen, Jürgen Pippig, Nicolaus Reichert, Eddie Roche, Claus Roedenbeck, Julie Rugenski, Alexander Safavi, Caroline Sambale, Oliver Schimpf, Mark Schneider, Torben Schröder, Armin Schwarz, Bernd Simmendinger, Albrecht Trautzburg, Hanno Vienken, Bernhard Voss, Kristina Weber, Jörg Weusthoff, Leo Wieland, Norman Winkler, Claus Witzeck, Sascha Wolfinger and many other people who helped to make this book happen.

Bibliographic information published by the Deutsche Nationalbibliothek
The Deutsche Nationalbibliothek lists this publication in
the Deutsche Nationalbibliografie; detailed bibliographic
data are available in the Internet at http://dnb.dnb.de.

ISBN 978-3-667-11327-6
© by Delius, Klasing & Co. KG, Bielefeld (Germany)

Texts: Jörg Walz
Photos: Alfa Romeo, Aston Martin, Audi, Audi Sport Auto-Medienportal, Auto-Reporter, AvD, Sandro Bacchi, Bentley, BMW, BMW Mobile Tradition, Brawn GP, Bugatti, Citroën, Chrysler, Deutsche Post Speed Academy, Dieter Dressel, FAG, Ferrari, FIA, Fiat, Ford, Lutz Gernert, Jaguar, Ferdi and Bodo Kräling, Thomas Kunert "Kuni Fotodesign", Lancia, LAT, Lotus, LuK, McLaren, Mercedes-Benz, Mini, Mitsubishi, Motorklassik, Motorsnaps.com, Motorsport aktuell, Museo Stanguellini (p. 81), NASCAR, Opel, Peugeot, Porsche, Renault, Schaeffler, Rainer Schlegelmilch, Skoda, speedpool, Lothar Spurzem, Spyker, Venturi, Volkswagen Motorsport, Gerhard D. Wagner, Jörg Walz, Wolfgang Wilhelm
Translation: Kaye Mueller, RWS Group Germany GmbH
Editor: Hanno Vienken
Design: Jörg Weusthoff, Weusthoff Noël, Hamburg
Lithography: scanlitho.teams, Bielefeld
Printed by: Himmer, Augsburg
Printed in Germany 2017

While all reasonable care has been taken in the publication of the book, neither the author nor the publisher takes any responsibility for the use, the complexity and the actuality of the information given in this book.

All rights reserved. The work may neither be entirely nor partially reproduced, transmitted or copied – such as manually or by means of electronic and mechanical systems, including photo-copying, tape recording and data storage – without explicit permission of the publisher.

Delius Klasing Verlag, Siekerwall 21, 33602 Bielefeld, Germany
Phone: +49-521-559-0, Fax: +49-521-559-115
Email: info@delius-klasing.de
www.delius-klasing.de

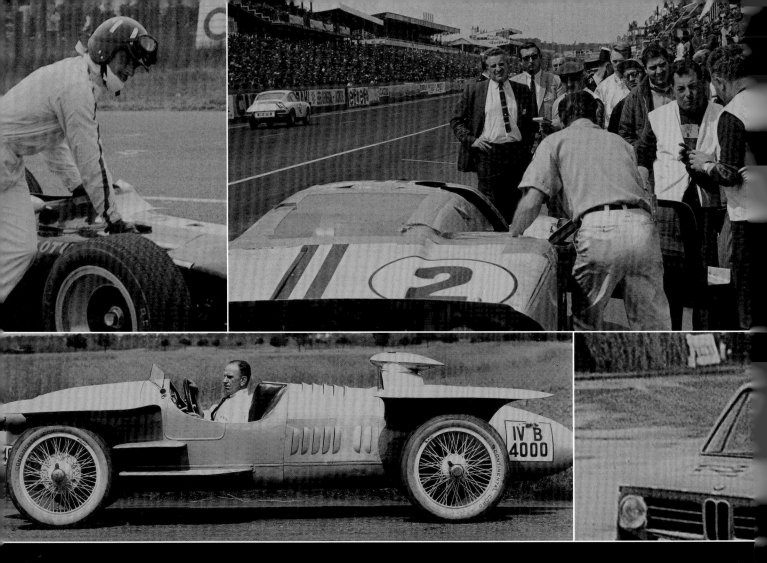

Peugeot, Pipe, Renault AK 90 CV, Fiat Taunus Corsa, Protos 17-30 PS, Blitzen-B
Austro Daimler Sascha, Bugatti T35, Alfa Romeo P2, Mercedes-Benz S, Opel RA
BMW 328, Alfa Romeo Tipo 158 »Alfetta«, Maserati 4CL, Ferrari 125 S, Veritas F
Porsche 550 A, Ferrari 250 Testa Rossa, Aston Martin DBR1, Bluebird, Lotus 25
Chaparral 2G, Porsche 917, Dodge Charger Daytona, Lotus 72, Lancia Stratos, B
Porsche 935, Volkswagen Iltis, McLaren-Cosworth MP4, Porsche 956, Brabham-
Audi V8 quattro, Sauber-Mercedes C291, Williams-Renault FW14B, Alfa Romeo
Indy V8, Mitsubishi Lancer Evo, Porsche 911 GT1, Mercedes CLK DTM, Audi R8,
Porsche 911 GT3 RSR, Brawn BGP 001, Venturi, Schaeffler Audi A4 DTM, Scha